Praise for
DARE to MATTER

"A stirring, hopeful reflection on life, faith, legacy, meaning, and love that will guide and encourage you to try just a little bit harder to let your reach exceed your grasp as you find your way to make a difference at home and in the world."
—**Walter Isaacson,** *New York Times* **bestselling author**

"An essential reminder that the greatest challenges of any age are no match for the goodwill, love, passion, and potential that abides in all human beings. I hope this superb book will inspire its readers to follow in Jordan's footsteps in making a difference for all."—**Madeleine K. Albright, former Secretary of State**

"By providing a road map to personal enlightenment, Kassalow encourages the reader to find professional success while simultaneously mattering to the world."—***Booklist***

"Whether we are seeking to be of service in our local communities or looking to make a larger global impact, Kassalow's experience and advice resonates and inspires . . . Challenging, informative, and inspiring, *Dare to Matter* invites us all to make our lives ones of true worth by serving our fellow man."—***Spirituality and Health***

"In an era when young people are compelled to find purpose yet they too often find themselves stressed and anxious, Jordan offers a sustainable and impactful path grounded in the clarity of his own experience with VisionSpring."
—**Sylvia Burwell, president, American University, and former Secretary of Health and Human Services**

"This book is an amazing gift. It shows us that the best way to develop fully who we uniquely are is to dare, repeatedly, over our lives, to change the world. Because that's what Jordan Kassalow has done, and because he's so very reflective/observant and clear, the reader's journey to this understanding is in rich comfort."
—**Bill Drayton, founder and CEO, Ashoka**

"*Dare to Matter* should be required reading for anyone who dreams of making a difference. The book shines with hard-earned wisdom embedded in spiritual ground and girded with practical advice. You will be inspired, enlivened, and possibly, forever changed in all good ways."
—**Jacqueline Novogratz, CEO, Acumen, and author of *The Blue Sweater***

"As feelings of cynicism, apathy, and hopelessness threaten to divide people and asphyxiate progress, *Dare to Matter* is a breath of fresh, hopeful air. This book will restore your faith in what is possible and inspire you to devote your personal power to making positive, meaningful change."
—**Darren Walker, president, Ford Foundation**

"Are you doing the things that make you most fulfilled in life? Are you having a positive impact on the people and the world around you? Jordan Kassalow has helped me answer these questions with the lessons artfully distilled in this important book."
—**Jeff Raider, co-founder and co-CEO, Harry's, Inc.**

DARE to MATTER
Your Path to
Making a Difference *Now*

JORDAN KASSALOW
and JENNIFER KRAUSE

CITADEL PRESS
Kensington Publishing Corp.
www.kensingtonbboks.com

CITADEL PRESS BOOKS are published by

Kensington Publishing Corp.
119 West 40th Street
New York, NY 10018

All Kensington titles, imprints, and distributed lines are available at special quantity discounts for bulk purchases for sales promotions, premiums, fund-raising, educational, or institutional use.

Special book excerpts or customized printings can also be created to fit specific needs. For details, write or phone the office of the Kensington sales manager: Kensington Publishing Corp., 119 West 40th Street, New York, NY 10018, attn: Sales Department; phone 1-800-221-2647.

CITADEL PRESS and the Citadel logo are Reg. U.S. Pat. & TM Off.

ISBN-13: 978-0-8065-3903-4
ISBN-10: 0-8065-3903-8

First Citadel hardcover printing: May 2019
First trade paperback printing: April 2020

10 9 8 7 6 5 4 3 2 1

Printed in the United States of America

Electronic edition:

ISBN-13: 978-0-8065-3904-1 (e-book)
ISBN-10: 0-8065-3904-6 (e-book)

*In memory of my beloved mother,
who opened up the world to me
through her light and love.*

—JSK

*For Jeffrey, Becca, Ben and Jenna,
who have given me a whole new way to matter.*

—JEK

For years to come the debris of a convulsed world will beset our steps. It will require a purpose stronger than any man and worthy of all men to calm and inspirit us. A sane society whose riches are happy children, men and women, beautiful with peace and creative activity, is not going to be ordained for us. We must make it ourselves.

—HELEN KELLER

Contents

Foreword

In 2003, I found myself working at a New York City think tank dedicated to coming up with policies for resolving deadly conflict. I was twenty-three, a recent college graduate. Like any fresh-from-the-quad young person plunked down into his first real adult job, I spent 50 percent of my time trying to navigate my nascent career and 50 percent of my time trying to figure out whether I'd settled on the right career to begin with. What I ultimately wanted was as straightforward as it was vague: to have a meaningful, positive impact on the world. And while I worked on puzzling out the specifics of that goal, I realized one thing pretty swiftly: the world of policy was not the quickest way to get there.

I quit my think tank job and started poking around my network of family and friends. One of those friends introduced me to her eye doctor, explaining that he always seemed to have fascinating side projects, including a project dedicated to distributing glasses in the developing world. She figured it might be useful for me to speak with him.

I met Jordan at his Upper East Side optometry practice, and we walked to lunch. Before we'd even ordered, Jordan sketched out some facts that got my synapses firing. Did I know that glasses had been around for about seven hundred years, and yet almost a billion people worldwide lacked access to this vital tool for living?

(I didn't.) Did I know that a single pair of glasses could increase an individual's productivity by 35 percent and her income by 20 percent? (Nope.) Did I know that 90 percent of individuals with vision impairment live in the developing world? (Also no.)

Over lunch, Jordan explained his vision to start a nonprofit that would make steps toward addressing these issues. The organization would train women in developing countries to give eye exams and sell glasses to members of their communities at affordable prices. Eyeglasses, Jordan explained, were one of the most cost-effective—and immediately useful—interventions available.

As we spoke, a couple of things struck me. Jordan's vision was remarkably ambitious, but it also made practical sense. We are so frequently confronted with sprawling, intractable, impossibly complex problems, with solutions that are overly expensive or difficult to scale or technologically infeasible. Jordan's idea was sensible and pragmatic. I could instantly see how it might work.

Rather than treat people as needy beneficiaries, Jordan's model approached them as value-conscious consumers. He was not interested in the paternalistic "we know best" rhetoric of many well-intentioned but under-effective nonprofits and nongovernmental organizations (NGOs). He was interested in treating people with dignity.

After all, everyone who has worn a pair of glasses knows that eyewear is a core part of your identity. A pair of glasses can be the most visible thing on your face. It doesn't matter whether you're a twenty-three-year-old kid in a Manhattan restaurant or a great-grandmother in El Salvador; nobody wants to sport an unattractive pair of glasses. Nobody knew this better than Jordan, who had catered to some of the choosiest customers in the world through his practice—as well as training on the ground as an optometric student volunteer in Latin America, and a development professional with Helen Keller International in Sub-Saharan Africa. He had truly seen both sides of the coin.

One thing led to another and Jordan asked me to come onboard and move down to El Salvador to work on the pilot program for what would become VisionSpring. It was there—having to prove out a model in a very challenging environment—that I caught the entrepreneurial bug and discovered the invigorating twists and turns (and headaches!) of boots-on-the-ground problem solving.

In the field, questions came at lightning speed: what was the best way to identify people who had the interest and capability to start (and run) their own businesses? What was the most effective way to train and incentivize them? How could the program maintain financial sustainability? Where should I spend money and where should I skimp? What was the best way to approach an unknown community and engage in a dialogue? What was the best way to build credibility and trust?

These were among the thousands—literally, thousands!—of lessons I learned at VisionSpring, which functioned as an incredible prep school for the business called Warby Parker, which I would go on to start.

Throughout my professional career, I've been fortunate to have Jordan as a boss, a friend, and a mentor. I look to him as an example of someone who has it "all figured out" and yet still has the curiosity to ask questions and keep learning. He has a thriving practice, a social purpose, and a beautiful family. At the end of the day, what Jordan taught me was not the importance of work-life balance, but the art of work-life integration. He can teach you, too.

Neil Blumenthal
Co-Founder and Co-CEO,
Warby Parker

DARE to MATTER

Introduction

In 2013, towards the end of my annual visit to the optometrist, Dr. Jordan Kassalow flipped on the exam room lights and did something I'd never heard him do in the entire ten years that I'd been his patient: talk about himself.

"So, I have this other work that I do," he said, "and it's taken me to a lot of places around the world over the last twenty-five years."

I was intrigued.

"Anyway," he continued, "I have a lot of stories from my experiences, and lately when I share them with people they've been saying, 'You should write a book.'"

"That's great!" I said.

"The thing is," Jordan explained, "I really prefer listening to speaking. I'm not a writer, and I don't even know if there's a whole book there."

That Jordan was a good listener had always been apparent to me as his patient. He is the kind of doctor who goes out of his way to know the people he treats. He asks real questions about you and your life, and remembers your answers the next time you visit the office regardless of how much time has passed.

Based on questions Jordan had asked me over time about my work as a rabbi and writer, and also because Jordan had noted that day that he sensed that his Jewish identity was an important part of his "other" work, I was honored when Jordan asked, "If you're not too busy could you tell me what you think?"

I said I'd be happy to, and Jordan handed me a business card that said VISIONSPRING.

Although my pupils were still dilated from the exam, when I got home from the appointment I immediately sat down at my desk and did what any normal person wearing sunglasses indoors in the middle of the day would do under the circumstances: I googled "Jordan Kassalow."

Of the many pages of links that appeared, I started with the VisionSpring website. From there I jumped over to YouTube, where I watched Jordan giving an acceptance speech on Vision-Spring's behalf for a social innovation award.

As I listened to Jordan talk about VisionSpring and tell the story of how he came to found it, I could see why some had suggested he write a book. When he spoke of his path, one clearly paved with a deep commitment to being part of something bigger than himself and shaped by moments shared with people of all backgrounds, cultures, colors, and creeds in places here and abroad, I could already envision the words on the page.

I emailed Jordan right away to share my thoughts about his book. A few weeks later, we sat down in the conference room at the VisionSpring offices to discuss them in greater detail. Somewhere in the course of the conversation, Jordan started referring to his book as our book. This took me by surprise because I hadn't gone into the meeting thinking I was there to be anything other than a sounding board.

As Jordan continued referring to his book as our book, I recalled one of the most striking things he had said in the video I'd watched following the routine eye exam that had opened my eyes to much more than I'd expected. In it, Jordan defined success as a series of significant moments—moments that, if you're open to seeing them, can guide you in the direction of something greater than you alone.

Then I thought of a favorite Jewish teaching that says that most of the time we walk through our lives with our hearts closed to much of the world around us, yet in singular moments created solely for us, our hearts open. If we can recognize these moments while they're happening, they have the power to change our lives forever. Sitting in the VisionSpring conference room, I sensed that this was one of them.

Six years later, after discussing everything from Tolstoy to Talmud, business models to baseball, poetry to public health; after six years of getting to know one another's families, sharing joyous milestones at bar and bat mitzvahs and weddings, and being present in times of sorrow, my sense about that moment has been reaffirmed again and again.

From the beginning of our collaboration, one of the things Jordan and I realized we share in our careers is that most of the people we encounter are searching for a way to make a difference. They want to create positive change for others and be changed for the better as a result. They want to help, do something that has an impact beyond just themselves and the ones they love, something that might even endure long after their lives are over, as the long life of the world goes on.

Jordan and I also have observed that almost everyone who wants to help doesn't know where to start or how. The remarkable thing I have observed about Jordan is that he does.

The reality for most of us is Jordan's reality, too. We lead busy lives. We have our own struggles and commitments and to-do lists that only seem to grow regardless of how much we accomplish in a day. We all know that living real life in the real world, with all of its complexities and demands, can leave us more often than not with little time to take a good look beyond our own small corner of the world and little energy left over to ask ourselves who needs us beyond the circle of the people we love.

What you'll come to know about Jordan in this book is that despite these challenges, he has found a way to turn making a difference into something more than a side venture or the subject of lingering regret due to lack of time or resources; to make changing the world a pursuit that doesn't have to eclipse the necessary pursuit of work that pays the bills or the enjoyment of life's pleasures. And while Jordan will be the first to tell you that the execution hasn't been seamless, that he doesn't have all the answers, and the task hasn't been—and isn't—an easy one, he will also say without a moment's hesitation that he wouldn't trade the life he's built for anything. Most important, he will show you that you can find a way, too.

As Jordan shares his stories, experiences, and the insights he has gathered along the way, he will encourage you to reflect on key questions that have helped him on his path, such as: What is my definition of "enough"? What do I do best? Where can I make the biggest difference? What skills and talents do I already possess that will allow me to connect what I do for a living with what I aspire to do to help change the lives of others? Who are the people in my midst who might be open to partnering with me to help make my dream of making a difference a reality? What am I willing to sacrifice for the opportunity both to have the basics I need and the creature comforts I want while living in service of something beyond my own personal needs and desires?

As you partner with Jordan in these pages to find a way to make a difference all your own, you will learn that Jordan has discovered a way to build an integrated life that knits together the hunger we all share to take care of ourselves and our loved ones, live our lives to the fullest, and live in service of something greater than ourselves. You will also learn that he hasn't made this happen by any sort of magic or power unique to him, but rather by choosing day by day, year by year, consciously and deliberately to make it so. And you will see that the power to make that choice, and the ability to live it, are in you, too.

I will tell you that working with Jordan, listening to everything that he has accomplished, and hearing all that he does with the same twenty-four hours in a day that you and I have makes it hard to resist comparison. The fact is, Jordan has helped millions of people. And as much as I hope that when I come to the end of my life, I, too, will have made a difference in people's lives, I'm also acutely aware that I am so not Jordan. I'm not even Jordan-adjacent.

While Jordan and I were talking one day I said as much. "I will never be able to do what you do."

"And I will never be able to do what you do," he answered without skipping a beat.

That brief exchange is, in a nutshell, what this book is really about.

Helping Jordan bring this book into being, working to help him inspire others to make a difference in the world, has been part of my path to making a difference for the last six years—using the things I know how to do, drawing on my own areas of study and interest, and based on what I believe I have been called to do in the world. It has also made me think in an entirely different way about how I will continue shaping my own path to create positive change in the years to come. This book will help you do the same, because this book isn't just about what Jordan has done, it's about what you'll do.

The true promise of this book isn't what Jordan has to teach you. The promise of this book is you.

Rabbi Jennifer Krause

The challenge I face is how to actualize, how to concretize the quiet eminence of my being. Beyond all agony and anxiety lies the most important ingredient of self-reflection: the preciousness of my own existence. To my own heart my existence is unique, unprecedented, priceless, exceedingly precious, and I resist the thought of gambling away its meaning.
—Rabbi Abraham Joshua Heschel

1 Dare to Matter

We are all something, but none of us is everything.
—Blaise Pascal

What do you want to be when you grow up?

Do you remember when you first heard this question? How old were you? Who asked? How did you respond?

From the moment we're old enough to carry on basic polysyllabic conversations, "What do you want to be when you grow up?" is the go-to icebreaker topic when grown-ups talk to kids. Chances are that before you could read, count to ten, or tie your shoelaces, people wanted to know what you wanted to be—meaning, what you wanted to do for a living.

I was in the second grade the first time I recall being asked the question, and I replied in the remarkably unremarkable way lots of kids do at that age. What did I want to be when I grew up? That was easy: a fireman. Firemen had everything you could possibly want in a job: a cool car with flashing lights and sirens, which you could drive as fast as you wanted; cool gadgets; cool uniforms; and you got to be a hero.

But as time marched on and I started to understand what firemen really had to do to earn the cool gear and hero status, I came to the sober realization that I didn't have what it would take to be a first responder. I also had embraced the fact that rocketing to earth from a distant planet, having first been endowed with special powers or being bitten by a radioactive spider, weren't things just anyone could do if they worked really hard and believed in themselves. With that, Superman and Spiderman were also off the table—my childhood dream no match for every kid's kryptonite: reality.

With high school came a more achievable career goal. What did I want to be when I grew up? A photographer for *National Geographic*. While I had no way of knowing for sure how solid my prospects in that field would be, at the very least I was optimistic that it was better suited to my talents and interests. And given the right training, determination, and commitment, success was within reach.

For a lucky few, the first "What do you want to be when you grow up?" answer never changes. There are people in the world who say they want to be a firefighter and who actually grow up to be a firefighter. Or a doctor. Or a chef. Or a Supreme Court justice. But for the rest of us, the answer changes and changes and changes again. And in this era when we've traded one-job-for-life gold watch retirements for second and third acts, the changes don't necessarily end in early adulthood.

The vast majority of us mere mortals do reach some turning point in our growing-up process when our circumstances and abilities insinuate themselves into our earliest childhood "What do you want to be when you grow up?" dreams. That watershed moment when what may have been an adorable answer at seven, if gone unchanged at seventeen, instead inspires sideways glances and furrowed brows in the adults who ask (parents in particular).

I think my son, Jonas, summed it up best when he addressed our synagogue community at his bar mitzvah. Gazing from the pulpit at the assembled group of friends, family, and synagogue goers—some Jewish, some of other or no religious backgrounds, Jonas said, "For those of you who are unfamiliar with this ritual, a bar mitzvah is the day in a thirteen-year-old Jewish boy's life when he realizes that he has a far better chance of owning an NBA team than playing for one."

Jonas got a big laugh, and not just because his observation was funny, but also because it was true. His words resonated with every person in that sanctuary who had ever shed a childhood dream for a grown-up truth: you can't be everything, but eventually you have to be something.

Yet when the time comes, how do you know what that something is?

Go West, Young Man?

If we're facing in the right direction, all we have to do is keep on walking. If it takes a year, or sixty years, or five lifetimes, as long as we're heading towards light, that's all that matters.
—JOSEPH GOLDSTEIN

When the time came for me to choose something, I was twenty-three and fresh out of college. "What do you want to be?" dogged me everywhere I went. Figuring it out was my central preoccupation and deep wellspring of anxiety—anxiety that was not helped by the fact that I was the only one of my friends who didn't have a plan. I was obsessed with choosing the right direction in my life; or as I thought of it, with whether to head east or go west.

As detailed by philosopher and naturalist Henry David Thoreau in his essay, "Walking," the bible of my youth, east and west aren't points on a map, but polar opposite states of being.

West is the future, while east is the past.

West is stepping boldly into the wild unknown without looking back, while east is retracing your steps to get back home.

West is setting up camp in the middle of nowhere; east is pitching a tent in your own backyard.

As someone who'd been hiking and mountain climbing since my early teens, far more at home in the great outdoors than I ever was in a classroom, whenever I read "Walking," I felt like Thoreau was speaking directly to me. But with college graduation in the rearview mirror and no strong sense of what I wanted to do with my future, a borderline manic manifesto dedicated to an existence unspoiled by commitments and basic social conventions wasn't going to cut it. I needed a plan.

It wasn't that I was completely lost. A few months before graduation, I'd been accepted to the New England College of Optometry (NECO). As the son of an optometrist, the operating assumption was that once I earned my doctor of optometry degree I would go to work for my dad in his practice.

I loved and respected my father, but the thought of being an optometrist didn't inspire me at all. It was retracing my footsteps, working just miles from the suburban New York home of my childhood, in the office I'd visited countless times on trips to the city with my dad. This was my east.

My west, on the other hand, was more in line with my passion for nature, travel, and adventure: spending a year climbing in Tibet, possibly followed by graduate school to become a tundra biologist, was the best idea I'd conjured in the way of a go-forward strategy.

Technically I'd already chosen west. I'd notified NECO that I wanted to defer admission and my plans for Tibet were partially underway. Yet while I'd made the decision, I hadn't made peace with it.

So when I set out on a two-month celebratory postgraduation trek through Alaska with my good friends, Rob and Mike, I carried a load of gear on my back and the NECO acceptance letter in my pocket.

To get to the starting point of our trek, we drove 210 miles on the Dalton Highway north of Fairbanks, parked our '78 Dodge Omni on the side of the road near the base of Sukakpak Mountain, and unloaded our monster packs. As we began our journey, I prayed that eight weeks in the most spellbinding wilderness in the country would bring me clarity.

As we took our first steps into the Gates of the Arctic National Park, an odd, yet familiar, combination of electricity and absolute peace guided me through nature's captivating antechamber. Venturing into the territory, sprawling west to east across northern Alaska all the way into the Canadian Yukon, was like collapsing onto a bed made for ten Goliaths. The guys and I were well trained to check in with a park ranger prior to heading into the wilderness, a practice that seemed all the more crucial given the enormity of the terrain.

With that, our first stop was a ranger station just outside Fairbanks, the very last one on the map, yet still hundreds of miles south of our destination. We spread out our map to share our planned route, pointing to some landmarks to help explain. It was quite challenging because almost nothing had a label or a name.

When we'd finished our presentation, the ranger looked up from the map and asked, "Why are you boys here anyway?"

We replied that we were exercising best practices and checking in before heading out for safety's sake. He laughed.

"Gentlemen," the ranger said, "we've got eight-and-a-half million acres of park and two rangers cover it. Appreciate the visit, but I'd be lying if I didn't say once you're out there you're on your own."

Rather than making us think twice about pressing on, the ominous sendoff made us more excited than ever. Clutching the barren map, we lit out like a band of explorers, and took great pride and pleasure in naming every new place we found along the way.

If I could have willed time to stand still, I would have wandered in the wilderness forever. For most of my young adult life, beginning in high school, the way Thoreau described it on the page was the way I felt on unmarked paths in untamed spaces. "Life consists with wildness," he wrote. "The most alive is the wildest." In the wildness I found comfort and confidence; in the wildness I was the most myself, the most alive. But I knew I could only seek refuge in the outdoors for so long.

Sitting at the edge of the water one afternoon at what we'd decided to call Cat Food Creek, I pulled the NECO acceptance letter out of my pocket and read it one more time even though I already knew its contents by heart.

I thought of my parents and all of the privileges and opportunities—more than most people get in a lifetime—that their hard work had afforded me, including a solid education, and now the offer of a guaranteed livelihood waiting for me on the other side of an advanced degree. If it wasn't for my dad and mom, I wouldn't even have had the freedom to ruminate about my future.

My thoughts then turned to a life spent day in and day out in dark, windowless exam rooms, with NECO as the gateway to that future—a vision I found terrifying. But the vision of one day being a person who could give the people I loved everything that my parents had given me and my sisters did inspire me. Holding that vision in my mind's eye, seeing optometry as the work I could do to help make that vision a reality, let in a little bit of light.

Dust in the Wind

When the soul asks, "What are you doing here?" its answer should be, "What needs to be done."
—Rumi

In the midst of a long trek somewhere above the Arctic Circle, the bright blue skies were graying fast. We still had a long way to go to stay on course for the day, but the weather made it clear that a change of plans was in order. Not long after we set up camp under a curious double rainbow, it started raining sideways and didn't let up. Rob, Mike, and I were trapped in a soaking wet tent, stuck in a frustrating waiting game for days.

After being cooped up and playing every card game we could think of for what seemed like forever, going into the pouring rain seemed like a far better deal than sitting around playing even one more hand.

The moment I stepped outside, the rain felt like a million tiny switchblades slashing my face, but I kept moving forward, slowly and not always surely making my way up, until I'd summited a nearby mountain with one of the most awesome views I've ever seen. Soaring mountains with bald gray caps sitting atop colossal pedestals of spring-green tundra stretched out before me for as far as my eyes could see. But standing there amid all that beauty, barely managing to stay on my feet in the wind and rain, I felt more anger than awe.

It felt like the wilderness was conspiring against me—from being stalled in that tent entirely at nature's whim to the soaring mountains surrounding me, making the one I'd just scaled look like a pile of rocks. It was as if the universe were saying, "Don't you see now that you are nothing? Surrender to insignificance!"

I call this my "dust in the wind" moment because I remember hearing the Kansas song on a loop in my head. Yes, it's true that nothing lasts forever, yet at that moment, something inside me felt like it would break if I completely surrendered to how small I was in the grand scheme of things. I had to believe that I was alive for a reason, even though this great big world was here long before I entered it and would be here long after I died.

With that, I shouted, "I will matter!" from the mountaintop and made a pact with myself that I would be someone who made a difference in the life of the world with the life that I'd been given. Although I shouted these words with great conviction, truth be told, I had no idea how I would make this bold proclamation a reality. What I did know was that whether I climbed mountains in the Himalayas or subway stairs in Manhattan, the focal point of my life and the hallmark of my success would be inexorably linked to my ability to live for something more than myself.

In the freezing rain in the middle of nowhere, I discovered a kind of wildness I never knew existed, and a new kind of dream for my life that remained totally consistent with the world according to Thoreau when he declared:

> The wildest dreams of wild men, even, are not the less true, though they may not recommend themselves to the sense which is most common among [people] today. . . . One who pressed forward incessantly and never rested from his labors, who grew fast and made infinite demands on life, would always find himself in a new country or wilderness, and surrounded by the raw material of life.

Daring to make my life matter, despite the fact that I had no idea how I would do it, became my new wilderness.

As the weather calmed, I came down the mountain with a different kind of focus and a quiet confidence I'd never experienced before. I felt that I'd uncovered my true answer to that nagging question. What did I want to be? A photographer? Possibly. An optometrist? Could be. A tundra biologist? Maybe. A person who mattered? Yes!

Being and Mattering

All people born into this world represent something new,
something that never existed before, something original and
unique. . . . The foremost task of all people is the actualization
of their unique, unprecedented and never-recurring
potentialities, and not the repetition of something another
person, be it even the greatest, has already achieved.
—MARTIN BUBER

When I talk about daring to matter, about making our lives matter, I'm not saying that each and every one of us doesn't already count. Regardless of who we are, where we're born, the color of our skin, our gender, or our circumstances, every human being is equal in value.

A passage in the Talmud emphasizes the intrinsic value of every created being by stating that God intentionally made each of us a descendent of Adam so that all people would understand that a whole world can come into being through one person. The text relates that because of this, all of us are obligated to consider how profoundly consequential the very fact of our existence and our actions can be, so much so that every individual should say, "The world was created for me."

With this sacred lineage in mind, no one person is better than another, more essential, or more precious. This wondrous admixture of sameness and uniqueness is the essence of our being from the moment we first draw breath until the day we die. Our inestimable worth remains with us throughout the course of our lives simply because we have been created human.

The main difference between being and mattering is whether

we actively participate in the ongoing work of creation by owning our uniqueness—understanding what it truly means to say, "The world was created for me." It means becoming aware that something we and only we possess has been implanted within each and every one of us that will never be replicated in any other human being who lives after we die. It's first connecting with the idea that our individual life could be so important to the life of the world that what we do—or what we don't do—can change everything.

My "dust in the wind" moment was the first time in my life when I awakened to the potential I had to make my time on this earth mean something. It was the first moment in my life that I said, in my own words, "The world was created for me." It was the first time I realized that being is a given, but being a person who matters is a choice.

The Jewish sages of old offered many ways to explain how we can be created the same and yet also distinguish ourselves from one another through action. They say, "In a place where there are no people, strive to be a person." Perhaps the best-known version of this teaching uses the Yiddish word *mensch*, which also just means "person." But when you say someone is a mensch, what you're really saying is that someone is a person who does good.

But how can you tell a regular person from a mensch? As someone who rides the subway pretty much every day, I think of it this way: a person has a seat on a crowded train, and when an elderly man boards, the regular person first looks around to see if someone else is about to give up his seat. A mensch is the person who doesn't look around to see if someone else is about to stand up, but instead is the first one to stand.

The only difference between being and mattering is believing and then acting as if the world depends on you—as if no one else exists who will step up except for you, even though you are well aware that billions of people, not just you, have been endowed with the unique potential to make the world a better place. And there are so many ways, large and small, to matter. You can matter to the people you love, change their lives for the better by giving them your best. You can change the life of a total stranger, even if it's just by expressing an interest, asking them a question about themselves. Mattering isn't about scale. It's a state of being: of being on call to heed a call however and whenever the moment calls for you.

Just imagine a world where everyone dared to matter. Imagine a world where all people acted as if the world's present and future lay in their hands, hinged on their choices, turned on the axis of their dedication and the courage to be as exquisitely consequential as they have been created to be. Imagine how we might feel about ourselves to wake up each morning knowing that today is a day when the world can be different because we are in it. It's a scary notion, having that much responsibility, but it's also an exhilarating one.

In that combination of great responsibility and possibility is where purpose is born, and where the seeds for a meaningful life are planted.

That Is the Question

A prudent question is one-half of wisdom.
—FRANCIS BACON

In January 2018, I read a *New York Times* article about a Yale University class called Psychology and the Good Life that had taken the campus by storm. Just three days into the winter semester, approximately 1,200 students (fully one-fourth of Yale's entire undergraduate population) had enrolled in the course aimed at helping them lead happier, more fulfilling lives.

As I read the piece, two things struck me the most. The first was how distressing it was that college-age students—young people at a stage in life when they have the least amount of responsibility and should theoretically be enjoying the most carefree years of their adult lives—needed a class to learn how to be happy.

The other was a comment offered by Alannah Maynez, a nineteen-year-old freshman enrolled in the class. She said, "In reality, a lot of us are anxious, stressed, unhappy, numb. The fact that a class like this has such large interest speaks to how tired students are of numbing their emotions—both positive and negative—so they can focus on their work, the next step, the next accomplishment."

At nineteen years of age, Ms. Maynez was describing the way that many professionals between the ages of forty and sixty, well into their working lives, including those who feel stuck and are looking to make a career change, reflect their situations back to me. I've heard the same thing from people in their midtwenties who are just starting out, many of whom already are in jobs they hate but where they are doing too well position-wise and salary-wise to quit. What they all share in common is precisely what Professor Laurie Santos, the creator and instructor of Psychology and the Good Life, has seen in students as both a professor and as head of one of Yale's residential colleges, where she encounters students in their day-to-day lives beyond the classroom.

Because Dr. Santos is on the front lines of the total undergraduate experience, she understands the deep disappointment that descends upon students who have seemingly done all the right things and checked all the right boxes to be at a top institution of higher learning. She says those students believed that they would find happiness in "a high grade [or] a prestigious internship," yet have not found happiness in these things at all.

Wanting to take a deeper dive, I decided to read a 2013 Yale Council College Report on Mental Health referenced in the article that revealed that more than 50 percent of Yale undergraduates utilized campus mental health-care services. The report mentioned that although *The Daily Beast* had dubbed Yale "the happiest school in America" in 2011, judging by the students' perspectives detailed in the survey, this was not the case. According to the report, students said the following:

> We work hard to succeed in school, and in this pursuit we incur considerable academic stress. Pressure to succeed applies not only in the realm of academics, but also in our extracurricular activities and social lives.

So these students, some of our best and brightest, at the "happiest school in America" not only aren't happy having attained the achievements that promised them happiness, but also feel pressure to demonstrate that they are happy, even though they are so confused about what happiness is that they flock to a class that promises to show them. A class so incredibly popular that the university has determined that it won't be offered again on campus because a course of that size taught on a regular basis would siphon off too many students from other classes and gobble up a disproportionate amount of human and financial resources.

Houston, we have a problem.

Precisely what the problem is may be impossible to fully understand because happiness is highly subjective. The exact definition of happiness evades even those who study it for a living, including Nobel Prize-winning behavioral economist Daniel Kahneman, who says, "The word 'happiness' is not a useful word anymore because we apply it to too many different things."

Despite the complexities, I think we can agree from a purely experiential standpoint that when the things we dedicate the greatest amount of our time, thought, and energy to leave us feeling empty and spent, something is wrong.

This doesn't mean you have to be in a good mood every day, whistling while you work, sliding down rainbows, and skipping through forests of wildflowers. This doesn't mean you have to live a stress-free existence, particularly when the right kind of stress and pressure can bring out the best in us, challenge us, and keep us from falling into a state of inertia.

It doesn't mean you can never be sad, either; however difficult it may be to say what happiness is, we surely cannot know how or when it presents itself to us, and appreciate its value, if we never know sadness at all. The valleys are essential in helping us recognize the peaks and what inspires them, and in encouraging us to enjoy the good stuff while it's happening (not only in retrospect). Nevertheless, living in a constant state of sadness, numbness (whether to joy or to pain), anxiety, hopelessness, and dissatisfaction is no way to live.

So how do we recalibrate our approach to living such that we can avoid the fractured relationship between achievement and gladness that Dr. Santos is attempting to help her students heal? I believe it starts with learning at a much earlier age in our lives how to answer bigger picture questions other than what we want to do for a living.

Five years ago, my friends, mentalist and educator Gerard Senehi, and his wife, Francesca Rusciani, founded an initiative called the QUESTion Project to encourage young people to do just that. The QUESTion Project empowers high school students to begin exploring the kinds of life questions that are not part of the conventional three Rs (the old school three Rs—reading, writing, and arithmetic; as opposed to the inarguably essential twenty-first-century three Rs—reduce, reuse, recycle).

Students who take QUESTion Project classes commit to a se-mester-long for-credit elective, in which they tackle topics such as choice, purpose, courage, and communal interconnectedness—all aimed at giving young people the tools to see a bigger picture for the lives they dream of leading. The primary goal of these classes is to empower youth to develop the foresight, skills, and awareness to take the steps that will help them make their dream lives—not just their dream jobs—a reality.

QUESTion Project classes are primarily taught in New York area high schools with the highest poverty levels, where the ma-jority of students come from some of the lowest income families in the country. These courses are taught by gifted teachers already teaching other subjects who train on their own time to learn the QUESTion Project curriculum, and who also work with students (called student ambassadors) who, having taken the QUESTion Project class themselves, volunteer to learn how to cofacilitate the courses for their younger peers.

Gerard and Francesca once invited me to experience the QUESTion Project classes firsthand at the Bronx Center for Sci-ence and Mathematics (BCSM). Located in the Morrisania sec-tion of the South Bronx, the poorest congressional district in the United States, BCSM consistently ranks among the top public high schools in New York City and nationwide according to U.S.

News and World Report. In fact, 78 percent of BCSM students are the first in their families ever to go to college. When I met BCSM's principal, Ed Tom, I knew why.

As chronicled in the 2009 documentary film *Whatever It Takes*, Tom began his career as a men's clothing buyer for Saks Fifth Avenue. His goal as far back as business school had been to make enough money to retire at the age of forty. He was on that trajectory, until Tom's girlfriend (now wife) commented that the only time she saw ever saw a smile on his face was when he was preparing lesson plans for the ninth grade Sunday school class he was teaching at his local church. That observation became a personal challenge. Tom decided that he would take a one week vacation from work, and if during that time he could earn a temporary high school teaching license and get a job offer, he would change careers. He did, and he hasn't looked back since.

During my visit to BCSM, I had a chance to speak to QUESTion Project students, talk with their teachers, and spend time with Tom. During our conversation, he shared why he believed the QUESTion Project classes were so important.

"I'm succeeding in preparing my students for college and career, but I also need to help them prepare for life."

When my co-author Jen and I were working on the book and talking about how much of our lives and the quality of our lives are shaped by the questions we are asked to consider as kids, I remembered Principal Tom's words and my day at BCSM. As I shared more about the QUESTion Project, Jen asked if it would be possible for her to see for herself how the program worked. I put her in touch with Gerard and Francesca right away, and they were kind enough to invite her to spend the day seeing their work in action at BCSM and at the Bronx High School for Law and Community Service (BHSLC).

At the end of the day of Jen's visit to both schools, she sat down with Kim Hudson, a fifteen-year veteran teacher at BHSLC who also serves as a QUESTion Project teacher, and two QUESTion Project student ambassadors. Together they had facilitated the day's topic, "Our Most Important Choices."

Sitting around a table in a cramped storage room (the quietest place we could find to chat), Jen asked one of the student facilitators, a young woman in her sophomore year, what question the class had inspired her to ask that she believes will have informed her most important choices in shaping her life ten years from now.

She replied, "I think asking myself every day what my purpose for being is and whether the choices I'm making align with that purpose."

I could never have formulated a question or a response like that at fifteen, and even if I had, I surely wouldn't have been equipped to grapple with it. It most definitely wouldn't have been a topic for discussion around my family's dinner table and never would have come up in conversation with my friends.

I marveled at the demands this high school sophomore already was thinking about making of herself and her life. She wanted to matter, as did every other student both Jen and I had the privilege of listening to and meeting during our visits. This young woman and all of her peers were creating visions for their lives that were about more than what they wanted to do for a living, but about what they wanted to do with their lives. And it was not borne of youthful exuberance or naiveté.

The stories the students shared during Jen's day at the high schools included the deaths of parents, murders of siblings, immigrating to the United States from West Africa without any money or the ability to speak one word of English, and, in the case of one young woman, electing to donate bone marrow to save a family member from cancer. These were not the stories of sheltered kids wearing rose-colored glasses. They were those of young people who have already seen a world that can be indifferent at best and cruel at worst, a world where kids exactly their same ages get up, go to school in the morning, and never make it back home, which is exactly what happened to fourteen high school students at Stoneman Douglas High School in Parkland, Florida, who were shot and killed the day before Jen's QUESTion Project class visits. These kids who Jen met were refusing to be dust in the wind, and who were asking the kinds of questions that would help them, as novelist Hermann Hesse describes, "discover [their] own destiny—not an arbitrary one—and live it out wholly and resolutely within [themselves]."

The QUESTion Project students are daring to matter. And while daring to matter will not inoculate them against pain or tragedy, will not liberate them from having to make important decisions about their education or from having to put food on the table, and will not guarantee happiness, in their daring lies a promise of something better and brighter than acceptance to a top school, a coveted internship, or a great job (even a job they absolutely love) can ever hold.

They are learning something now that I wish I'd known at a much younger age: when you ask the right questions, you get the life that's right for you.

Redefining Achievement

The truth of human being is the love of being alive.
—RABBI ABRAHAM JOSHUA HESCHEL

So here's the point in the story where I tell you that later that night in the Brooks Range, on the heels of my mountaintop moment, while sitting around the campfire with Rob and Mike, I fished the NECO acceptance letter out of my pocket, unfolded it for the umpteenth time, tore it into tiny pieces, and dropped each one into the flames with great ceremony.

But that isn't my story.

At the end of our trip, I emerged from the wilderness, acceptance letter still very much intact, and the first thing I did when I got home was reverse my deferral. Six weeks later, I was in optometry school.

My dust-in-the-wind experience had changed everything and nothing. My desire to one day be able to support a family stayed the same, and the need to lay a solid foundation for making a living hadn't magically disappeared. My aversion to, and strong ambivalence about, becoming an eye doctor hadn't vanished, either. In fact, it remained a near constant throughout my training and for decades to come.

But something about having dared to matter made the question about whether or not to go to optometry school feel not unimportant, but less of a make-or-break proposition. I was less obsessed with my east/west decisions—far less anxious about choosing the wrong direction because I had found my life's true north. As long as I pressed on intently following that star, while I might take some wrong turns and make a bunch of mistakes, I would never be completely lost when it came to what I cared about most.

A few years ago, nearly thirty years since earning my degree, I returned to NECO to speak to the graduating class. I chose to speak less about the field they were entering and focus more on the lives they were about to lead.

I told the graduates how vividly I remembered sitting in their seats, and what the central questions on my mind and on those of my classmates had been. Am I going to find a job? Will I be able to pay off my student loans? The east/west questions. The real and practical ones that not only had to be asked, but also would have to be answered with hard work, perseverance, and action. I assured them that the answer was yes.

While I knew that they wouldn't believe it was true until they'd seen things work out for themselves, I hoped I might be able to get them to shift their focus in that space to set their sights on mattering.

For as much as they may have been frightened of failing at finding the right job, paying off those loans, being successful in whatever way they were determined to be, I told them that the source of their greatest fear shouldn't be of failing at those things, but of succeeding in things in life they may realize (and realize too late) weren't as important as they thought.

So even as they sat there on that day, having solidly decided what they wanted to do, suspended between one achievement on their chosen path and the next, I wanted them to imagine a different kind of achievement by asking the question they'd heard a million times before—what do you want to do?—and suggest an alternative answer: "I want to matter." I wanted to make this peak day in their lives a mountaintop moment for them, too. Because when I dared to matter, I came to life; and from there I set forth on a path to making a difference—a path that has been, and continues to be, one of the great loves of my life.

Making a commitment to making a difference is like any lifelong love. You commit with your whole heart, sign on for a lifetime, and because it's a lifetime commitment that comes with a lifetime of changes, challenges, and surprises, it captures your being in a way that little else can. Even, if not all the more so, when things get hard, when you lose touch with the good and maybe wonder if it might be easier to walk away. Because if the love is big and real and rewarding and exciting, and sometimes a comfort, and sometimes what allows you to explore the territory well beyond your comfort zone, where unexpected treasures lie that without that love would otherwise go unnoticed and their riches unrealized, you have something sacred. It may frustrate in one moment, make you happy the next; it may make you sad, cause you pleasure, cause you pain, be your shifting sands and your solid ground. But ultimately what you've got is something that will engage your whole self for the whole of your existence. It will always need the whole you, always call upon the infinite potential in you, and will never end with any one achievement. This kind of love is its own unceasingly ample reward. And unlike when the mortar board falls to earth, when the bonus hits the bank account, when your name is on the door, when the wish you made when you blew out the birthday candles one year comes true the next, this love won't leave you wondering, "Is that all there is?"

We must and can have dreams of all kinds, including academic and professional ones. Yet if these are our only aspirations, each time we achieve one, something ends; and with it often comes the letdown—the "Is that all there is?" feeling. The buildup to success at one thing places demands on the achievement that it alone, no matter how momentous, can deliver. We ask that the achievement itself meet too many needs, including happiness.

We even imagine that should our wildest dream come true, we'd never need anything more. But even under those circumstances, the happiness it brings (when and if it does actually yield it) fades, and there is a hole where the dream used to be. And if the hole gets filled, it often gets filled with despair.

Yet making our lives matter is a meta-dream that we don't ask to meet our needs, but rather one that reminds us that we are needed, and then demands that we discover how and where, for a lifetime if we let it. As philosopher and theologian Rabbi Abraham Joshua Heschel suggests, happiness can be defined as "the certainty of being needed in the world."

Perhaps, then, the antidote to disappointment and despair, to numbness and anxiety, is not to look only to achievements in our lives to make us happy, but to seek a need in the world that makes us come alive—something that, as Gerard once put it beautifully, "puts who we are at the forefront of what we do, not in the background."

Things Are Looking Up

I learned this, at least, by my experiment: that if one advances confidently in the direction of his dreams, and endeavors to live the life which he has imagined, he will meet with a success unexpected in common hours. . . . If you have built castles in the air, your work need not be lost; that is where they should be. Now put the foundations under them.
—HENRY DAVID THOREAU

So, who are you? As author and theologian Frederick Buechner taught, "When you wake up in the morning, called by God to be a self again, if you want to know who you are, watch your feet. Because where your feet take you, that is who you are."

Dare to make your life matter, dare to serve a need greater than yourself, and you will, over the course of a lifetime, not only find where your feet take you, but you also will find happiness, fulfillment, and meaning as you go. Dare to matter, and your feet will not fail you.

Because mattering, unlike becoming a professional basketball player or a world-class musician or a Nobel Prize–winning physicist, is something every single one of us can do at any age or stage in our lives if we will it, want it, and work hard at it. All daring to matter takes are two beliefs: that the future can be better than the present, and that you have the power to make it so.

From there, choose your mountaintop. Your mountaintop could be your living room, the park, the parking lot of your workplace, your car, or walking down the street. Wherever you choose, simply say, "I will matter!" Say it out loud and say it with conviction, even if it feels a little weird. Say it more than once if you want.

Next begin a dialogue with yourself by reclaiming the question, "What do you want to do?" Make it a practice to ask yourself every day, and answer, "I want to matter."

And the next time you're on a blind date, sitting next to a stranger on an airplane, chatting in a Lyft, or meeting new people at a party, try a little something different when asked, "What do you do?" Instead of answering by saying what you do for a living, say, "I'm trying to matter." Then get ready to explain what you mean, knowing that what you mean is a work in progress while you figure out how you're going to do it. Also prepare yourself for a far more interesting conversation than you might otherwise have had if you'd stuck to the usual script.

This may seem simple (albeit awkward at times), and I'll admit it is the easiest part. However, you can't get to the work of mattering unless you dare to matter first. Daring is where it all begins.

Don't quit your day job, don't stop looking for a job, don't quit school or stop trying to figure out whether you need another degree. Don't stop wrestling with your east/west questions, especially if they have an expiration date on them. Don't ditch other dreams you may have already in progress. Just add another dream to the mix.

Dare to make mattering the big dream for your life. Make it your life's commitment and obligation—to yourself and the world. Then spend your life putting the foundations underneath it. And one day when the gray hairs on your head are too numerous to count, when more years lay behind you than lie ahead, and when the kids you call kids are children no more ask, "So, what did you do?" you can confidently say, "I mattered." Then ask them what they're going to do to matter, too.

Take the Dare

Now it's your turn. Consider this a warm-up as you practice connecting the awareness of how much you matter to the world to actively declaring your intention to activate your uniqueness and put it to work in the world.

This doesn't have to mean making declarations from mountaintops, but doing little things that remind you that your being here is no small thing, but rather is as big as you decide your presence can be.

To jump-start the process, commit yourself to one conscious moment of menschiness every day. Wherever you are, when something or someone you observe moves you to act, and you notice that you and others around you are waiting to see who will jump in to help, don't be the spectator. Don't hesitate. Don't imagine what you could do, but instead just do. Think about how taking action makes you feel. Does it change your outlook? Does it move you from a sense of insignificance to significance, powerlessness to powerful? Build on that momentum. That momentum is the birth of your daring to matter.

As you move forward, also ask yourself what question you believe will inform the most important choices that will shape your life ten years from now. Or twenty or thirty.

I also challenge you to have awkward exchanges with new people by saying, "I'm working on mattering," to the next five people who ask, "What do you do?"

And the next five times you're about to ask someone what they do for a living, I similarly challenge you to replace that question with, "If you could dedicate your life to changing one thing in the world, what would it be?"

Be not the slave of your own past—plunge into the sublime seas, dive deep, and swim far, so you shall come back with new self-respect, with new power, and with an advanced experience that shall explain and overlook the old.

—Ralph Waldo Emerson

2 Meet Your Miracle Halfway

Óyeme con los ojos—Listen to me with your eyes.
—Sor Juana Inés de la Cruz

In a small village about an hour south of Mérida in the Yucatán Peninsula, thousands formed a serpentine line that stretched through the town square and coiled around corners of hidden side streets. Young mothers in intricately embroidered Mayan dresses shifted their babies from hip to hip in a seesaw ballet, while eighty-year-old *campesinos* in white pants and sombreros with patches of straw pulled this way and that sat sturdily on their haunches just as they would at work in their corn and agave fields. Some were barefoot, while others wore leather sandals of their own handiwork. All were prepared to wait for as long as it took in the stubborn blistering heat for free eye exams from a visiting group of American doctors. It was hard to believe that barely twelve hours before I'd landed at the Cancún International Airport with a group of American optometrists and ophthalmologists from Boston's Back Bay and Forest Grove, Oregon. When the plane door popped open from the outside, like a champagne cork finally coaxed from a bottle, and we spilled bleary-eyed onto the tarmac, I had no idea what to expect. I'd been at NECO for three months, and I was one of six students joining a group of seasoned eye doctors on a five-day volunteer medical mission.

I thumbed through my passport during the long wait in line at Mexican immigration. Scavenging through blank page after blank page, I came across a few stamps—vestiges of family vacations long past. Other than a climbing trip to Europe with Rob, I'd never been out of the country on my own before.

At the window, the agent looked at me, at my passport, then at me again. I smiled the way my sisters and I used to when our dad corralled us for a photo with an enthusiastic "Say cheese!" It's the smile that starts out human and slowly begins to resemble a Madame Tussauds wax figure in the eons it takes for Dad to get the lens to blink and deploy the flash that leaves us with polka-dot vision.

After clearing customs, our hosts from El Sistema Nacional para el Desarrollo Integral de la Familia (DIF), a government service agency dedicated to providing social assistance to Mexican families, herded us on a bus for the three-hour journey to our home-away-from-home. These incredible volunteers, almost all women, were with us every step of the way during our time there, making sure we had everything in the way of transportation, food, and lodging; they also functioned as translators and worked crowd control during eye clinic hours. We couldn't have done our job without them.

It was 1984, and Club Med was one of the few conquistadors in what's now known to tourists as the glamorous Riviera Maya. Club Med's vibrant ads in the in-flight magazine promised winter-weary visitors an escape from civilization, where they would live in "villages" with buffets and swim-up bars, and where the local currency was resort-issue beads. It was exactly the kind of place my parents took us on Christmas breaks, after which we'd return with tans and souvenir trinkets to the comfortable, decidedly less exotic Village of Scarsdale.

It was strange to think of people escaping from civilization to what had once been womb and cradle to one of the most advanced civilizations in human history. Mayan mathematicians and astronomers gave us the 365-days-a-year calendar; their scientific calculations yielded accurate predictions of solar eclipses and the precise positions of planets in the firmament. They were master builders, gifted artisans, and agrarian innovators, and the architects of one of the first written languages in the western hemisphere.

Our bus blew past the well-lit sign for the turnoff to Club Med in short order, and we flew down Highway 180 on the first leg of our journey. The welcome warmth had quickly turned hostile. Even with every window down, the bus was a movable greenhouse. I climbed up the aisle using the backs of the seats like rungs on a ladder toward the front of the bus to a cooler filled with bottles of water and Coca-Cola. The driver laughed when a couple of potholes knocked me sideways as I attempted to grab a soda. We chatted a bit, which mostly involved a lot of pantomime to bridge the language gap. All the while I noticed him squinting as he kept his eyes trained on the road.

As we neared the hotel, the highway gave way to much smaller, narrower, and darker dirt roads. I mentioned my concern about the driver's vision to one of the doctors on the team, who talked him into an eye exam upon arrival at our hotel. Much to our horror, she discovered that he had 20/200 vision—legally blind by US standards, and far less than the 20/40 visual acuity required to obtain a driver license in America. Anything our driver should have been able to see from two hundred feet away had to be twenty feet in front of him before he could actually see it.

We learned that our driver had never had his eyes tested, which turned out to be the case for most everyone we examined during our time in the Yucatán. With no local optometrists, only one or two ophthalmologists at least a two-hour drive away, and eye care in general far from a priority, it made sense. We fit him with a pair of the donated glasses we'd brought for the clinic and said a little prayer of thanks that we made it to our destination safe and sound.

Although I was exhausted from the trip, I didn't sleep a wink that night. A combination of nerves and excitement kept me wide-awake. As a green student, my knowledge base was lacking, to say the least. By all accounts I shouldn't have been on the trip, where the student spots were generally reserved for seniors. But when a group of students came to one of my classes a few weeks into the beginning of school and gave a presentation about this mission, getting on the team became my chief objective.

During the presentation they'd explained that an organization called the Volunteer Optometric Services to Humanity (VOSH) was sponsoring the mission, but it was on us to raise all of the money to go. We also were responsible for collecting used eyeglasses.

Thanks to the Boston-area chapters of Lions Clubs International, one of the largest local and global service organizations in the world, the eyeglass donations were easy. In fact, we had so many that it gave me an idea for a plan to sell the excess frames and direct the proceeds to picking up the shortfall on the funds we still needed to make the mission possible.

Once I got the go-ahead to try, I separated the used frames into three types: nonprescription sunglasses (like old-school Ray-Bans), a little worse for the wear but still solidly in possession of the cool factor; vintage frames popular with the hipster set; and gold antique frames that were actually made of real gold. Then a few of my classmates and I popped the lenses out of the vintage frames, gathered up the shades, and fanned out onto T platforms on the Red and Green lines near the Harvard, Boston University, and Boston College campuses. We spread out our wares on blankets and opened up shop. We also went door-to-door on fashionable Newbury Street to every high-end boutique and optical store we could find interested in purchasing the frames from us for resale. We took the gold frames that weren't in good enough condition and sold them to a smelter, who in turn gave us cash for the value of the gold.

The business plan worked. We raised $5,000 and received a matching donation from Newman's Own, thanks to my dad, whose patient, Ursula Hotchner, was married to the cofounder. Since I helped raise almost all of the money for the trip, one of the spots went to me. Yet with the beginning of our work on-site just hours away, the elation I'd felt having secured a place on the mission vanished in a magician's puff of guilt and self-doubt. I lay in bed locked in the awareness that my primary motivation for going was to see the world, not to save it. NECO (not to my surprise, yet still to my chagrin) felt claustrophobic, and I needed an adventure to let some oxygen in—to visit a place I'd never been before, experience new people, a different language and culture. I went out of curiosity, not a calling.

What's more, the no-holds-barred honesty that cagily cloaks itself in the darkness and waits to reveal itself when your head hits the pillow confronted me with a reminder that I'd arrived with a skill set so rudimentary I was certain I'd forget even the little bit I'd learned. It was a surety that my inexperience would lead to failing the people who'd given me the chance to be there, and, even worse, would make me the weak link on our team who'd fail the people who were counting on us.

Although I was in a new place and a strange setting, I was no stranger to this thinking. I'd never been much of a student, and growing up alongside my whip-smart, diligent, overachieving sisters for whom report card time was like Christmas and the Fourth of July rolled into one, had cemented my role in our family as kid least likely to succeed. Regardless of anything I achieved or how old I got, I saw myself as that kid—the dumb one, the one who had to work ten times as hard to do half as well at the things that seemed to come so easily to everyone else in my family.

Yet our first morning, there were so many people to see that I had no time or energy to waste sifting through the contents of old baggage and clutching souvenirs of insecurity and self-doubt. We worked ten-hour days, ate dinner, collapsed at the hotel, then got up and did it all over again. But no matter how hard we worked or how many patients we saw, the line never got smaller. And these patients were nothing like those I watched come in and out of my dad's practice when I drove with him into Manhattan and he'd set me up in the outer office behind a glass partition organizing charts and updating files.

We saw babies missing eyes; children who'd been born with microphthalmia (also known as small eye syndrome), where the eye is so small that it appears nonexistent; people with skin lesions and tumors inside their eyes; older folks with end-stage glaucoma, their eyes white as stones and forced beyond the lids from the extreme pressure of unhealthy fluid built up inside. Never once did one of my father's patients walk through the door with anything even remotely resembling these kinds of problems because none of them had ever gone without eye care or been exposed to the myriad, imminently curable diseases that people in the developing world routinely suffer from due to lack of access to doctors, vitamin deficiency, or the absence of inexpensive pharmaceuticals widely available in Europe and North America.

When we officially opened the clinic, a boy named Raúl was my first patient—not just of the day, but my first patient ever.

Raúl's mother held his hand and helped him up into the exam chair across from mine. A translator gave me a sheet of paper with his basic stats:

> **Gender:** *Male*
> **Age:** *7*
> **Chief Complaint:** *Blind*

Raúl's mother explained that her son had been blind since birth, and his expressionless gaze reflected as much. I leaned in and shined my penlight in his eyes. A healthy eye's exterior is like the silken surface of a still pond, and the boy's eyes, both left and right, were perfectly smooth: no scars, no signs of trauma, disease, or congenital abnormalities.

"*¿Puedes ver a esta luz?*" the translator asked, as I moved the instrument in searchlight fashion from side to side. Not only could the boy perceive the light's presence, but he also discerned which direction it was coming from.

When I waved my hand, he saw me waving. I held up three fingers, and he gave an accurate count. After these simple tests, one thing was certain: Raúl was not blind. I called one of my professors over to take a closer look just to be sure. Five intense minutes of additional examination later, she turned to me and said, "Jordan, this child has -20 diopters of myopia." In layman's terms, Raúl was just about as severely nearsighted as a person can be and still have their vision restored with glasses.

With my assessment confirmed, I raced over to a bunch of crates filled with hundreds of those used glasses my classmates and I had collected back in Boston. I dug through dozens with the strongest prescriptions I could find until finally a pearl of a pair caught my eye—a 90 percent match for Raúl's eyes. I sat back down opposite him, fastened the frames about his ears, and brought the lenses to rest on the bridge of his nose. Instantly his eyes came alive and a smile spread across his face. It was a moment that transformed both of our lives. I gave him his vision, and for the first time he gave me a clear vision of how I could matter.

On our last night of the mission we had a big party back in Cancún to celebrate the culmination of our trip. Together with the volunteers, we prepared a feast where tequila flowed. We danced and listened to the voices and haunting guitar harmonies of the *trovas* Yucatecas with the echoes of the Cuban, Spanish, and Guatemalan cultures that course through Mayan history and linger in its sights and sounds.

As the party wound down, my friends and classmates, Tom and Dory, and I had a brilliant idea. For five days we'd been within driving distance of the ancient Mayan ruins of Chichén Itza— one of the wonders of the world. We didn't know if or when we'd return to this place and decided we'd be crazy to leave without seeing it.

It was late, but we weren't tired at all. We figured if we hopped in a car right away, we'd have more than enough time to visit Chichén Itza and get back to Cancún to catch our 1:00 P.M. flight to the States.

Somehow we managed to rent a car, took off, and were at Chichén Itza by 2:00 A.M. Only one hitch in our inspired plan: it was 2:00 A.M. and the site was closed. The sign on the gate said it wouldn't reopen until 10:00 A.M., but if we waited that long, we were sure to miss our flight home. Our adrenaline supplies totall depleted, we decided it would be best to catch some winks in tl car before we attempted the drive back. When we awakened at 5:00 A.M., we spotted a security guard and with the help of a few pesos talked him into opening the gates.

For the next three hours we wandered first by flashlight and then by the rising sun through three thousand years of history—through Chichén Itza's vast plazas and stepped pyramids, mile-long arcades with elaborate stone columns, sacrificial altars, and the graves of high priests.

We lingered at the Platform of Venus in front of a massive relief depicting Quetzalcoatl, the Aztec god of science—part serpent, part bird, part man—said to have cured the blind. I stood at the Cenote Sagrado, a watering hole and pilgrimage site. On the informational placard set there, my eyes fell upon the words from one of the most sacred Maya texts, named for the prophet Chilam Balam: "I am nothing in myself alone." It reminded me of a saying I learned as a child in Hebrew school: "If I am only for myself, what am I?"

Tom, Dory, and I raced to the top of El Castillo—Chichén Itza's main temple. We made it most of the way up the 365 steps and had a spectacular view of the sun rising over the ancient city once teeming with life and then mysteriously abandoned. While we didn't want to abandon this moment, our flight home beckoned.

On our hurried trip to the airport, we stopped once to gas up and get some water. While Tom was inside paying, a big flat-bed truck pulled up alongside us carrying what had to be at least seventy-five pigs on the long, wooden flats in the back (probably on their way to market). I walked over to get a better look and one pig stared straight back at me. It was like looking into the eyes of another person; its gaze felt human. (It suddenly made sense to me why we studied the anatomy of pigs' eyes in school.)

After five days of playing charades, if I wanted to communicate directly with our patients without a translator, I'd become more aware than ever that every pair of eyes has something to say, and there are some things that only the eyes can make heard. I thought about how one look, whether from a person who knows you best or from a complete stranger, can say everything without one word.

What You See Is What You Get

If you believe it can be broken, then know it can also be fixed.
—REB NACHMAN OF BRATSLAV

As a kid, I loved puzzles and attacked them with relish. It usually didn't take more than a sitting for me to piece one together.

I remember that when I was around the same age as Raúl, I got a little cocky and asked my mom if she could find me a puzzle that was more challenging. A few days later she handed me a box, smiled, and wished me luck.

The puzzle was called Little Red Riding Hood's Hood. The box boasted, "506 Pieces—Every One Different," but from the picture each piece looked exactly the same. The finished product was a solid red circle. Without any hard edges or the slightest variation in hue, it was a puzzler's nightmare, but I was as excited as ever to dive in. I removed the top, turned the box over, and spilled the pieces onto the table.

For months I spent every spare moment I had on that puzzle. Just sorting through the pieces to find some way to organize them and cobble together the outside border, which with any other puzzle usually was the easiest part, took weeks. It was several weeks more before I was able to work my way into the center. Finally, through a crazy amount of trial and error, I was looking down at a perfect crimson sphere matching the picture on the box that had been staring up at me for months.

That's why when my mom got a phone call from my teacher, Mrs. Solomon, asking her to come in to discuss some concerns she had about my schoolwork, it was a surprise. Mrs. Solomon told my mom that my grades hadn't been particularly good, I wasn't completing classroom assignments, and I was having—as she described it to my mom—"self-control issues." She suggested that I might have attention deficit hyperactivity disorder (ADHD).

Mrs. Solomon's observation wasn't entirely without merit. Although I could spend tons of time at home focusing on difficult puzzles from chaos to completion, many of my issues in school were consistent with ADHD symptoms: I had trouble paying attention, following instructions, and sitting still. I often failed to follow directions on worksheets or the chalkboard, and I frequently gave up on homework assignments before I'd finished. If I had reading to do, I constantly lost my place on the page and found myself returning to the same sentence or paragraph over and over; and if you asked me to talk about what I'd read, I struggled to remember.

Unfortunately as time marched on, even with extra help and tutors, my academic challenges only got worse. Looking back, I spent a lot of my childhood well into my teenage years becoming increasingly depressed, although that wasn't something I would have known to call it at the time. And in my Jewish, yet oddly stereotypically WASP-y family that believed feelings were best left unacknowledged and unarticulated, even without labeling it as depression it still wasn't something I would have shown or shared at home.

Although I knew on some level that I was smart, nothing I did—not my grades or exam scores—demonstrated any native intelligence. And if you've ever had a tough time in school, you know that when you repeatedly try to do better and still don't get results, it's only a matter of time before you lose interest in studying and stop caring about school.

It's also only a matter a time before you start feeling bad about yourself, ashamed, and you settle in to your worst thoughts about yourself. Mine were that I was dumb, nothing special, certainly nothing remarkable, and since no one expected a whole lot out of me, I expected even less of myself. I spent most of my time feeling angry, started hanging out with kids who definitely weren't bringing out my best (in large part because I didn't think there was a best hiding out in me). By my teen years I was doing a fair amount of drinking and smoking pot—going from numb to number. And even though I had plenty of friends, it didn't stop me from feeling increasingly isolated and alone. Somewhere along the way, I lost my sense of wonder and the color drained from my life.

While I can't remember precisely when things went from color to black and white, I do remember the first time I was aware of seeing the world in living color. (As is the case with anything of value, the only way we know we've lost something is to have had it in the first place.)

It was the summer after Mrs. Solomon first alerted my parents to my academic troubles. We were on a family vacation in Switzerland, where we spent the whole month of July touring around from place to place and getting to know the country. On one of our excursions, we took the train from a little village in the Bernese Alps called Grindelwald through the Jungfrau, a popular ski destination where it's not unusual to see snowfall in summertime.

Our hotel was near the top of a mountain accessible only by train. Ninety-nine percent of the ride was through a long tunnel that had been carved deep in the rocks. When we left the train station at the base, it was a cloudy day. By the time we arrived at the hotel just twenty minutes later, resurfacing high above the valley floor, we were smack in the middle of a whiteout blizzard.

Once checked in, the snow continued to blanket the land in seemingly endless amounts. It was so mesmerizing that I sat in front of the window watching the snow fall for hours. When it came time for bed, I crawled beneath the down comforter, nestled my head in the puffy pillows, and instantly fell asleep.

My parents woke us up at first light, rushed us to the window, and threw open the curtains. While we slept the blizzard had stopped and the sky had turned a deep navy that stood in stark contrast to the pure white of the snow covering every square inch of ground. In the distance I spotted three mountaineers, specks on an endless glacier that filled a deep valley surrounded by mountains that looked like giant marshmallows. I remember thinking that if there was a heaven, it probably looked exactly like this, and those lucky climbers were smack in the middle of it.

My fascination with the mountains began then, and it was the mountains that saved me in high school when I was still flailing academically as the pressure mounted with SATs and college applications on the horizon.

In the fall of my junior year, Rob and Mike (of Brooks Range fame) invited me and our other friend, Bruce, to go climbing in the Shawangunk Mountains, also known as the Gunks, in upstate New York. The Gunks, a long band of cliffs up to three hundred feet high, are a popular destination for climbers from the New York area and across the country.

As Boy Scouts, Rob and Mike's love of the outdoors grew throughout their childhood and into their teen years as they attained Eagle Scout status. In the process they'd taken a National Outdoor Leadership School (NOLS) course where they learned technical rock climbing and wanted to share the experience with me and Bruce.

With the guys' help and encouragement, I clung to rocks by little hand and footholds, many less than half an inch wide, as we scaled the cliffs, my mind dancing between thrill and fear. Gone were anger and frustration and feelings of inadequacy that regularly occupied my being. Instead I felt competent and connected, lifted by the camaraderie of my climbing buddies, and reunited with the sense of wonder I'd known as a boy. Whereas I'd mostly become accustomed to focusing on my limitations, in nature I felt like anything was possible.

In school I was always afraid—afraid of not knowing the answer, afraid of looking stupid, afraid of the next report card. But the fear I felt on the mountain was different: it was exhilarating. It didn't make me anxious about what was coming, but instead made me excited about what I'd yet to experience and how much there was to encounter.

Until that first VOSH mission to Mexico, I hadn't felt that plugged into the possible anywhere else other than in the mountains. In fact, that first night after we opened the clinic in the Yucatán and every night of the trip thereafter, although I lay awake in bed, it wasn't out of insecurity and imposter syndrome. Instead, what kept me from sleep was a constant buzz, like I'd drunk ten cups of coffee. My brain was crowded with thoughts from the work of the day and filled with anticipation of the work that lay ahead; my heart pumped pure adrenaline instead of blood. I thought of our patients, their lives, and the stories they shared. And before sheer exhaustion invariably bested me, no matter how many people we'd treated on any given day, the last patient I always thought of was my first patient—Raúl.

Over the course of those five transformative days, we saw two thousand patients. And even though Raúl's exam was but one of those two thousand and had lasted just minutes from start to finish, and although I never saw him and his mother again, my eyes had recognized something deeply familiar in Raúl's.

Like many blind children in the Yucatán, and in fact in many countries throughout the developing world, before we realized that Raúl needed nothing more than a pair of glasses to see, he had spent his entire young life labeled "a mouth without hands." That's what people in communities like Raúl's call the blind. A human being reduced to a list of needs—food, clothing, shelter—with no perceived ability to contribute in the present or future to the family's financial well-being.

Age-old Mayan superstitions and strong beliefs rooted in astrology, including the notion that blindness is a punishment for the sins of one's ancestors or is an everlasting, even contagious, curse of bad luck for having been born under the wrong sign, still come into play in the Yucatecos' day-to-day existence. This is despite the fact that four centuries have elapsed since the Spanish conquered the Yucatec kingdoms. In societies such as these that rely on subsistence farming and crafts, no family can afford the possibility that others will cease buying their crops or wares to avoid "catching" blindness. As a result, and out of an overall sense of shame, people often hide blind family members for fear that they will be ostracized by their communities and rejected in their religious congregations. Because of these taboos, even with the availability of some social or governmental aid for the blind, families generally won't risk seeking it.

And the blind themselves, the "mouths without hands" viewed year after year as a drain on family resources, see themselves as punishments and not people and often fall into deep depressions, forced as they are into lives of isolation, bullying, humiliation (both inside and outside the home), and inattention to their physical and emotional health. And even when parents elect to send their blind children to school (as opposed to those who do not because they see no good reason to do so), teachers often completely ignore them in the classroom, treating them as a waste of time and school resources.

As a result, it's said that some blind Yucatecos die young, not from poverty or disease, but due to purposelessness, depression, and neglect. (Several studies have also explored whether the severely visually impaired are at greater risk of suicide in the developing world.)

Fortunately, nothing about Raúl indicated that he'd fallen victim to this kind of stigmatization or maltreatment, and perhaps even if his mother hadn't brought him to the clinic and everyone had continued assuming that Raúl was blind, he never would have experienced the worst of what a blind person can face in his culture.

Nevertheless, I had to wonder how Raúl thought of himself, his abilities, his possibilities. How much of his self-worth would have been dictated by others' well-intentioned low expectations at best, and complete social irrelevance at worst? How might he have come to expect precious little of himself, to count himself out of so much of life, and to accept his place on the sidelines?

I wondered these things because while Raúl and I could not have been more different, what we did have in common was a vision problem that left undetected could have significantly changed the course of our lives.

After years of failed tests, below average grades, and feeling like a puzzle no one could solve, in my sophomore year of high school a colleague of my dad's who knew about my troubles in school asked if I had ever been evaluated for an eye condition still relatively obscure today called convergence insufficiency.

Convergence insufficiency is the inability of the eyes to focus simultaneously for a sustained period of time—kind of like looking through a faulty pair of binoculars all day every day. When you have convergence insufficiency, your eyes have to work extra hard to perform basic tasks, and they fatigue quickly. In young people these diminished capacities eventually lead to frustration, poor self-esteem, and avoiding schoolwork entirely, which is why parents and educators sometimes assume that kids with convergence insufficiency have ADHD or label some students as lazy.

The problem is compounded by the fact that convergence insufficiency almost always goes undetected in regular eye exams. As the son of an optometrist who most definitely never wanted for regular vision screenings, I was a rather absurd case in point. Because our eyes' ability to focus in a normal, coordinated fashion technically has nothing to do with how well we can see, even a person with 20/20 vision, like me (I've never needed glasses) can suffer from convergence insufficiency without anyone, including her optometrist, being the wiser.

When Dr. Kavner diagnosed the problem, I was relieved not only to finally understand why school had been so hard, but also relieved to know that convergence insufficiency was 100 percent treatable. Every Tuesday for a year after my first office visit, I rode the train into Manhattan for corrective vision therapy with Dr. Kavner. (I remember often sitting near Chuck Scarborough, a local newscaster, who used to take the same train into the city to anchor the evening news. The presence of a hometown celebrity added a little cachet to the trips.) During these sessions I basically learned how to read all over again using exercises intended to strengthen the medial rectus muscles in my eyes—the muscles that help our eyes converge so we can see things clearly up close. We also worked on my saccadic eye movements, which are also essential to reading and following words on a page. And I did exercises at home every day to retrain my eyes to focus.

With the daily exercises and weekly therapy, studying came much more easily and my grades went up dramatically. I stopped showing up late to classes and handed my work in on time. It was a whole different world. But I still saw myself the same exact way as I had before Dr. Kavner pinpointed the trouble with my vision.

By my senior year, my GPA was more than solid and every bit of empirical evidence told me that I was a reasonably intelligent person who could do well in school if he worked hard (maybe still not punching in the same academic weight class as my sisters, but no slouch, either). Yet I didn't think of myself as a student, per se—not "book smart." I also remained disdainful of academics in general; I hung on to the whole "school is a waste of time" thing, a detached stance I'd had most of childhood and young adulthood to compensate for my embarrassing grades. I was so invested in that image of myself that I recall selecting the words of naturalist David Polis for my high school yearbook quote: "Must we always teach our children with books? Let them look at the mountains and the stars up above. Let them look at the beauty of the waters and the trees and flowers on earth. They will then begin to think, and to think is the beginning of a real education."

These lines appeared beneath my senior class picture, and that's how I pictured myself: the adventurer, the outdoorsman. And it was true to who I was, but it wasn't my entire truth. Learning that there might be more to me, more for me, was almost more frightening than the panic I used to feel when the teacher would call on me in class or ask me to read out loud. In a strange way, I longed for the safety and certainty of knowing what I couldn't do.

Dream a Bigger Dream

Rabbi Yonatan said: A person is only shown in his dream the thoughts of his heart when he was awake.
—Babylonian Talmud, Tractate Berachot 55b

While neither my challenges nor my circumstances ever compared to Raúl's or to those who live in places like his in the developing world, you don't have to be blind or live in a faraway land with significantly limited resources or perilous social taboos to be at risk of being relegated—or relegating ourselves—to lives that are a speck of what they could be. Human hardships are by no means created equal, and far too many people in every part of the globe, including our own, are born into valleys of challenges so deep, they end up spending the majority of their lives just trying to climb out before the journey to the heart of themselves and the excavation of their potential can really begin. But every one of us is vulnerable to succumbing to the labels we've been given by others; and each of us is imminently capable of buying into the stories we've told ourselves that rob us of our true promise and potential, choosing self-imposed limitations forged out of habit and fear instead. It's the ultimate inside job.

However, if we do choose to stay shackled to stale internal narratives or settle into existences that are safe, yet mere shadows of the promise we possess, we aren't the only ones who lose. I told you that daring to matter begins with two beliefs: that the future can be better than the present, and that you have the power to make it so. But getting down to the actual business of mattering requires that you move from believing you have that power to behaving like you do. Because the future can only be better than the present if you push yourself to build a better life for yourself tomorrow than you're living today. Until and unless you liberate yourself from the narrow straits of self-perceptions well past their sell-by date, you will shortchange the world. When you give away your power to transform your own life, your power to transform the world, no matter how much you genuinely yearn to do so, is diminished.

Every year when my family gathers around the table to celebrate the Passover holiday, I'm reminded of that inextricable link between claiming our own transformative power and achieving collective social transformation. During Passover we both recall and are called to re-experience the Israelites' journey from slavery in Egypt to life as free people. As we tell the story, it is far more nuanced than the CliffsNotes style summary we sometimes humorously use to describe many of our holidays: they tried to kill us, we survived, let's eat. But the Passover narrative is not a simple one of good guys and bad guys and overnight transformation from slavery to freedom. Much of inherited Jewish wisdom on this seminal moment in the Jewish imagination encourages us to think about the internalized emotional, psychological, and spiritual impact that four hundred years of slavery (the length of time tradition suggests we remained in Egyptian bondage) has on the individual and the community.

For instance, an eighteenth-century Hasidic rebbe, Rabbi Hanoch of Aleksander, taught, "The real exile of [the Israelites] in Egypt was that they had learned to endure it."

While being physically enslaved is not a choice any human being makes, seeing ourselves as slaves on the inside, allowing our hearts and minds to be held captive along with our bodies, is. To refuse to relinquish the power we possess within, even as we are stripped of our power by those who traffic in gross injustice, often is what not only preserves our humanity and allows us to survive even the worst possible conditions, but also inspires us to reject the notion that we are less than. It strengthens our resolve to demand more than the meager portion dealt us by some other hands, and to keep our lives and our futures in our own. By refusing to give away our power and potential, we are constantly preparing our hearts to seize opportunities to break through when they present themselves, to allow these minor miracles into our lives.

When I talk of claiming our transformative power, I use the word *miracle* on purpose because I believe that miracles are more than jaw-dropping supernatural events—more than never-before-seen phenomena that we look upon and marvel at, that we observe in stunned silence. I believe that miracles are the beginning of a story, not the end. They are the gateway to something bigger than anything we could have imagined—extraordinary occurrences that don't exist for their own sake, but that are meant to point you in the direction of something just as extraordinary: a greater goal, a hidden strength, an undreamed dream. Miracles are a gateway that remain largely incomplete if we don't step through.

The great miracle of Passover, for instance, is known to us all whether through the Bible or popular culture (thank you, Charlton Heston and DreamWorks): the parting of the Red Sea. Yet the sages of old added their own Hollywood-style flourishes to suggest that the parting of the sea was also just a beginning. As Pharaoh and his men drew ever closer and the Israelites were stopped dead in their tracks by a raging, impassable sea, it appears to be the end of their mad dash to freedom. Then, in the chaos and panic, the waters part, leaving a wide path of dry land and a way out of slavery. But rather than move forward, the Israelites look askance at the parted sea. They begin discussing whether to keep going, whether they can trust the path, or whether they might be swallowed up by the waters the second they try to walk in. Even Moses hesitates. No one wants to be the first to go in. It is here that the sages introduce a man named Nachshon ben Amina-dav, the head of the Tribe of Judah, who pushes through, moving without hesitation toward the edge, and walks right into the sea without looking back. Once the others see that the path is steady, they all follow.

Had Nachshon not stepped forward, that miracle might have amounted to little more than a magic trick. Had he not chosen to seize the opportunity to cross over to something new, Pharaoh and his men would have overtaken the Israelites and kept them enslaved perhaps for another four hundred years, maybe more. And the story might have been told to their children by a still enslaved Israelite people about a strange occurrence at the sea once upon a time.

Yet because the Israelites took Nachshon's lead and did walk forward onto the dry land before them, this story has been told from generation to generation by a free people. It is a story not just about being freed from slavery, but about having been freed for a purpose: to protect the strangers in their midst because they once were strangers in a strange land, and to build a world where no one person is lord over another—where all people are equal and all people are free.

I believe that the experience I had in the Yucatán when I met Raúl, a moment that changed me and everything that happened after that moment in my life, was a miracle—not of biblical parting of the sea proportions, but of the sort where the universe pointed to a future I would never have envisioned on my own and I had to choose whether to move forward or stand still.

Survival Is Not Enough

Security is mostly a superstition. It does not exist in nature, nor do the children of men as a whole experience it. Avoiding danger is no safer in the long run than outright exposure. Life is either a daring adventure, or nothing.
—HELEN KELLER

When I returned to Boston after the VOSH mission, the first winter chill made me long for the Yucatán's stubborn heat. I sat in my apartment and analyzed the data we had collected from the trip. The numbers told me something I'd suspected while we were in Mexico: Out of the two thousand patients we had seen, 1,400 of them were exactly like Raúl. All they needed was a simple pair of glasses to have a greater chance at a better future—to get an education, stay safe on the road, to work, to put food on the table and a roof over their heads. Not medicine, not surgery. Just glasses. I wondered how many more people existed elsewhere, not only in Mexico, who needed the same. This was a puzzle I wanted to piece together.

But if I was to do this, I also really had to decide whether I wanted to keep seeing myself as the kid least likely to succeed, always a few steps behind, afraid of getting laughed at for having the wrong answer, or was I really serious about making my life matter? Because you can't stand still and move forward at the same time.

This struggle we face between known and unknown, between breaking even and breaking through, and the voice inside us that keeps us from moving forward even when life has parted the sea and is waving us through is our lizard brain. It's the voice that bestselling author and marketing guru Seth Godin suggests we must quiet if we want to unstick ourselves and get somewhere truly new.

The lizard brain, or amygdala, is the oldest part of our brain ... t controls, among other things, fear. And while the amygdala ... reat at telling us when to be afraid, it isn't quite as good at tell-... us when not to be. If it's different, it's terrifying. End of story.

Godin explains that when we take on something that coaxes us out of our comfort zone, even if we claim that's exactly what we want, the lizard brain is the voice inside our head screaming a long list of perfectly valid reasons why not to do it. The lizard brain sabotages and harangues, turning your biggest disappointments, greatest blunders, and worst projected outcomes into sleek montages that play endlessly in your mind.

Go ahead. Pick any one of the greatest hits from your personal hit parade of reasons you've ever come up with to keep you from taking on a challenge: I'm not smart enough. People will laugh at me. I'm too old. I'm too young. Any of these ring a bell? When was the last time you heard your lizard brain? When was the last time you listened?

Of course the lizard brain exists for a reason. Sometimes we do need a "danger, Will Robinson!" to keep from doing something stupid that could put our lives or the lives of others in jeopardy. Yet as Godin reminds us, "The lizard brain is . . . fighting for your survival. But, of course, survival and success are not the same thing."

The lizard brain is alive and well within us all the time. And had I listened to it, had I put the data I collected on the VOSH trip away in a drawer and never looked at it or thought about it again, then there's no doubt that the moment when I put the glasses on Raúl's face would have been little more than a passing rush of satisfaction and later a cool story to tell.

If I'd listened to my lizard brain, I don't know whether I would have followed through with my dare to matter or whether that, too, would have fallen by the wayside, dismissed as the silly idealism and grandiosity of youth. I certainly never would have continued doing VOSH missions throughout optometry school or pursued the many experiences that took me far from home and well beyond the comfortable confines of myself that ultimately led to my founding VisionSpring. All this took a matter of decades, but that one moment changed my entire life because I saw it and claimed it as the miracle it was. From there, it was as if I had no choice. Even when I wasn't sure I could do it, I was absolutely sure I had to try. Reverend Victoria Safford describes it best: "Once you have glimpsed the world as it might be, as it ought to be, as it's going to be (however that vision appears to you), it is impossible to live compliant and complacent anymore in the world as it is."

On some fundamental level, the world is a reflection of the way we see ourselves. If we can see our potential, then we can see the world's. If we demand more of ourselves, then we'll demand more from the world. If we have the courage to take on our limitations, real or perceived, and the will to exile ourselves from inertia, then we'll move the world beyond the bounds of the status quo. It all boils down to this: we can live in a world that merely survives, that coughs and sputters along, that neither completely self-destructs nor totally soars. Or we can build a world that succeeds, where people are free to flourish, and where what is broken can be healed. But we can't participate in that wondrous human enterprise if we're too scared to heal what's broken in ourselves and too frightened of our own power to be extraordinary enough to step forward when the seas part.

Take the Dare

As you begin to add how you'll matter to your dare to matter, I encourage you to open your heart so you can recognize and meet your own miracles that beckon to you and invite you to step forward into unknown territory with untold possibilities.

This doesn't only include moments that may come in the future. A revelatory moment may have already occurred in your life that held your miracle, and it isn't too late to claim it. With that in mind, I encourage you to reflect on a time in your life that was so profound that it stopped you in your tracks or maybe even moved you to tears. As you reflect on that moment, did you believe that it would change your life, and, if so, has it? If it did move you to change something in your own life, how did you change? If it came and went, what stopped you from taking the moment and turning it into action that gave it life long after the moment passed?

As you reflect on that same moment, think about whether it might have hinted at something you could do to make a difference. Hold it in your mind's eye now and view it through the lens of these questions: What was it about this moment that distinguished it from others? If I mine this moment for meaning, could the impact it had on me reveal something inside of me that I can use to make a difference?

You also might want to think of a time when your lizard brain talked you out of taking bold steps. Did it succeed? Why? How did things turn out as a result? If you had it to do over again, would you talk back and push back and do things differently? If so, consider preparing for your next bold move by imagining what you will tell your lizard brain if it attempts to stand between you and forward progress again. As you strategize, think not only about how it will affect you if you allow your lizard brain to prevail, but also how it will affect others as you begin consciously trying to make a difference in the world. What do they stand to lose if you fail to put your lizard brain in its place?

As you strategize, it also might be helpful to examine what old stories about yourself you're still telling yourself that are out of step with who you are now. How are they holding you back? How can you help yourself fully embrace your new life story? If you need help doing this, who can you seek out to assist you?

Shmuel said to Rav Yehuda, his beloved student: Keen scholar, grab and eat, grab and drink, as the world from which we are departing is like a wedding feast, whose joy is only temporary, and one who does not take pleasure in it now will not be able to do so in the future.

—BABYLONIAN TALMUD, ERUVIN 54A

3 How Much Land Do You Need?

Before I go I really want to be here.
—CHRISTINE PRICE

In a *Forbes* magazine article by career coach Kathy Caprino called the "Top 5 Regrets of Mid-Career Professionals," regret number one was, "I wish I hadn't listened to other people about what I should study and pursue." Number two was, "I wish I hadn't worked so hard and missed out on so much."

When Caprino pressed people to be more specific, their answers ran the gamut from missing out on time with spouses and children to missing the opportunity to have children itself; from regretting they didn't take more time to smell the roses and savor life's pleasures to forgoing opportunities to expand their intellectual and spiritual horizons.

And then there were finances. Nipping at the heels of two, regret number three was, "I wish I hadn't let myself become so trapped about money."

Regarding the money trap, Caprino reports that some people, fearful of earning less than what they had been earning, elected to stay in positions that significantly diminished their quality of life. Others feared they were not earning enough and had gone after jobs guaranteed to bring home the paycheck they thought they needed, all the while knowing full well that they would dread how they had to spend their days in order to bring home the desired amount.

While listed as separate line items, these regrets are wholly interconnected. When we make choices about the remunerative work we do, we also make choices—albeit mostly unconsciously—about what we value and are willing to sacrifice in other facets of our lives. We forget that time is finite, resources are finite, and the amount of energy we have, particularly as we grow older, also is finite. We cannot be everywhere at once or do everything at once. Something's always got to give, and whether we want to or not, if we don't observe the way we prioritize wants and needs, life forces us to give up on some of those things we say we cherish the most because at a certain point we're so overloaded and overwhelmed that we have nothing left to give.

This type of focused observation, of being accountable to ourselves for how we allocate our time, how and on whom we expend the greatest amount of effort, and whether we are living in line with what we say we want and believe we value, begins with a story that is yours and yours alone to create. Your central narrative.

Caprino touches on this when she says, "I've learned that our relationship with money goes very deep, and stems directly from our wealth programming and what we learned from childhood about it. The negative, fear-based stories we tell ourselves about money keep playing out in our lives, despite all our best efforts. If we don't get to the bottom of our own money story, and heal it, we remain trapped in unhappy, desperate situations for the entirety of our lives."

Money is never all about money. Although it boils down to dollars and cents in one sense, the bottom line is the numbers only work if at the same time you're always working to align what's in your pocket with what's in your guiding vision for your life. Because although we know that you can't take it with you, that money doesn't buy happiness, that the best things in life are free, and that on our deathbed we won't say, "I wish I had spent more time at the office," these stock phrases and aphorisms, while true, aren't the whole truth.

Money matters. It may not guarantee joy and well-being, but it sure can make life a lot easier. And while we can think of lots of things—our closest relationships chief among them—upon which it is impossible to put a price tag, this doesn't mean that material things have no value or add nothing to our overall enjoyment of life. And as to work, although more time at the office may not be anyone's deathbed wish, in our efforts to make ends meet, we may not always have a choice; it's just a necessity.

I'm sure if we all were to gather in a room and write down how we'd like to fill our days and then compare notes, most of us would have similar answers regardless of age and stage of life. In fact, many studies exist that demonstrate how aligned most people are in what they value and wish to pursue over the course of their lifetime. For example, a few years ago, the IBM Institute for Business Value conducted a cross-generational study of about two thousand employees from six different industries in twelve countries. The study revealed that the millennial, generation X, and baby boomer professionals they surveyed were strongly aligned in their chief values and aspirations. According to the study, 22 percent of the millennials, 20 percent of the gen X-ers, and 24 percent of the baby boomers expressed a desire to help solve social issues (including the environment). Slightly more than 20 percent of each cohort also identified doing work they are passionate about as important. The same percentage across generational lines—approximately 17 percent—also expressed the desire to achieve financial security.

Similarly Bruce Pfau, a partner at KPMG (one of the biggest global business advisory companies in the world), recently wrote a *Harvard Business Review* article called, "What Do Millennials Really Want at Work? The Same Thing the Rest of Us Do." In it he shared that in the last fifteen years since he and his colleague, Ira Kay, published findings from their extensive research on what people generally want from work, the same four factors still figure into their decisions—regardless of gender, age, or race—when weighing the possible opportunities. One of them is "the desire to draw a sense of meaning and purpose from what they do every day."

A recent *New York Times* piece exploring how human beings can cultivate a sense of well-being revealed the same thing. Highlighting the findings of Dr. Martin E.P. Seligman, Director of the University of Pennsylvania Positive Psychology Center, the article notes that years of research on the subject have shown that a critical component of well-being (which Seligman is careful to differentiate from our old and enigmatic friend happiness, in that as he defines it, happiness is a feeling that comes and goes and not a state of being) is "experiencing a sense of contentment in the knowledge that your life is flourishing and has meaning beyond your own pleasure."

The truth of the matter is, though, that while we may hunger for meaning and impact, and while that hunger may be absolutely genuine, unless we think consciously about how to make it happen, unless we approach building a life of meaning and impact like a job, we remain far more likely to look back with regret upon all we wished we'd done. The better option is to put ourselves in a position to call the shots and stomp out those regrets before they have a chance to multiply.

As we design the lives we say we want to lead, we have no choice but to face the financial bottom line. However, if we are methodical about fashioning the blueprint, our other priorities and most cherished values needn't fall to the bottom of the list. And when one of those priorities is making your life matter in the bigger picture of the life of the world, you don't have to be a billionaire philanthropist or make a pile of money early on in life so that you can retire in order to be the kind of change agent you dream of being.

If I Had a Billion Dollars

I am God's creature and my fellow is God's creature. My work is in the town and his work is in the country. I rise early for my work and he rises early for his work. Just as he does not presume to do my work, so do I not presume to do his work. Will you say that I know a lot and he knows a little so I am better than he? We have been taught: One who brings a large sacrifice and one who brings a meager sacrifice have equal merit, provided they direct their heart to heaven.
—Babylonian Talmud, Tractate Berachot 17a

While we know intellectually and hear constantly that you don't have to be rich to make a difference, somewhere along the line money, and more to the point, having lots of it, got tangled up with the power to create real change.

In centuries past, we once called people with a certain net worth "rich." In the twenty-first century we might now refer to them as the "Merely Rich," so as to distinguish them from a new category of bionic net worth individuals called the "Mega Rich" or "Super Rich." With the Super Rich's super riches growing each year, we also have seen an unprecedented kind of charitable giving power as evidenced by the creation of the Bill and Melinda Gates Foundation, which took off in 2000 with a multibillion dollar runway for effecting social change. The wide-reaching work of the Gates Foundation and the way that Bill and Melinda Gates have inspired others, like billionaire businessman Warren Buffett, to allocate their considerable financial resources to changing the world are tremendous.

But being a Gates or a Buffett isn't the only way to make a difference, and since the world's Super Rich population is but a sliver of the total global population, the world urgently needs the rest of us to jump in and dedicate some part of our lives to making change just as much, if not more. It's not an either/or, to be sure. We just have to work on the both/and.

Philanthropic dollars on a massive scale play a significant role in the work of healing social problems in numbers too staggering to count. But when being Bill gets tangled up in our collective unconscious with being a significant builder of a better world, too many of us relegate ourselves to the sidelines of social change.

I was reminded of just how tightly this line of thinking has lassoed our individual and collective worldviews while reading an opinion piece by *New York Times* columnist David Brooks called "Giving Away Your Billion."

In the op-ed, Brooks explained that he'd spent some time looking at Giving Pledge letters. Giving Pledge letters are written by high net worth families and individuals (many of whom have remarkable rags to riches stories) who have joined the Giving Pledge Campaign. Founded by Warren Buffett and Bill and Melinda Gates in 2010, the billionaires who join the effort pledge to give more than half of their wealth to philanthropic efforts while they are alive. In addition to writing these letters and making public declarations of their commitment to dedicating their more than considerable resources to social change while they are alive, Giving Pledge Campaign members also come together periodically to discuss the causes they support and to learn about those of others, creating a community and sense of cohesiveness in their giving missions.

Brooks shared that reading these Giving Pledge letters had inspired him to think about how he envisioned making a difference, and then he outlined a plan both practical and moving for how he would do it. Yet the last line of this elegant and passionate articulation of how he envisioned mattering read, "Now all I need is a hedge fund to get started."

We've all been there. We care about the world. We care about people. And even if we don't yet have a clear vision of how to translate our care into action, we do have a sense of what a better world looks like to us. And even if we, like Brooks, have constructed a thoughtful, detailed approach to making it so, our soaring vision almost reflexively lands with a thud on the heap of all those other things we would do if we had a billion dollars.

While it's true that to achieve something on the scale of what Brooks described would take significant financial resources, vast coffers of money are neither the precursor to nor a guarantee of success in any effort to make a difference. Yet waiting for 2,208 people—the billionaires census as recorded on *Forbes* magazine's 2018 list—to make all the difference in the world most definitely is a guaranteed way to see none of our visions for positive change become reality, billionaires included.

We cannot and will not all be billionaires, but we can all be resourceful, resolute, creative, motivated, and kind. Fueled by enthusiasm and elbow grease, we all can identify a change that we want to bring about in the world. We can take a careful look around to identify efforts already in progress that may be addressing our "if I had a billion dollars" issues. If no efforts of the kind yet exist, we all can convene groups of like-minded folks with different skill sets to come at the challenge that speaks to us together.

This sense that it is possible, if not necessary, to begin your impact work in the here-and-now is at the core of the Giving Pledge Campaign. And although it exists for an infinitesimally small percentage of the human population, encouraging those with virtually limitless assets to invest in change today, the Giving Pledge Campaign's message is universal.

By committing to give away more than half, if not all, of their total net worth in their lifetime, Giving Pledge Campaign participants are actively thinking about how much they really need, about what constitutes enough, about how money figures into their lives and the lives of their families, and how it connects to their core values.

In this sense, what inspires me about the Super Rich Giving Pledge Campaign members isn't what I could do if I had billions of dollars. What inspires me instead is the way that they, having made the decision to dare to matter in the here and now, are making the conscious effort to define how much money is enough money for them, so that they can do something with their time on this earth on a scale far greater than themselves or their net worth. This is a process from which we all can benefit, and one in which anyone can participate simply by choosing to do so. No membership required.

Value Added

Try not to become a man of success but rather try to become a man of value. He is considered successful in our day who gets more out of life than he puts in. But a man of value will give more than he receives.
—Albert Einstein

Net worth aside, we're all programmed to think about how much we can get as opposed to thinking about how much we need. Even those of us who may say we are content with what we have and need nothing more could find that if more were to fall into our laps we wouldn't exactly complain.

It's a little like going to a big-box store: intellectually you know that you don't need a restaurant kitchen–size tub of mayonnaise (especially if, let's say, everyone else in your household but you hates mayo), but the price is so good that you just have to buy it anyway. When more is throwing itself at you, it's exceedingly difficult to resist.

Nowhere is the potential peril of letting how much we can get override how much we need depicted more brilliantly than in Leo Tolstoy's short story, "How Much Land Does a Man Need?"

The story opens with a woman of means who is married to a businessman in the big city coming to visit her sister, a country mouse and the younger of the two, who is married to a farmer.

The two sisters sit down to tea, and before the steam ceases rising from their cups, the older sister begins bragging about her wealthy husband and their lush life. To save face, the younger sister glorifies her own circumstances by disparaging those of her sister, engaging in her own humble brag by extolling the virtues of subsistence, including asserting that she and her husband have a far more, as we would call it now, stress-free existence due to how little they have and how little they want. "Though a peasant's life is not a fat one, it is a long one," the younger sister opines. "We shall never grow rich, but we shall always have enough to eat."

As the sisters continue arguing the merits of their respective lots, the younger sister's husband, Pahom, eavesdrops, and as he reflects on his wife's statements also feels that he leads a life superior to that of his sister- and brother-in-law.

Pahom goes on with his daily routine filled with the certitude that the life he has chosen for himself is the superior choice for all. Until one day, a neighbor lady with a desirable parcel of land decides to offer it up for sale, and Pahom looks on while the other villagers flock to gobble up the rarely available extra acreage. The more Pahom sees the others investing in a share, the more he feels that he is missing out and should enter the fray himself. And so it is that he manages through some complicated dealings to secure forty acres.

Pahom has no more than finished putting in his first wheat crop when he hears a rumor that people are selling their land and leaving his village. He wonders what they know that he doesn't, and begins torturing himself with the idea that he needs more land in a new place, better land (or land he imagines is better), and so he pulls up stakes and does as the others.

Yet no matter where Pahom goes and how much land he acquires, he no longer can survey his fields and think of anything other than how much more land he might be able to get.

Finally, a rumor leads Pahom to a seller who makes him an offer he can't refuse. The owners of the latest piece of land upon which Pahom has set his sights tell him that for 1,000 rubles (the land parcel equivalent of the giant tub of mayonnaise), they will sell him as much of their land as he can walk in one day, as long as he returns by sunset to the place where he first set out at dawn. And that they will continue to do the same each day at the same price for as many days as Pahom wishes.

Pahom cannot believe his good fortune and sets out the next morning ready to return at nightfall in possession of more acreage than he ever dreamed. He gets going at a good clip, but as the day wears on and the heat grows more intense, his energy starts to wane. He's already amassed quite a bit, yet each time he considers calling it a day and making his way back to the starting point, he simply cannot resist the urge to capture another magic parcel.

Before Pahom knows it, the sun is approaching the horizon and he is farther from the starting point than he realized. He tries to find that second gear, gutting it out all the way, pushing himself harder and harder until finally he sees the point. He lunges forward and manages to slide into home plate just in the nick of time, face in the dirt, but safe.

When Pahom's servant comes to help lift Pahom off the ground, he finds that Pahom is dead. The servant then begins to dig a grave and give Pahom a proper burial. And as the story winds to a close, of his tragic hero Tolstoy writes, "Six feet from his head to his heels was all he needed."

While not a feel-good story, the central questions that Tolstoy poses to every reader are the same questions we must ask ourselves if one of our life's goals is to make our lives matter:

> What is your ideal material sweet spot?
> How much money do you want?
> How much money do you need?
> What does it or will it take for you to reach your financial goal?
> What are you willing to sacrifice to reach it?
> Are you willing to have less if having less affords you the time to dedicate yourself to something bigger than you and your loved ones?

Somewhere between six feet from your head to your heels and everything under the sun is your portion, but only you can decide how much is enough.

As Caprino wrote in her article about regrets, "To live a happy, rewarding life on your own terms, it's critical to start saying 'yes' to your authentic beliefs and values." Of course, we have to clarify what those authentic beliefs and values are, and get just as good at saying yes to them as we are at saying no to those things that keep us from the life we say we want to lead.

Yet knowing how to say no and mean it hinges on knowing how you conceive of what it means to have enough, and then asking yourself whether what you're doing will make you sufficiently financially successful by your own calculus and also make you the person of value you wish to be.

The Good Dishes

Repellent attire, unkempt hair, slovenly beard, open scorn
of silver dishes, a couch on the bare earth, and any other
perverted forms of self-display, are to be avoided. Do not wear

too fine, nor yet too frowzy, a toga. One needs no silver plate,
encrusted and embossed in solid gold; but we should not believe
the lack of silver and gold to be proof of the simple life. . . .
If [men] visit us at home, they should admire us, rather than
our household appointments. He is a great man who uses
earthenware dishes as if they were silver; but he is equally great
who uses silver as if it were earthenware. It is the sign of an
unstable mind not to be able to endure riches.
—SENECA

Suresh was a forty-seven-year-old husband, father, and tailor living in Andhra Pradesh, a state on the southeastern coast of India, one of the great hubs of sari production for centuries. Like his father, grandfather, and great-grandfather before him, Suresh was part of that grand tradition, known throughout his village and in neighboring towns for fashioning the finest saris around.

Like any sari maker, Suresh's process began with designing the fabric for each garment, dyeing every single thread to match a customer's chosen pattern. And because a distinct feature of a traditional sari in Andhra Pradesh is a highly detailed border, getting the fabric just right the first time without wasting time or material required an even higher degree of precision in the dyeing phase. All this before the painstaking weaving and sewing work could begin.

As is the case most everywhere in the developing world, although up-close work like Suresh's demands great skill and attention to detail, it yields low wages. This makes accuracy, efficiency, and peak productivity all the more crucial to make ends meet.

For some time, Suresh's productivity had been in rapid decline. He had gone from producing fifteen saris a month to ten. The significant decrease in yield, as well as the accompanying difficulty Suresh was having maintaining the quality and beauty of the saris he was known for, were threatening his livelihood. Word had already spread that Suresh's work wasn't what it used to be, and loyal customers were taking their business elsewhere. Suresh was but a few weeks away from closing his doors for good.

In addition to the specter of shuttering the business, the mounting financial burden wasn't only affecting Suresh's balance sheet, but was also driving a wedge between him and his wife and creating palpable tension at home that he could no longer hide from his children. The combination had eroded Suresh's self-esteem, dignity, and pride as an artisan; as a man capable of supporting his family; and as a highly regarded businessman in the community where he'd grown up and lived his entire adult life.

When things were at their most dire, a thirty-two-year-old woman named Aarti wandered into Suresh's shop. She wasn't there for a sari, but as a VisionSpring Vision Entrepreneur (VE). A wife and mother, Aarti was the sole breadwinner in her household who had participated in one of VisionSpring's three-day training programs. She was equipped with what we called a "business in a bag"—a backpack with the necessary supplies to go out into her community, conduct basic eye exams, and sell affordable nonprescription reading glasses if the screening revealed that a person could benefit from them.

Like all VEs, Aarti earned a commission for every pair of glasses she sold, and she happened to be particularly talented at it. Within three months of becoming a VE, Aarti became Vision-Spring's number one salesperson in her region.

With her excellent people skills and business savvy, Aarti succeeded in getting an initially reluctant Suresh, who had never had his vision tested in his life, to agree to have an eye screening on the spot. Within minutes Aarti concluded that Suresh didn't have any complicated issues with his sight, but he did need a simple pair of readers to correct his vision.

With that, Suresh selected a pair of readers he liked and purchased them from Aarti for 170 rupees—about $2.50. In short order Suresh not only rebuilt his business, but also increased his earnings by 20 percent more than he'd been making before he first noticed his decline in productivity and in the quality of his work. He also rebuilt his reputation, restored harmony in his home, and felt like himself again.

In the meantime, Aarti was earning $100 a month and was doing so well that she began developing a strategy to expand her territory and increase sales. This included investing some of her profits in a motorcycle and hiring her husband to drive her to conduct vision screenings in towns she otherwise wouldn't have been able to reach on foot.

On a visit to India, I had the good fortune to meet Aarti, who graciously invited me to her home. She took me on a tour, showing me some of the home improvements she had made with her earnings: her previously thatched roof had been replaced with a metal one, and in the kitchen sat a refrigerator where a few months before there had been no refrigerator at all. More than anything, though, Aarti's greatest source of pride was that her children were now enrolled in a local private school and not out working to help her and her husband put food on the table.

It was during that visit, as Aarti spoke animatedly about the people she met each day as a VE and about how much she enjoyed those encounters, that I asked, "Do you have a favorite patient?"

Aarti replied, "Suresh."

These two people, who might otherwise never have met, had become bonded not through money but through the things that mattered to them most in life that they wanted to make money for—their vision for what a good life was for themselves and their family: getting an education, putting food on the table, sustaining a family legacy, providing a safe and comfortable home. They had their money stories straight, knew the role money occupied in their lives, and understood how it fit into a much bigger picture for them, the people they loved, and their community.

Meeting Aarti taught me a great deal about money and about my own relationship with it. In many ways, we're taught that money is dirty. We're not supposed to talk about it. We're supposed to wash our hands after touching it. But in my work with VisionSpring I've come to see something pure when money changes hands.

When I'm in India at one of VisionSpring's eye camps, and I see a locally trained community member who is comfortably supporting three generations under her roof, with the equivalent of an additional fifty dollars a month she makes as a VE, touch hands for the briefest moment with a local farmer who has reached into his own pocket to pay for a brand-new pair of high quality glasses he has tried on and chosen just like anyone I see in my practice, it's more than just a sale to me. When the man tells me that with those glasses he'll be able to spot an insect that, if left undetected, can devastate an entire crop on the land his family has been farming for generations; that he'll once again read to his grandchildren; and that when he catches a look at himself in the mirror he feels young again, I see more than the frames on his face—I see the life in his eyes.

Ella Gudwin, VisionSpring's president, once told me a similar story of meeting an older Indian man with many working years still ahead of him who pointed to his VisionSpring glasses and said, "Without these, I would be retired."

Just as we don't have to be billionaires to make our lives matter, we don't have to take vows of poverty, either. We don't need to reject money or be disdainful of material things. In fact, deriving pleasure from the things that money can buy needn't be disconnected from the rest of our values and life's goals. As the great Greek philosopher Aristotle observed, in order for us to pursue a life of greater purpose we must also be "sufficiently equipped with external goods not for some chance period but throughout a complete life."

The Color of Money

Life is precious, so I should give everything away except that I live in the world. And in the world, I actually have needs and wants, and I value my needs and wants.
—JONATHAN SAFRAN FOER

During a family snowshoeing trip to Maine over New Year's, I was speaking with my nephew, Ben, who was a senior in high school at the time. As we worked our way through the snow, Ben mentioned that he was thinking about taking a gap year to work before starting college. His hope was to get a better grasp on what kind of learning would best suit his career goals once the tuition meter started running.

Ben was drawn to engineering and economics, and he also has always been a socially minded person. And because if he took the gap year he wanted to use the time wisely, he wasn't sure whether he should get his feet wet with an internship at a hedge fund or somewhere in the social entrepreneurial space. He asked me what I thought he should do.

Given his stated goals and interests, I told Ben that he should think of the different ways he could go about earning money as if each were a separate color—kind of like having a small box of crayons and pulling out of the box whichever one you want to write with. I suggested that he spend his gap year dedicating three months to working in an environment that lets him see what it's like to write his life story with each color.

The color green, I offered, was making money solely for the purpose of creating wealth in the tradition of Nobel Prize–winning economist Milton Friedman, who said, "There is one and only one social responsibility of business—to use its resources and engage in activities designed to increase its profits so long as it stays within the rules of the game."

Orange, as I described it to Ben, signified making money partially for the purposes of wealth creation in a business model that also exists to create a better world, like B Corporation (B Corp) companies. B Corp companies, like Etsy, Kickstarter, and Patagonia, are for-profit businesses that make public pledges not only to have market impact, but also to effect social change.

Purple was the color I designated for social enterprises like VisionSpring, that exist to address a social issue. Social enterprises make money utilizing traditional business principles and practices in order to create a revenue stream like any other traditional business. However, they often run at a loss and require philanthropic subsidies to balance the books.

And yellow signified the traditional nonprofit philanthropic approach—an approach also aimed at addressing a social need, but one that relies wholly on grants and charitable contributions to do its work to effect change.

When I finished describing the colors of making money, Ben and I walked in silence for a while, just the sound of our snow-shoes shushing and crunching through the patches of ice studded with twigs and the fresh powder not yet marked by the presence of footprints, animal or human.

After a while, Ben said sheepishly, "Uncle Jordy, to be perfectly honest, I'm really only interested in spending my gap year writing in green and orange." I told Ben he had no reason to be concerned or embarrassed about sharing his answer honestly. As a matter of fact, I told him that honesty was key. As he processed the possibilities I suggested he consider, asking his mind to produce what he believed were the most compelling options and instantly getting the answer, it was crucial for Ben to listen. His mind had spoken in an entirely unvarnished way. His silence wasn't him waiting to hear it; it was being afraid to share out loud what he knew to be true to him.

Listening to your mind speak about money, not being afraid to hear it, and listening without judgment is an absolute must if one of your core objectives is to dedicate some part of your life to making a difference in the life of the world around you. Having the courage to say how you feel about money out loud and without shame will allow you to engage in the ongoing, compli-cated, yet completely worthwhile exercise of keeping money and the pursuit of money from eclipsing the other core components of your life's vision.

You can't be afraid to write the story of your life in the Cray-ola rainbow of your choosing, however you determine what each color is and what it represents. And before you can truly commit one part of your story being about making your life matter, you have to know what color you want to write with the most. Ask yourself:

Do I want to make a lot of money so that I can have complete freedom from financial burdens and demands?

Do I want to take care of myself and my own now and give thought to those beyond my immediate circle of friends and loved ones later?

Do I want to serve others without the burden of supporting anyone other than myself?

Do I want to do well enough to take care of myself and my own, enjoy some of the good things in life up to a point, and still have room to serve others beyond myself and my immediate circle of friends and loved ones?

There cannot be any judgment on your answers. You must get real with yourself about where money factors into your vision, your life—the only one you get—without overcomplicating it with what you think you should think or feel about money. You must begin with this kind of transparency if you want to begin paving your path to making a difference, and you want to start now.

If you ask, and most importantly, if you listen, chances are you will have more clarity about your priorities than you think you do; and you already have the power to draft your life's story rather than to allow the random unfolding of life to dictate your story to you.

Get Your Story Straight

Rabbi Elai said: In three matters a person's true character is ascertained; in his cup, i.e., his behavior when he drinks; in his pocket, i.e., his conduct in his financial dealings with other people; and in his anger. And some say: A person also reveals his real nature in his laughter.
—Babylonian Talmud, Tractate Eruvin 65b

Once you've been honest with yourself about money, what it means to you, how much you want, and how much you need, you can begin to write your story of how you're going to make your life matter and make ends meet. This will be your central narrative.

A central narrative is a framing story for your existence. When you set out to develop it, you start out with a list of things you desire the most out of life. Start by asking yourself what you care about most:

Is it love and a long-term relationship?
Is it family?
Is it travel and adventure?
Is it making a difference in the life of the world?
Is it making enough money to live well—however you define well?

Further, ask yourself:

What makes me see my cup half full?
When do I feel the best and most confident that I have spent my money well?
What, and who, make me laugh out loud and smile without effort, even when I don't think I have a laugh or a smile inside me?

Surely your answers to these questions will change as you change, and as your life changes along with you. And while it's impossible to live a regret-free life, creating a list of what we care about most, with which we can measure the quality of our days, can make our list of regrets far shorter and less painful. As long as we still have runway ahead of us, by allocating time to reflect honestly on how we want to live, we'll spend much less of the precious time we have in our lives focusing on regrets.

For the most part, my central narrative has stayed the same since my early twenties. I have always wanted to do well enough to provide for me and my own, but up to a point. I want to take care of the fundamentals as I define them: the ability to send my kids to good schools; provide my wife and children with a safe and comfortable home; make sure that my family has good health care; and, time and budget permitting, be able to take special vacations together every once in a while.

And then, of course, serving a driving purpose in life that extends well beyond me and my own also has been a vital part of my central narrative. I want to leave the world better than it was when I entered it, and exit the world knowing I spent my time doing something that hopefully will transcend my lifetime.

Once you've created a rough draft, your central narrative will look great on paper, yet be far more complicated when it's put to the test in the daily round, with every aspect competing for its own share of real estate, never following a straight line and never playing out precisely the way you thought it would when it was neat and tidy and clear in your head.

Nevertheless, if you want to get certain things out of life, and if one of those things is that you want to change the world, a central narrative will help you do it.

I backed into constructing my central narrative in 1991. I was thirty years old and had begun discussions with my father's partner, Dr. Barry Farkas, about becoming a partner in the practice myself. At the outset, Barry and I'd had a frank conversation about what he needed from me if I was to become a partner. His expectation was that I dedicate five days a week to the practice—nothing surprising or unreasonable, but not a contribution I could commit to, given what I hoped to also be able to achieve in my commitment to mattering.

Going into that first conversation, I was already aware that Barry and my dad had expected that in my first few years out of optometry school I would get this idea of changing the world as a co-vocation out of my system and let it become an avocation. And while both men were outwardly always supportive of me, I knew in sidebar conversations between the two of them they had to be saying, "What's Jordan doing? He's still marching to the beat of his own drummer, which is all well and good, but didn't you think by now he'd have grown out of this phase?"

It also was tough sitting across from Barry, especially as my father's son. My dad was the first one in his family to go to college and the first ever to become a doctor. He'd never "reflected" upon his existence and the meaning of his life—this was all woo-woo stuff that didn't make sense to an old-school guy. He went to school, graduated, got married, had a family, went to work, and put everything he had into the practice. In that way, he and Barry were completely aligned. They'd both killed themselves to get where they were.

So I got why Barry was more than a little bit cautious about taking on a partner who he couldn't be sure he could count on, let alone understand. And knowing that Barry had a healthy amount of skepticism about the wisdom of putting me in a partnership role, before our next meeting I decided to sit down and create a worksheet for how I would schedule my time in the office to uphold my responsibilities to the practice, while also apportioning time to my work outside the practice, and how our profit sharing could reflect my dedication to both.

I wanted to show Barry in firm facts and figures how exactly I would put in the time he needed me to spend in the office seeing patients, how I could also spend time working on management and administrative matters, and how I would take less vacation time than would otherwise be given a partner in order for me to pull my full weight and have time away from the practice to work at making a difference.

I prefaced the nuts-and-bolts details with a clarification of some of the values that were the driving force for the proposal. As I got deeper into the project, I found myself trying to help Barry understand why earning a living and having an impact on the lives of others beyond the practice were integral to my being. As I did, the one-page worksheet became a two-page letter to Barry. The hard numbers were still there (they migrated to page two), but the first page was a clarification of what I held most dear, and my commitment to spending my life honoring through deeds what at that point were only words.

I talked about the place of money in my life, about one day

wanting to give my wife and family (I hadn't yet met Erica) the same gifts that my parents had given me. I shared how important having financial security was to me, and that my entrepreneurial spirit made me want to partner with Barry in the business and be in a position to shape the practice and continue helping it grow. After the fact, I realized that in writing a letter to Barry I'd also written a letter to myself.

The figures and profit-sharing percentages that I'd originally set out to present to Barry to convince him to invite me into the practice as a full partner worked out as I'd hoped. To this day the practice remains the financial rock that has enabled me and Erica, whom I met two months after writing the letter, to invest in our home in New York City, provide our children with private school educations, and now college tuition for our eldest son, Bryce.

In addition, the practice has been the solid financial footing that has afforded me every opportunity I have had over the course of my career to engage in a wide variety of experiences (from pursuing advanced degrees to working in the public health arena, and more), all of which, and without any of which, I could never have built VisionSpring or continue growing it now.

More than a partnership pitch, the letter also became the first draft of the central narrative for my life, one that I still keep on hand and read when I find myself getting lost in the chaos of living.

First Things First

Who can be called pious? One who does not make what's primary secondary, and what's secondary primary.
—RABBI MENACHEM MENDEL OF KOTZK

Before you get down to facts and figures, nuts and bolts, budgets and spreadsheets, first take some time to get your own central narrative in order. Start by writing yourself a letter. You don't have to do it all in one sitting. It may come to you in pieces spanning weeks. However long it takes is as long as you need because this will guide you for a long time to come.

As you write, define what you believe constitutes "enough." Ask yourself what doing well means to you. What does financial success look like to you? What does a life of value look like to you? Are those two things connected? Are they in conflict?

Also as you write, keep a log of how you spend your time, and at the end of a week ask yourself if the way you've spent your time is aligned with your emerging central narrative. If you notice that you're not allocating as much time as you would like to paving your path to mattering, can you restructure your schedule as is to create that time? If so, what will you have to sacrifice, and are you willing to make that sacrifice?

Focusing on sacrifice is key because dedicating real time to the business of mattering, structuring your life in such a way that your efforts to make a difference don't fall to the bottom of the pile, and guarding that time diligently the same way you already do your remunerative work—as if you've no choice but to show up—is one of the only ways you will have the impact you want to have.

You have to know your limitations and have a strong sense of what kind of discomfort you can reasonably tolerate.

For instance, I know that although I have an entrepreneurial spirit, I am not a person who can deal with a great deal of financial insecurity. I always like having a plan and a budget, and I am allergic to taking on debt.

However, for the sake of doing my mattering work, I have learned to live with a certain degree of financial insecurity because that is the trade-off for having consciously chosen to reduce my earning power by not dedicating myself solely to private practice. What this means is that Erica and I rarely have much of a financial cushion, and that is scary. It also guarantees that in a little over a decade, we, like so many Americans, will take our place among the more than 20 percent of Americans sixty-five and older who are working well past what used to be considered retirement age.

But when I look at my central narrative and what matters most, I know I can't make a difference in the way I want to without trading some of the peace of mind I'd like to have, all things being equal.

What are you willing to trade to know at the end of your life that you spent some portion of your life making your life matter? Whatever your answer, arming yourself first with your own truths about money, and placing that truth within a realistic context of all else that you truly care about, will be the difference between regretting how much you could have done to change the world and reflecting on what you actually did to change it.

The Do Good Discount

The citizen must have high ideals, and yet he must be able to achieve them in practical fashion.
—THEODORE ROOSEVELT

With your truths in order, you can begin to create the calculations that make sense for your life to allow you to focus on remunerative work and on working to make a difference. I call this the Do Good Discount.

The Do Good Discount is the practical foundation for how I structure my life so that I can pay the bills and build a better world without being a multimillionaire (or billionaire) and without living on instant ramen in a yurt.

Once you've made your own determinations about how much is enough, it's time for you to put the numbers where your aspirations are: how much money do you need to live, and how much money can you leave on the table in exchange for the time you need to make a difference with your life?

When I started out, my answer essentially came to me earning 70 percent of what I would otherwise have earned dedicating all my time to the practice. I would cram all my obligations to the practice into three days a week in the office, reserving two days a week for doing good.

For the first seven years of VisionSpring's life, for instance, I worked most nights starting from 9:00 P.M. until 1:00 A.M. Although I formally allocated two full workdays to VisionSpring, I spent at least another fifteen to twenty hours of work each week over that to get it off the ground. I made that a priority because I knew VisionSpring wouldn't grow without that level of output on my part.

Yet as is the case for all of us, some of the things we are willing and able to do when we're younger or have fewer responsibilities change over time. Whereas in the past I was willing to work fourteen- to sixteen-hour days, the reality is that I'm older and have less energy now, so I've had to come up with a different structure that still allows me to maintain my practice and Vision-Spring work but that is consistent with who I am in this stage of my life.

Currently, I work two twelve-hour days and one seven-hour day at my practice, and I also work on management and administrative tasks from home. My VisionSpring days are also lengthy and highly structured because making a difference has to be treated as a job just like any other.

Guarding your making-a-difference time is one of the key elements in making the Do Good Discount work. Because the work most of us will do to do good is either totally nonremunerative or far less remunerative than the work that keeps us doing well financially, and anything that doesn't come with a paycheck always is the most vulnerable to quickly falling by the wayside, you need to be realistic in your commitments. It is because I designed a model that was realistic for me that I have been able to guard those two days a week designated for doing good consistently ever since I finished optometry school, even though much in my life has changed since then.

With this in mind, be conservative as you crunch your own numbers, and consider allocating less time to making a difference at first. You can always add more, but this way you won't put yourself in the position where you're borrowing more and more of your making-a-difference time in order to play catch-up in times when finances are tight. This will set you up for success to dedicate a consistent part of your life to making a difference over time, which is far better than doing everything all at once (which is unsustainable) or doing nothing at all (which is what will happen if your calculations are great in theory but clash with reality).

My Do Good Discount and yours won't be the same, and they shouldn't be. If you want making a difference to be an integral part of your life, all you have to do is:

1. Create a realistic structure that works for you.
2. Start by allocating a specific amount of time per week that you'll dedicate to making your difference.
3. Be prepared to try multiple approaches before you find a structure that fits your life. Don't be afraid to experiment to make your Do Good Discount work for you and the people who count on you. The point isn't to get it right the first time, but to build something that changes with you while you continue to work for change.
4. If you find that your Do Good Discount isn't working financially, rather than asking yourself how much of your make-a-difference time you can reallocate to your remunerative work, first ask yourself how you can potentially reduce some aspect of your cost of living in order to retain some, if not all, of the time you want to dedicate to doing good. If you can't find a way to be more profitable and creative with your professional time allotment as is or come up with a way to reduce your monthly nut before resorting to using your difference time to make up the monetary difference, accept that this is a reality of the here-and-now and adjust accordingly.
5. Once you've begun allocating a consistent amount of your time to making a difference, even if you have to dial that time back significantly, don't stop completely. If you have an hour, use the hour, and protect the hour. It has value, you have value, and the difference you can make over the arc of your lifetime by integrating making a difference into your life is invaluable.

Take the Dare

Just as your Do Good Discount won't be the same as mine, your timeline for designing it will be totally unique to you. So please bear in mind that while I've listed the steps you can take in chronological order, it doesn't mean that these have to come in precisely that order for you. In fact, you may go back and forth between steps or skip to the one that makes more sense for you right now.

The one place I will encourage you to start, though, is with your central narrative. It is something you should do now because everything else will flow from it. It also is something you can do now because it requires no concrete changes or sacrifices yet, so it is a low stakes action that will guide you in the present, as well as in the future when the stakes are higher.

On this one step I challenge you not to wait. In fact, before you start the next chapter, open up a file on your computer or take out a piece of paper and a pen and write only the words, "Dear Me." Add a little bit more each day, even if it's just two or three sentences, but also give yourself a deadline to finish. You can always edit and revise, but give yourself a deadline for revisions, too. Once your central narrative is complete, pick a next step and keep going from there, also setting deadlines for each step's completion so that you don't lose momentum.

I can lay down for mankind a rule, in short compass, for our duties in human relationships: all that you behold, that which comprises both the divine and the human, is one—we are the parts of one great body. Nature produced us related to one another, since she begot us from the same source and to the same end. She engendered in us mutual love and made us prone to friendships. She established fairness and justice; according to her ruling, it is more wretched to commit than to suffer injury. Through her orders, let our hands be ready to assist. Let this verse be in your heart and on your lips: "I am human; and nothing human do I believe alien to me." Let us possess things in common; for birth is ours in common. Our relations with one another are like a stone arch, which would collapse if the stones did not mutually support each other, and which is upheld in this very way.

—SENECA

4 Be Spontaneous

Douglas Steere, a Quaker teacher, says that the ancient question, "Who am I?" inevitably leads to a deeper one, "Whose am I?" . . . To ask "Whose am I?" is to extend the question far beyond the little self-absorbed self, and wonder, How wide is the circle of your caring, the circumference of humanity, the bright ring of life, the holy perimeter, within which you live and move?
—REVEREND VICTORIA SAFFORD

In my work and travels I've been blessed to meet people who have come into my life for just a flash, but who have become part of me forever. María Lopez is one of them.

María arrived at a pop-up vision screening site in rural Mexico where I was volunteering while still in optometry school. Clutching a well-worn Bible to her chest, she had one simple request. María was in her sixties, and she said it had been a decade since she'd last seen a page of Scripture with her own eyes. All she wanted, she explained, was to be able to open her Bible and read it again.

When I examined her and put a pair of glasses on her face, sure enough the first thing she did was open her Bible. She reconnected with the words on the page in an instant, as if she were picking up a conversation with a long lost friend exactly where she'd left off. Then she dropped to the ground, hugged me around my knees, and cried.

As we were setting up the next morning, I saw María standing at the head of the long line of patients. She spotted me and determinedly made her way through the early morning chaos, a small army of people trailing behind her. As she drew closer, I grew anxious. I was sure that I'd screwed up somehow and that she'd returned with reinforcements.

Finally we were standing face to face.

"Doctor," María said, "perhaps to you these are just a pair of glasses, but to me, you've given me back my God." Then she reached into a wicker basket, grabbed two handfuls of chickens by the feet, and offered them to me as a gift. Seeing that I had no experience handling live chickens, a quick-thinking volunteer took them from María and graciously accepted them on my behalf.

It wasn't the chickens, though, that had left me silent and more than a little stunned. It was a combination of relief and embarrassment: relief because I hadn't sent María home with the wrong pair of glasses. And also because the crowd she'd brought with her was hardly an angry mob, but rather members of María's church congregation whom she'd convinced to have their vision tested, too.

The embarrassment stemmed from María calling me doctor, even though I still had years to go before earning the title. I also felt kind of stupid, as I'd done little to deserve the depth and poignancy of her gratitude. If María had been one of my New York patients or if she'd lived most anywhere else in North America, she wouldn't have needed me or any other doctor to get the exact same pair of glasses that had made all the difference for her in the blink of an eye.

María was one of the billions of people in the world who have an eye condition called presbyopia, which sounds like something complicated but in fact is the easiest vision problem to diagnose. Presbyopia is a decline in up-close vision, and is something that everyone over the age of forty eventually experiences (even those who have 20/20 vision). I use eye charts and instruments to detect signs of presbyopia in my patients, but it doesn't take an office visit to determine whether your up-close vision is diminished.

For instance, you can just as easily open your morning paper at breakfast or read a news alert on your phone. Are you struggling to read the smaller print? Or grab a sewing kit. Does it take you longer than it should to pull a piece of thread through the eye of a needle? If your answer to either or both is yes, but you can still see things at a distance well, your up-close vision is the problem and presbyopia is the only diagnosis.

To correct the problem all you need are glasses in the +1.00 to +3.00 prescription range—the kind we call readers. If María were one of your neighbors, she would have been able to walk into any number of nearby drugstores and try on an array of readers in multiple styles and strengths until she found a pair that worked best for her, plunk down five or ten dollars at the register, and walk out the door. Instead it took ten years and a team of volunteers who'd randomly shown up in María's village to create a life-altering moment out of something that should have been matter-of-fact.

In fact, it's because of patients like María in particular that I founded VisionSpring. Beginning in school when I started my volunteer work, no matter where I was in the developing world, consistently 70 percent of the people who came for vision screenings who needed glasses only needed readers, just like María's. But María's story and its relationship to VisionSpring is just one of the reasons why she has remained part of my life to this day.

Oftentimes when I'm in synagogue, I think of María, her hands curled around her Bible, as I gaze up at five words etched in the burnished wood of the Holy Ark that houses the Torah scrolls: "Know Before Whom You Stand."

This adjuration comes from a Talmudic tale in which a rabbi named Eliezer has fallen ill, and his students have gathered around him as he prepares to die.

"Rabbi," they say, "teach us the paths of life, some guidelines by which to live."

Rabbi Eliezer replies, "Safeguard the honor of your fellow human being . . . and when you pray, know before Whom you stand."

Jewish prayer requires that ten people, called a "minyan" in Hebrew, be present for the public recitation of certain prayers, such as the Kaddish prayer, said by those who are in mourning or on the anniversary of a loved one's death. The public reading of the Torah scroll, during which time special prayers are offered for the sick, also requires the presence of a minyan. Without a quorum of ten, none of these public observances can occur.

While I'm certain Rabbi Eliezer was referring to God when he told his students to know before whom they stood, when I pray I often think of the people standing next to me and around me. I think of people living their lives thousands of miles away. People I've met and people I will never know who are going about their daily lives, carrying their happiness and their heartache, their worries, their wonder, and their fear, just like all of us.

I think about how somewhere, someone is holding a newborn and welcoming her into the world, while someone else is standing at a graveside unable to pull himself away from the place where he has laid a loved one to rest. Somewhere, someone is getting a clean bill of health from her doctor, while another person is hearing the doctor say, "We're going to need a few more tests."

My synagogue community is a large one, and I by no means know every person in our congregation. Yet when people in my community rise to recite the Kaddish prayer or our rabbi reads the names of those who are in the hospital before the prayer for healing, although most of them are complete strangers to me, for a moment they aren't strangers. As part of the minyan, I'm called to hold these people in my prayers as if they were my own family or friends.

As part of a minyan, I'm reminded that we live in the presence of people's deepest pain, their greatest hopes, triumphs, dreams, and disappointments every day—not just in church or synagogue, in a temple or mosque. But everywhere: on the bus, in traffic, on the sidewalk, at the grocery store, in class, at work, and at home.

In this sense, the world is one giant minyan. Every day, as members of that minyan, we have the ability to be present for one another just by taking a moment to stop whatever it is we're doing, look up, and look at the faces around us. Take in the expressions, imagine the stories behind them. What's making him smile? What's making her laugh? Why does he seem worried? Why does she seem down? Without even having a conversation, we're encouraging ourselves to value all of the life in our midst, to honor the lives within our midst—lives no less real or important or significant than our own. By drawing ourselves out of the bubbles of our own lives, we remind ourselves of the billions of other lives going on right alongside our own.

And when we do have real opportunities to meet and talk with people in our midst who may be strangers or relative strangers, if we encourage ourselves to listen carefully and be witnesses to their lives, rather than spectators, we might begin to understand what and whom they value and care about most.

When María stood in front of me the first time, she told me instantly why her vision mattered to her most, and when I put the glasses on her face, it was special and gratifying to have been in her presence. However, I'm not sure that I was present enough to grasp what was really at stake for her when she arrived.

Yet when María and I stood in each other's presence again with members of her church community standing behind her, I got a rare second chance to know before whom I stood: a woman whose connection to her Bible was her connection to God and to the people she worshipped with, the people she cared for, and who cared for her. I stood before María's touchstone for living, caught a glimpse at what imbued her days and her life with meaning.

I often wonder what the world would be like if in interactions large and small we could know before whom we stand—if we could see the people we encounter for what they cherish and what they fear—and remember that they, too, are loved by family and friends whose own circle of caring would be broken without them.

Leading Buddhist teacher Jack Kornfield describes an exercise that can help us be part of the minyan of humanity. He says, "There is a . . . practice in which you look at another person and you try to picture their happiest moment as a child, laughing and running and playing. You see that there's an inviolable spirit in them that cannot be touched by the traumas and the sorrows of life. To be able to see the original innocence and goodness born in everyone, and to foster that as you move through the world, is kind of a blessing."

Imagine how much more generous of spirit we would be if

we stopped long enough to see a person as they were before the stresses and strains of adulthood set in. How much more difficult it would be to ignore someone, turn our back, and walk away if we felt as if we were turning our back on a child in need.

We share this in common with everyone: we were all children once. We had an innocence about us, a lack of awareness of pain and suffering, a whole world open to us free of limitations. Although for too many people, childhood ends sooner than it should, we were all once wide-eyed and hopeful. We were the most trusting even though we were the most vulnerable—not yet capable of caring for ourselves, but abundantly kind and caring to others without thinking twice.

When Opening Your Heart Hardens Your Heart

There are some who agonize over whether to give or not give.
—SIFREI DEUTERONOMY 116:10

As beautiful as Kornfield's practice is, there is such a thing as being too aware of all those we encounter. In seeing them, we also see how much we can't do for them. And with so many people in our lives counting on us already—at work and at home—to look out for them, the combination of our existing commitments and the knowledge of our limited ability to help everyone can cause us to circle the wagons—to parse out our caring rather than offer it freely. This certainly was the case for me in the early days of my career.

In 1990, two years after graduating from NECO, I'd decided that in order to expand my commitment to making my life matter, I would pursue an advanced degree in public health. After some research, I determined that the best way for me to join the battle was to apply to a program at Johns Hopkins University for a master of public health degree and a fellowship in preventive ophthalmology.

I shared this plan with my father and proposed that I spend the next year in New York with the practice and then take a one-year leave the following year to earn my degree at Johns Hopkins. He was completely on board.

Two years later, with a freshly minted graduate degree, Helen Keller International (HKI), a not-for-profit global health organization dedicated to combating diseases of the eye, malnutrition, and other conditions that cause blindness in adults and children in the developing world, along with a low-income health-care initiative called Andean Rural Health Care, sent me to Bolivia to conduct an ecological survey of an eye disease called xerophthalmia.

Xerophthalmia, or vitamin A deficiency, each year causes more than a quarter of a million children to go blind and almost three quarters of a million children to die. But a simple twice-yearly vitamin A supplement given in infancy is all it takes to provide lifelong immunity to it. My assignment was to help identify those areas where vitamin A deficiency was a significant public health problem so we could get the supplements to all of the populations in need.

I had a great deal of territory to cover to make my assessments, screening children in the high-altitude plains of the Altiplano (a mountain plateau second only in size to that of Tibet); on the shores of Lake Titicaca, the largest lake in the Andes; in the midaltitude Mediterranean environs of Cochabamba in central Bolivia; and in the lowlands in the peri-urban neighborhoods surrounding the eastern Bolivian city of Santa Cruz. This meant many lengthy rides in the most crowded buses I'd ever seen. Sometimes they were so jammed that we'd pass people overhead down the center aisle, like they were crowd surfing at a rock concert, to get them to a tiny open nook where they could stand.

While the scenery changed dramatically everywhere I went, the scenarios I encountered were the same: malnourished children, most of them under the age of five, many of whom already showed early signs of xeropthalmia, and others who had already been blinded by the disease.

Although we could still give the vitamin A supplement to those already suffering from xeropthalmia to prevent the disease from claiming children's lives, once the disease has caused scarring in the cornea, the blindness is irreversible. In this sense, one of the hardest parts of the trip was talking to the parents of those children who had been robbed of their vision forever, telling them we could do nothing to change it, and seeing the pain in their eyes.

I had this conversation with a man named Anselmo when he brought his infant son to see us. The baby was already blind. I explained that the cause was a lack of vitamin A, but Anselmo pressed me further with the question I'd quickly learned to dread.

"What can I do?" he asked.

"Unfortunately there isn't anything you or we can do," I said.

"What could I have done?" Anselmo inquired.

When I told him about the supplement, he was devastated. Like any parent who wants anything and everything that will make his child's life better, Anselmo would have made sure his baby had that supplement in a heartbeat had he known its importance to his son's development. Yet even then, with conditions as they stood, where would Anselmo have gone to get the supplement?

The sad fact was that although HKI had sent me to Anselmo's town to make questions like the one he asked unnecessary, for Anselmo and his infant son, it was too late.

On the plane ride home, I cracked open a copy of Fyodor Dostoevsky's *Crime and Punishment* that I'd brought with me on the trip. I read a line that made me think of Anselmo: "Do you understand, sir, do you understand what it means when you have absolutely nowhere to turn?"

I imagined that Anselmo knew exactly what it meant to have nowhere to turn. Having never experienced anything close to what he felt, having been in Bolivia in some part because I had a father who had the freedom to give me options, I surely didn't understand. And while I couldn't begin to fathom the depths of Anselmo's pain, I could see how much pain he was in and it pained me, too.

Even after returning from this trip and getting back into my regular life, the acute suffering I'd seen stayed with me and weighed heavy on my heart. Entering my cushy Upper East Side practice, I instantly resented the sterility, perfection, and predictability of it all. Objectively, the ocular problems of patients in the developing world, not to mention the accompanying issues— poverty, no access to health care or basic medicine of any kind— were far direr than those on the island of Manhattan.

With that it was easy for me to keep my attention focused on the poorest parts of the world where I had just been—the real world, as I saw it. I saw the struggles of the people like Anselmo whom I'd encountered there as real struggles. As a result, I'll admit that sometimes when I sat across from my New York patients in the exam room, part of me would be thinking, "If you only knew what a real problem looked like."

My arguably sanctimonious attitude never changed the standard of care I gave my patients, but I did begin to see caring as a currency reserved for those in real need. Just like a monthly budget for food and rent and bills, I began to budget my compassion, too.

You probably have your own compassion budget. Too little time, plus too much work, plus too many people to whom you have committed your time and attention, starting with family and friends and moving outward to those who are also part of your circle of care who periodically need more of your attention: friends who aren't close friends, extended family members, and coworkers, to name a few. All this, plus a world awash in trouble, people plagued with problems beyond your comprehension, and strangers suffering right in your midst. At the end of the week, how much discretionary care and attention do you have left? How about at the end of a month? A year?

The balance sheet of true presence, of who we can and are willing to help, proves ever complicated to manage, and all the more so when we're dedicating some portion of our time and energy to being a force for positive change. While working to make a difference in the lives of some, we must guard against allowing ourselves to become, or give ourselves an excuse to be, indifferent to the pain of others.

A Distinction with a Big Difference

We should not take sorrows on ourselves upon another's account; but we ought to relieve others of their grief if we can.
—CICERO

I once thought that compassion and empathy were one and the same, and we do often use them interchangeably, but some psychologists who study human emotion suggest that they not only are different, but also that too much empathy is not a good thing.

Yale professor of psychology and author of *Against Empathy: The Case for Rational Compassion* Paul Bloom explains, "People mean different things by empathy. Some people use the term as a catch-all term for everything good—compassion, love, morality, wanting to make the world a better place, and so on. I'm certainly not against it in that sense. In fact, it's because I'm for all those things that I'm against empathy."

Bloom goes on to share that the type of empathy that concerns him is "the capacity to put yourself in the shoes of other people and feel what they feel." The obvious response to Bloom's assertion is to wonder what possibly could be wrong with putting ourselves in another's shoes. It stands to reason that if we thought more about what it was like to walk a mile in someone else's shoes, as the saying goes, we might be more attuned to the suffering of others and therefore be more motivated to help.

As it turns out, neurological research has shown that empathy and compassion stimulate different parts of our brains. Based on these findings, feeling someone else's pain may not yield the positive outcomes we imagine; rather, the studies suggest that walking a mile in someone else's shoes leaves everyone with blisters.

For instance, in a 2007 study, Dr. Tania Singer, then director of the department of Social Neuroscience at the Max Planck Institute for Human Cognitive and Brain Sciences in Leipzig,

Germany, gathered thirty subjects to study the neural responses to empathy and to compassion. Using a functional magnetic resonance imaging (fMRI) scanner, Dr. Singer and her colleagues monitored their subjects' brain activity as they participated in exercises designed to trigger empathic responses.

To do so, the study participants sat and viewed news footage of people suffering. This triggered the part of the brain that feels pain. The researchers concluded that feeling the pain of others resulted in emotional exhaustion, burnout, and a sense of powerlessness. This is why so many people in helping professions leave their jobs. And when people in helping professions internalize so much pain that they bow out in droves, society as a whole suffers the loss.

Case in point: A Mayo Clinic Proceedings study published in 2017 conducted to examine the correlation between burnout and the career plans of US doctors, showed that one in fifty plan to leave medicine altogether to pursue different careers. The study's authors concluded that if the doctors they surveyed follow through with their intentions, the burnout could contribute to what many fear is a coming doctor shortage. (The Association of American Medical Colleges projects that based on a precipitous decline in medical school applications, we will have at least 100,000 fewer doctors in the United States by 2030.)

To counter this dim view, when Singer and her colleagues directed their subjects to engage in guided meditation exercises, what they called "compassion training," the results were surprisingly positive. In this compassion training exercise, subjects were encouraged to think of a loved one, someone for whom it is easy to conjure up feelings of love and care, and then slowly to extend those feelings to other human beings, including those whose faces they saw in the news footage.

When subjects focused on extending their natural feelings of concern to others well beyond their circle of care, it stimulated the parts of their brains that generate feelings of warmth, friendship, and connection. The fMRI data revealed that the more the subjects triggered their compassion responses, the more they triggered their brains' reward responses. Hence feeling compassion generated more compassion.

Singer's findings led her to a partnership with Buddhist monk and author Matthieu Ricard, who engaged in the same empathy and compassion exercises as Singer's subjects. Ricard's brain imaging produced the same responses as those in Singer's study. Ricard, too, observed his responses from the inside out and marveled at the difference in his attitude and outlook when he focused his meditative practice on compassion.

In his book, *Altruism: The Power of Compassion to Change Yourself and the World*, Ricard writes about the experiment and what he and Singer called "empathy fatigue." He notes, "While I observed that meditation on empathy came up against a limit, that of burnout, on the contrary it seemed to me that one could not tire of love or compassion. In fact, these states of mind both fed my courage instead of undermining it, and reinforced my determination to help others without increasing my distress."

Ricard goes on to say that even though the reality of the suffering in his midst remained, approaching suffering with compassion made him more eager to help. Whereas overidentifying with the pain of others, Ricard explained, left him feeling emotionally spent and more wary of reaching out to those in need.

These findings resonated with me and my early experiences. It would have been impossible, but also not human, to have stood stone-faced in Anselmo's presence. It would have been similarly impossible for me to have left behind my experiences abroad in the direct line of extreme human suffering and jump back into life as I knew it at home without skipping a beat. Yet focusing only on the extreme suffering of Anselmo and people like him and becoming mired in their pain was causing me empathy fatigue. Rather than opening my heart, it was hardening it.

A symptom of my empathy fatigue presented in the way I had made myself judge and jury in deciding whose suffering was true suffering, determining whose problems were real problems. But this approach wasn't going to make me any better at making a difference in anyone's life in any part of the world. At best it would have made me less effective, leaving me drained, frustrated, cold; at worst it might have sent me into an irretrievable state of empathy fatigue and forced me out of working for positive change.

This is the distinction between empathy and compassion. While empathy can drain us, compassion sustains us. It costs us nothing. The more we give, the more it grows.

If empathy is walking a mile in someone else's shoes, compassion is resisting the urge to walk away from someone you deem less worthy of your care. The fact is that we want to stand still. Isn't this the reason why we want to make a difference in the first place? Because we care. Because we don't want to move through our lives focusing solely on ourselves and our own.

Since this is our natural state, it takes more energy for us to mete out our compassion, to vet its recipients, than it does to, as Kornfield describes it, "reach [our] hands out in spontaneous compassion to do what [we] can to alleviate the sorrows of others."

It costs us nothing to be present with another, to let someone know that they are not alone. And it takes nothing away from our efforts to help those whom we've chosen to make a conscious effort to help on our individual paths to making a difference to extend our compassion in small ways to anyone we encounter on our life's way. If anything, being free with our compassion strengthens and renews our ability to do more.

Whatever She Lacks

Respect is not fear and awe; it denotes, in accordance with the root of the word (respicere = to look at), the ability to see a person as he is, to be aware of his unique individuality. Respect means the concern that the other person should grow and unfold as he is.
—ERICH FROMM

Like most members of the indigenous Chocó tribe in Colombia, Noka made her home in a village at the headwaters of the Río Atrato. She had traveled by canoe to our screening location—an entire day's journey from her village and back. That she'd managed to navigate the rough waters and surrounding jungle terrain safely was a wonder in and of itself, given that a quick vision assessment revealed that no Department of Motor Vehicles in the United States would ever have let her walk out the door with a driver license. By US standards, Noka was legally blind.

After examining her eyes, however, I was able to find the one pair of used frames we had that were a 100 percent match for the prescription she needed. When Noka set out for home, she did so with complete use of her sight.

But a few days later Noka reappeared in her canoe at the screening site. She moved through the crowd to find me just as deftly as she'd crossed the river. Holding—not wearing—her glasses, she explained via translator that when she'd returned to her village wearing the eyeglasses, her friends and family made fun of her and hadn't let up since. Staring at the frames she'd thrust back into my keeping, I had to admit I understood why.

I'd sent Noka home with a pair of 1950s-era cat-eye frames with rhinestones and Coke-bottle lenses. Needless to say, they were not a style she would have chosen for herself. We explained that due to her unusual prescription, this was the only pair we had that was what she needed. Her next move blew our minds. Noka took the glasses, placed them on a wooden table, got back in her canoe, and rowed back to her village blind once again.

When a person with 20/800 vision basically says, "I'd rather be blind than be bullied," you have to hear it. I especially had to hear what she was saying to me with her actions. After all, Noka certainly didn't have to spend a second full day on the river to return the bedazzled Coke-bottle glasses. She could have gotten rid of them, and I never would have been the wiser. But she took the time to show up to show me something I needed to see.

Noka was no different than any of the people who walk in and out the door of my practice, who take time and care to select glasses that reflect the way they want to be seen, not styles that make them feel terrible about themselves to the point of wanting to be invisible. Her glasses, just like theirs, were tied to personal pride, confidence, and dignity. They were about the difference between what it feels like to have to take whatever someone has to give and having the power to choose for yourself.

Noka showed me that glasses were about more than the ability to see the world around you, but also about how you see yourself from the inside and how you wish to be seen by others. It is in this way that putting glasses on people's faces and in their hands that Fromm's definition of respect comes into play. Noka, just like every human being, deserved to be seen as the person she was, to be treated with the awareness of her unique individuality, and to be able to grow and unfold as she was.

In his 1991 book, *Emotion and Adaptation*, psychologist Dr. Richard Lazarus, one of the first in his field to study how stress affects our emotional responses, defined compassion as "being moved by another's suffering and wanting to help." The next step is to give the person what they need, rather than what you think they need. This, too, requires awareness and understanding.

In Deuteronomy, the Bible tells us to open our hand and "lend that which is sufficient" for whatever a person lacks. But if we are to follow this prescription, how exactly are we to determine what's sufficient for the person we encounter?

A rabbinic commentary explores the question and tells the story of a once wealthy nobleman who had fallen upon hard times. The man was accustomed to riding on a horse with a servant running ahead of him, yet with his fortunes reversed he had neither horse nor servant anymore. In the spirit of upholding the biblical precept set forth, the community bought the man a horse. And Hillel, one of the greatest scholars in the whole of Jewish history, volunteered to go and run in front of it.

At first glance the community's response and Hillel's efforts appear absurd. While we could understand making sure that this man and his family had a roof over their head, clothes on their backs, and food in their bellies, a horse and a servant hardly make for essentials. But I think this case is one shared by design to highlight how acts of compassion are intentional acts, based not solely on replacing lost or absent material things, but upon being present enough to understand what a person has lost of themselves in their struggles—their dignity, safety, confidence, personal agency, resilience, hope.

I not only learned this from Noka, but also from Ember, the head of the local service group hosting our mission in Colombia. During our six-day trip to Quibdó and the neighboring town of Istmina, I spent practically every moment working side by side with him.

Ember was in his late twenties, and having been born and raised in Quibdó, he knew the area's dangers and demons as well as he knew himself. Like most everyone I met there, Ember had a warmth and openness you would never imagine thriving in a place where survival demands a suit of armor of suspicion, caution, and a general mistrust of strangers. But Ember, with his sheltering smile and reassuringly unfurrowed brow, was our true standard-bearer. His absolute dedication to his people and excitement to be part of a team working to help them made the constant presence of the two Uzi-packing paramilitary guards who accompanied our every movement almost magically disappear.

Ember showed me that local heroes exist in every corner of the globe—individuals eager to improve their lives and those of their family, friends, and communities. He protected us from the stresses and strains of each day by getting us on our feet dancing at night, keeping our cups running over with anise-flavored aqua ardiente ("firewater"); filling our plates with fresh papaya and guanabana (a cross between a pineapple and a banana); and making certain we didn't lose sight of the orchids and lilies everywhere around us, their beauty nature's perennial rebellion against a region overgrown with man-made ugliness.

One day our team had an opportunity to travel on the Río Atrato with Ember as our skipper and guide. As we drifted by the Chocó houses lining the water, which are open on all sides, I took my camera out and began snapping pictures. As I did, a man emerged from one of the homes and began yelling at me as he chased us up the river. Ember translated, explaining that the man was shouting for me to give him back the pictures I'd taken because according to Chocó tradition, when you take a picture of a person, you take a piece of his soul.

I felt terrible for having caused the man distress. As we continued along the river, I thought more about the Chocó tradition that I'd inadvertently violated. It occurred to me that the heart of the tradition also was about the difference between looking at a person and seeing them. When we're in another's presence we have the chance to glimpse a bit of their soul if we pay attention. If we ditch the lens through which we've chosen to look at people from the outside, we allow them to show us who they are from the inside out. They open a window onto the essence of who they are.

I thought again of Noka. When she returned with those terrible frames, she offered me a second chance to see a bit of her soul, a bit of her true self, even though I'd missed the chance the first time. I have tried to honor the great lengths she went to then by working each day to see others the way she taught me to.

We cannot fix people, and we can't give people every single thing they lack. But we can be with people where they are in the moment. With respect and understanding we can see them, not as we see them, but as they want to be seen. With respect and understanding, we can be a temporary mirror that reminds them of who they are on the inside when life's trials separate them from the best of themselves. With respect and understanding, we can show them that no one is invisible.

Don't Forget Yourself

The circle of compassion is not complete if one person is left out. You know who that person is? Yourself. As the Buddha said, you can search the entire tenfold universe and not find a single being more worthy of love than the one seated in your own home—you.
—JACK KORNFIELD

We say it all the time. After sharing with a close friend or partner something difficult we are facing, something that is causing us pain, we punctuate what we've said with, "But, whatever. My problems are nothing compared to others.'" Or we say, "Hashtag FirstWorldProblems."

Let's not minimize the truth in that awareness. If we compare our struggles with those of billions of others around the globe, or even with people in our immediate orbit who are terminally ill, who are caring for elderly parents while at the same time raising children with special needs, who are out of work and running out of resources, who have a chronic disease that requires treatments that health insurance won't cover—it is easy to dismiss whatever problems we may be facing that pale in comparison. We aren't wrong to put our troubles in perspective.

Yet it is neither right nor helpful to minimize our own struggles or diminish our own pain. If we can't treat ourselves with compassion, we are poorly equipped to help others, and if changing the lives of others is a priority, our ability to be kind and caring to ourselves is a key to our success.

Part of our own compassion training is not reserving our compassion solely for others, but also sharing some of our compassion with ourselves. If we believe that compassion is a renewable, healing resource, then being kind to ourselves when the moment calls for it won't decrease our ability to be kind and caring to others.

Part of being compassionate with ourselves is allowing joy into our lives, whether it be in the simple pleasures or in the rare and memorable ones. Seeing what is good and glorious in our experiences doesn't hinder our ability to do good for others. Guilt doesn't make us more effective as we work to create change in the lives of others. As Kornfield explains, "We may feel it's not right to be happy when there is so much suffering in the world. The free heart is one that can experience joy and well-being and then extend it to others."

We often think of doing good in relationship to "the other." Yet doing good is a practice—a state of being that we hone daily, some days succeeding more than others, but always in the process of trying. Practicing compassion in every relationship, beginning with our relationship with ourselves, only adds to our power to change the world.

The evidence of a change-maker's work in the world is not in how much guilt we collect and store in the gloomy recesses of our inner world; it isn't in the joy we deny ourselves, somehow thinking that joy, too, is a nonrenewable resource—that joy for you means less for others. The only evidence of a change-maker's work that matters is change.

We Are One

We resemble one another in what we see together, in what we suffer together. Dreams change from individual to individual, but the reality of the world is common to us all.
—Albert Camus

The first time I met Chitra, I was seated at one of several stations at an eye clinic in the South Indian state of Tamil Nadu screening people for cataracts. With thousands of patients to see each day, my job was to do a preliminary assessment to search for the milky white pupil that is the telltale sign of a cataract.

Sure enough, when I examined Chitra's pupils, each one was milky white. With that kind of severe ocular impairment, not only was she blind, but as I continued the exam I also learned that she had been blind for seventeen years. Before I sent her to the next station, where she would be assessed further and scheduled for surgery, I had to check to see if there was any healthy tissue left all the way in the back of her eyes.

Searching for healthy tissue in the deepest recesses of the eye requires an instrument called a direct ophthalmoscope. You've probably been examined with one dozens of times in routine visits to your eye doctor. The ophthalmoscope lets you see into the fundus to examine the retina and optic nerve. The ophthalmoscope has a mirror that reflects a light source into the eye to aid in the process.

The ophthalmoscope gets the job done, but it isn't the most advanced tool, and to use it properly you have to get particularly close to the patient. You start from far away, and slowly draw closer, your hand on the patient's brow, until you are practically forehead to forehead, touching the patient's cheek with the outside part of your palm, almost cradling the patient's head.

The closer I got to Chitra to peer into the furthest recesses of her eyes, the more I became aware of a scent. At first I thought it was leather, but then I recognized it as the scent of earth. It transported me to my mountain climbing days and evoked the same feeling I had in the wilderness when all barriers vanished between me and the ground—when I feel not that I am standing on it, but that I am of it.

I thought, Chitra also is of the earth—both of us are descendants of the first human being, formed from dust, given the breath of life, whose shared destiny is to return to the dust from whence we came.

Even though I was looking into the eyes of a person who could not have been more different than I was in appearance, age, gender, or background, we were inextricably and eternally connected through the simple fact of being human, and in our humanity we were exactly the same. For a sliver of a second, I was Chitra and Chitra was me.

Part of daily Jewish practice is saying the words, "God is One." These words are part of a prayer called the Shema—Hebrew for "hear," "listen," "learn," and "understand." Traditionally we say these words three times daily, plus once more at nighttime before bed. They also are intended to be the last words we speak before we draw our very last breath. Ask any Jewish person of any age if she knows the Shema, regardless of whether the last time she saw the inside of a synagogue was seven days or seven years ago, and she will say them as naturally as she speaks her own name.

Yet speaking the words and knowing their translation is not the same as understanding them. Grasping the true meaning of oneness is like trying to hug the wind, because it is more than a theological statement. It is a proclamation and a prayer for the unity and interconnectedness of all people and things—something that cannot be captured in words alone, but must be felt. We're fortunate if we get the chance to feel something that big, that all-encompassing, that elusive even once in a lifetime. And even when you've experienced a sense of oneness, the even greater challenge is hanging on to it. Memory fades and these kinds of moments are impossible to replicate. But you do at least retain the knowledge that oneness is real.

Having been fortunate enough to have felt that sense of oneness in Chitra's presence once in my lifetime, and as a result knowing that this unity is real, has changed the way I look at everyone around me. The certain knowledge that we are connected at a soul level through our humanity and in our very humanness—in our strength and our fragility—is with me everywhere I go now, including anywhere in the world that I see patients, whether at home or abroad.

I recall returning from South America once and walking into the practice early the next morning to find an impeccably dressed twenty-eight-year-old banker named Melissa waiting in my office. Melissa had been having some eye problems, and it was an emergency appointment.

As I asked her about her symptoms, all of the polish and confidence she emitted vanished. She started to cry and told me she was terrified that she was going blind.

Upon further examination, I determined that Melissa had a large corneal abrasion, a treatable condition, but one that many patients I've seen over the years have described as being more painful than giving birth or getting shot.

Seeing Melissa's tears and hearing the panic in her voice, she looked no different to me than any other human being I'd encountered anywhere in the world in physical pain and emotional distress. She was a human being who was hurting and reaching out to another for help, a person who deserved the most compassion I had to give. And she deserved that I give it just as freely as I would to any other person in any other city, town, or village in the world.

No human being escapes life unscathed or without struggle. Without compassion we are alone. With compassion, we are o

Take the Dare

Now take the opportunity to expand your circle of care by teaching yourself how to see compassion as a renewable resource. Think about who falls regularly into your compassion budget. To whom do you readily allocate compassion? When you have identified your existing circle of caring, try to extend it to include one more person each week. It doesn't have to be cumulative. It can be one more person each week who is different from the previous one.

When you identify these people, try to be present with them in the same way that you endeavor to be present with the people who inhabit your inner circle of caring. This can be by listening to them more intently, and asking questions based on what you hear, perhaps extending what might have been a brief exchange into a real conversation, at the end of which you don't need to have solved a problem, but by the end of which the people you encounter know that you see them and that you care.

Just as you commit to expanding your circle of care, also practice turning inward to make certain you include yourself. Commit to one practice that takes anywhere from 1-5 minutes daily that sustains and restores your energy. Be just as present with yourself as you hope to be with others. Take stock of yourself from head to toe. Where is your stress? How can you let it go? Recognize your own pain and don't discount it. What small thing can you do for yourself today to heal?

No matter how small, if you have a conviction that this is something that is going to change your community, if you have a conviction that this is something that is going to change your family, if you have a conviction that this is something that is going to do some good, step out and do it.
—LEYMAH GBOWEE

5 Discover the Need That Needs You Most

There will never cease to be those in need in your land, which is why I command you to readily open your hand to your brother, to your afflicted, and to your impoverished in your land.
—DEUTERONOMY 15:11

As you look at the world around you, and you try to find where you fit in the effort to change it, you will encounter suffering overload. You will encounter need everywhere you look, and you will see no shortage of problems that need you.

Social media and the ubiquity of screens of every size and shape have done wonders for giving us a window onto the world's problems and keeping us informed about issues we would never have known about even a generation ago. Yet our total access reality also has created what a 2018 Pew Research Center survey called "news fatigue." The findings included that some seven in ten Americans feel worn out by the sheer volume of news available to them each day.

British psychologist and mental health researcher Graham Davey has conducted studies over the course of more than two decades demonstrating that news fatigue is a global issue, not solely an American one. His work has demonstrated that prolonged exposure to negative news, particularly of the digital variety when stories often include disturbing audio/visual components, can cause consumers of content to lose sleep and experience mood changes. Moreover, Davey explains, television news can cause viewers to worry not just about the topics of the negative stories they see, but can also intensify viewers' worries about problems in their own lives wholly unrelated to the news itself.

Given that exposure to too much news isn't good, and that a goodly portion of the news we consume is about how bad things are the world over, we know that much of what constitutes news fatigue could also be described as need fatigue—the stress, anxiety, and exhaustion that ensues from being in the near nonstop presence of how much help so many people need and how many problems need fixing.

But let's say you decide to give yourself a breather and swear off Twitter or ditch your tablet for a day. With your newfound free time and energy you amble over to your mailbox to clean out several months' worth of catalogues from stores you've not only never shopped at before, but that you've never heard of. There amid the alarming amount of snail mail you still get despite having gone paperless, you also find that your mailbox overfloweth with requests for donations to countless worthy causes. Upon further inspection you find that many of these envelopes are stuffed with personalized, self-adhesive, return address labels that you then must struggle to decide which is worse: using the labels, even though you won't be making a contribution to fill-in-the-blank organization, or throwing the labels away, which is wasteful given that said fill-in-the blank organization already spent its resources to print them. Fatigued and guilt-ridden by all you can't give, you slump down on the couch, grab your phone, tap the CNN App, and let the "breaking news" fill the silence.

You know you can't fix it all, you know you can't change it all, and you may be inclined to chuck the whole change thing because, hey, what's the point. Add to this only so many hours in a day, jobs to do, bills to pay, relationships to nourish and sustain, and a whole lot of life to enjoy (joy and pleasure being vital to existence for us all and not to be neglected), and you have every reason in the world to let changing the world fall to the bottom of the priorities list.

When I feel myself caving to the avalanche of problems and the

demands of my day-to-day life, I think of the line from Deuteronomy that I used to find more than a little bit troubling: "There
will never cease to be those in need in your land, which is why I
command you to readily open your hand to your brother, to your
afflicted, and to your impoverished in your land."

There will never cease to be those in need in your land? Could
there possibly be a worse advertisement for making a difference?
Hey, people, knock yourselves out, but at the end of the day nothing will ever get better.

A third-century Jewish commentary called Sifrei Devarim
(Devarim being what Deuteronomy is called in Hebrew) explores
the dystopian reality the biblical text portends. Yet what bothers
the commentator is not the declaration of the guaranteed eternal-
ity of need, but rather why the verse has to mention who specifically we're to open our hand to. He reasons that the verse could
just as easily have said, "There will never cease to be those in
need in your land, so readily open your hand." Yet because the
text goes to great pains to be more detailed than that, the commentator suggests that the specific designation of each potential
recipient of aid tells us that not every person in need will need
exactly the same thing. He explains, "One whom it befits to give
a loaf, give a loaf; one whom it befits to give dough, give dough;
one whom it befits to give money, give money; one whom it befits
to be fed, feed him."

I take from this that there will never cease to be needy in your
land unless you realize that you have to carefully divide the labor:
those who are best at offering a loaf should give loaves; those best
positioned to give money, give money; those who can feed, feed.
The only way we are going to chip away at the world's problems,
not fade away when the problems are dizzying in their size and
volume, and also be there for our families, our friends, our neighbors, and ourselves is by finding the need that needs us most.

Your task in making your life matter is not to solve all problems, but to find the problem that you are best positioned and
best prepared to help fix. When you do, the only thing about

working for change that will feel impossible is not doing what you realize you have been created to do.

Staying Alive

Don't ask what the world needs. Ask what makes you come alive and go do it. Because what the world needs is people who have come alive.
—HOWARD THURMAN

I once texted my nephew on his birthday and said, "Did you do something today that connected you with your aliveness? If not, make sure to go for it this weekend."

He responded, "I'm going sailing this weekend, so it will be an opportunity to do just that."

I guess it wasn't your usual "many happy returns of the day" type birthday greeting, but it seemed to me that celebrating the anniversary of the first day of your life should include doing something that makes you feel alive. Something that animates your spirit and makes you feel like everything is possible.

You start finding the need that needs you most by noticing what makes you come alive. Travel has always been one of those things for me, but I knew that while traveling around the world simply for adventure's sake might have made me a more interesting person it wasn't going to turn me into a person who makes an impact. I needed to figure out how I could marry my interest in seeing the world with my commitment to changing it.

Finding the need that needs you most also requires an active awareness of what, and who, inspires you. For me, one of those people was a pioneering ophthalmologist, Dr. Govindappa Venkataswamy. When I was less than a year away from starting to work in the practice and still in full-blown angst mode trying to figure out how I was going to make my life matter, a family friend told me about Dr. Venkataswamy (or "Dr. V.," as he was known to all), who was doing groundbreaking work in Nadu.

Dr. V. had seen a simple need with a simple solution: of the ten million blind people in India, he determined that half could see again with cataract surgery. Moved by this observation to take action, Dr. V. founded the Aravind Eye Institute, where he dedicated the rest of his ninety years of life to making cataract screening and affordable cataract surgery available to millions in underserved rural communities.

When I heard what Dr. V. was doing I knew I had to meet him and see Aravind for myself, so I wrote him a letter asking if I could come work for him in exchange for room and board. Dr. V. obliged, and I spent six invaluable months learning from one of the most gifted physicians and compassion-driven people I've ever met.

Not only did I admire the kind of caring practitioner and brilliant social entrepreneur Dr. V. was, but I also appreciated his ongoing dedication to studying the wisdom of his own faith and that of others—of creating a lens through which he saw the world, his work, his family, community, and patients as its own interconnected universe, each part essential to the other.

Dr. V. meditated daily and encouraged me to explore the practice of meditation as well. He was a follower of the teachings of the philosopher and guru, Sri Aurobindo, whose ashram has been a destination in the union territory of Pondicherry, not far from Aravind's home, for almost ninety years.

When Sri Aurobindo founded this ashram where Dr. V. drew inspiration, he had a partner named Mirra Alfassa. Mirra's parents were Sephardic Jews; her father grew up in Turkey, her mother in Egypt. Mirra took a different path, leaving her native France for India, where she became known as The Mother and helped spread Sri Aurobindo's teachings long after his death. It was Mirra, or The Mother, who said, "The Divine is everywhere, in everything, and if He is hidden . . . it is because we do not take the trouble to discover Him." Dr. V. showed me by example what it meant to see the Divine in all things.

In addition to his skill and special talent for welcoming wonder and connection in his life, no matter where he was or what he was doing, Dr. V. inspired me because he was always so utterly and completely himself.

It is no exaggeration when I say that in India, Dr. V. was

treated like a god everywhere he went, revered as he was for his remarkable impact. Yet whether he was with high-ranking officials, foreign dignitaries, or his patients, he was the exact same guy: humble, levelheaded, abundantly kind.

While Dr. V.'s ease with being Dr. V. was readily apparent during my time at Aravind, I remember being the most impressed when I saw him in New York about a month after I returned from working with him in India. Dr. V. was in New York on Aravind business and I went to meet him at a typical New York diner.

Dr. V., his colleague Thulasiraj (a remarkable individual in his own right), and I had barely squeezed into a booth and begun perusing the encyclopedia-length menus in front of us when a gum-popping waitress came over to our table. Barely looking up from her order pad, she gestured toward Dr. V. and said, "What d'ya want, hon?"

I watched Dr. V. as this scene unfolded—the god greeted as "hon" in a greasy spoon. Of course the waitress didn't know who Dr. V. was, nor should she have, and Dr. V. didn't need to be known. As long as he knew who he was, knew what he had been created to do, and was doing it, he required little else to feel totally at home in any place and with anyone in the world.

Still so uncertain at the time of how I would make a difference or if I could, trying on different selves, seeing every path that I wasn't on as the path I should be pursuing, that day in the diner I hoped I might one day know, like Dr. V., what I had been created to do and that I would be doing it. That one day I would feel just as at home in the world because of it, just as Dr. V. did.

As much as Dr. V. inspired me as a person, a problem I saw while working with Dr. V. motivated me as a change-maker. At Aravind I helped conduct countless vision screenings; and on a near weekly basis, I noticed again, just as I had noticed at that point on dozens of VOSH missions, that one of the biggest bottlenecks in the long screening lines had nothing to do with cataracts. Instead the long waits consistently came as a result of the many people there who just needed glasses, most of whom also required nothing more than nonprescription readers. Encountering this phenomenon over and over again got under my skin. I kept thinking how ridiculous it was for a problem with such a simple solution to go unnoticed and unaddressed; how needless it was for people to suffer when the solution didn't require anything fancy or complicated.

That feeling, the feeling of being moved by the senselessness or the injustice of a situation, is your clue. Whether it's anger or disgust or a sense of outrage you feel, if it pisses you off enough that you can't easily shake your indignation, that's your motivation pointing you in the direction of the need that needs you more than any other. That's you telling yourself where to match your pique with whatever skills and talents you have to start solving the problem. Maybe you're reading this and thinking, okay, but I don't know where to start. Or okay, but I'm not just starting out in life, and I don't have a couple of spare decades lying around to get going on doing good. Whatever your reaction, set the "buts" aside for a second (don't worry, you can have them back later). Try something that starts with "okay, so," and fill in the blanks. Something like this:

Okay, so I read this article the other day that I haven't been able to stop thinking about because I never knew that _____.

Okay, so I met someone last month who told me the most amazing story about _____, and it made me wonder, what if _____?

Okay, so I was listening to this podcast and I was shocked to learn that _____. When I think about _____ it makes me wish that I could _____.

Rather than anticipating what the obstacles are to finding the need that needs you most first, try thinking about people, conversations, experiences, and issues that move you the most—possibly without your even realizing it. If nothing comes to you right away, that's fine. As you go through your days, try to pay attention to people and issues that capture, and hold, your attention.

If it makes you come alive, follow the inspiration, follow the motivation, follow the quickening of your pulse, and don't be afraid to see where it leads.

This Time It's Personal

But the experience of suffering, it's often noted, is not effectively conveyed by statistics or graphs.
—PAUL FARMER

Living in a place like New York City makes trying to escape the scope of need impossible. You can't walk one block without encountering someone who is homeless, either sleeping on a bed of cardboard boxes under a storefront awning or standing with a paper cup in hand asking for money to get something to eat. If I stopped for every person in need between home and my office, I'd have a waiting room full of patients whose appointments I was late for, and no money left in my own pocket.

So I do what most New Yorkers do—pause once, maybe twice, to put a bit of change in a cup, and avert my gaze most of the rest of the way, forcing myself to feel numb to it all to justify my inaction.

Oftentimes I'm so caught up in everything I have to accomplish that admittedly I don't notice anyone or anything around me. My thoughts turn to the twelve-hour workday ahead, administrative responsibilities I have in the office, calls I have to make for VisionSpring, and trying to figure out how I can make it home if not in time to sit down to dinner with Erica and my kids, then at least to see them and ask about their day before they go to bed.

Yet while walking with Jonas one morning when he was about eleven, deep in my daily routine and on autopilot, he did something that stopped me in my tracks. When I looked over at Jonas expecting him to be at my side, he wasn't there. I did a 180 to find him, and he was behind me talking to a homeless man we pass on the same corner most every day. That day Jonas had decided that rather than walk past the man whose condition troubled him, he would walk toward him. When I doubled back, Jonas was mid-conversation asking more about him and his life, where he was born, his family.

The personal connection Jonas made that day motivated him to explore how he could be part of the solution to the widespread problem of homelessness in the city we call home. Soon thereafter, he began volunteering at a men's shelter in our synagogue that hosts ten guests, five nights a week, nine months out of the year.

Each night that the shelter is open, volunteers transform one room in the synagogue building into a place where homeless men can sit down to dinner, shower, sleep comfortably, and have breakfast the next morning. People in our community, like Jonas, make this possible in a variety of ways: some come early in the evening to prepare dinner for the men, and some come to sit, eat, and talk with them. Others donate food and supplies. Some stay in the shelter overnight to make sure things go smoothly and make sure breakfast is on the table in the morning.

Not only has Jonas been volunteering at the shelter now for years, but moved by his example and inspired by his commitment to being a small yet vital part of the solution to this problem, we often volunteer together as a family.

Jonas's efforts to matter also reminded me that doing good starts not by identifying a problem, but by first getting close to one person alone. This simple act of connection is what Bryan Stevenson, executive director of the Equal Justice Initiative (EJI) and author of *Just Mercy: A Story of Justice and Redemption*, calls "getting proximate to a problem."

In 2016 I was privileged to hear Stevenson speak at the Skoll World Forum in Oxford, England, where social entrepreneurs from more than sixty countries throughout the world gather to share best practices, learn, and be inspired by one another. That year Bryan was a recipient of the Skoll Award for particularly outstanding and innovative work to change the status quo. During his acceptance speech, he talked about the EJI, which he founded in 1989 with the goal of eradicating mass incarceration in the United States. With EJI, Stevenson has created a vast army of change-makers dedicated to social justice and racial equality, and to transforming criminal justice in this country.

The impact Stevenson has had over the last three decades is dazzling and incredibly moving. Yet of all the things that stayed with me long after hearing him speak was that his path to making a difference began with people, not with the problem that he came to understand needed his efforts the most.

Stevenson was a philosophy major at Eastern University in Pennsylvania. As his college career was drawing to a close, he realized there wasn't much in the way of solid job prospects for a philosophy student, and he somewhat randomly applied to law school.

He said that when he began his graduate studies, he still had little interest in the law and had difficulty imagining a life as a lawyer. Yet when a course he took required him to visit prisoners on death row in a Georgia correctional facility, something clicked. The moment Stevenson sat across from the first inmate he met, speaking with him, really seeing him, and listening to his story, he knew what he had been created to do. In that meeting with one person he was changed, and being changed by one man pointed him in the direction of the need that needed him most.

Settle In for the Long Haul

It's not that I'm so smart, it's just that I stay with problems longer.
—ALBERT EINSTEIN

Thinking about the process of finding the need that needs you most, and then putting your whole heart into making a difference in that one small corner of your universe of change, calls to mind a trip I took in the fall before my board certification exams.

I'd planned to meet my friend Scott in Hong Kong, where he was working in his father's business, for a three-week trek through Nepal, followed by one week exploring India before beginning my six months of intensive work with Dr. V.

First I flew to Moscow, where I boarded the Trans-Siberian Railway for what is still known today as the longest ride (roughly six thousand miles) you can take on the same train. For seven days I survived on terrible food (most of which I'd brought—the Orient Express this was not), and as the only person onboard who didn't speak Russian, Chinese, or Vietnamese endured far more of my own company than I liked, as the train wended its way through multiple countries and time zones at the breakneck speed of about thirty miles per hour until I arrived in Beijing.

From Beijing, I took a series of more trains, each time folding myself into tiny sleeper cars that made me long for the luxury of the Trans-Siberian and traveled for three more weeks until finally making it to Hong Kong.

A life dedicated in some significant part to doing good is not like those hop-on/hop-off bus tours, but much more like that series of long, slow train rides I still remember as if they were yesterday. To have an impact in any meaningful way, you have to take the slow trains and keep riding. I know because I've been riding them for thirty years; as long as I have life I don't intend to stop.

Jim Collins, author of *Good to Great*, has come up with one of the best descriptions of what a lifetime goal of making your life matter looks like. Collins has spent his entire career studying what makes some businesses merely average and others wildly successful, if not total game changers (he profiles Amazon as one of the latter). The difference between the two is what Collins calls "the flywheel effect."

In Collins's conception, the flywheel is "a massive metal disk mounted horizontally on an axle, about thirty feet in diameter, two feet thick, and weighing about 5,000 pounds." He asks us to imagine having our own flywheel in front of us and to think about the initial push—how much effort and time it will take to eke out one rotation. Collins encourages us to keep thinking about continuing to push the wheel, turning it over and over again, regardless of how hard we have to exert ourselves, without stopping. The more muscle we put in, the faster the flywheel turns until finally all of the time and sweat we have expended becomes a force so great that the flywheel spins almost effortlessly under the power of sheer momentum.

"Now," Collins says, "suppose someone came along and asked, 'What was the one big push that caused this thing to go so fast?' You wouldn't be able to answer; it's just a nonsensical question. Was it the first push? The second? The fifth? The hundredth? No! It was *all* of them added together in an overall accumulation of effort applied in a consistent direction."

Mattering is your flywheel. Getting started is difficult, staying with it just as hard. But as long as you keep pushing, eventually your efforts will generate more and more momentum. Through trial and error, you will understand how to pair your superpowers with a problem; you will be drawn to a person or people who are broken by a particular social ill that will make you feel simultaneously called and crazed by the injustice you have seen—a problem you cannot turn away from or walk past. You will make it your business to get close to like-minded people who feel as you do, and within that community of doers you will roll up your sleeves and uncover the fragment that you are uniquely suited to mend within what will be something even more broken and complex than you originally thought. And then, as Collins says, "Whoosh . . . !"

Don't get me wrong: you don't have to pick a problem at twenty-one that you'll still be working at solving when you're ninety-one. But you do have to stick with your commitment to doing good, even when the good you're doing isn't flashy or the cause of the moment; whether it's something you do every day, once a week, or once a month, as a volunteer or for a living. Nothing you do with your whole heart will ever be small.

Seek and You Will Be Found

Finding the right work is like discovering your own soul in the world.
—Thomas Moore

Many of my years of trial and error in discovering the need that needed me most had everything to do with my search for *the* big problem to which I could be part of the solution. What compelled me to get the Hopkins degree, in fact, was about wanting to make a big splash in social change.

When I began my work in the 1980s, the greatest amount of attention and the greatest number of resources in the eye-care field were going to global efforts to combat diseases of the eye in the developing world. I was chasing the action, chasing the funding, and, yes, chasing the prestige that came with working on issues garnering more of the spotlight.

By comparison, refractive error of the eye, which is a fancy way of saying correcting people's vision with glasses, could not have been less sexy. As such, the medical community not only didn't see the enormous need for glasses and its deleterious effects as an important issue; it simply wasn't anywhere on its radar screen at all.

This is why despite the fact that at nearly every turn in my adult life, working first as a student volunteer and then as a public health professional in the developing world, the need for glasses was always there staring me right in the face, it wasn't on my radar screen, either.

Even while training with Dr. V., I spoke so animatedly about the outsize need for glasses and how it was affecting individuals and entire communities that he suggested that I do the same with glasses as he was doing with cataract surgery. Dr. V. kept encouraging me in that direction the entire time I was at Aravind, and even though Dr. V.'s approach did ultimately become the foundation for VisionSpring's, for the longest time I ignored what anyone else, including this giant of a man who I respected so much, could see was so clearly meant to be my path to making my life matter in the way I'd set out to.

As I continued my social justice equivalent of storm chasing, after the work I did in Bolivia with vitamin A deficiency, I had the opportunity to expand my engagement with HKI. This time I was sent to Cameroon to aid in HKI's efforts to combat another insidious disease called onchocerciasis, also known as river blindness. River blindness is a dreaded parasitic eye infection that, like xeropthalmia, causes blindness.

River blindness, as was also the case with xeropthalmia, is entirely preventable. A one-tablet dose of a drug called Mectizan administered annually for at least ten consecutive years keeps the disease permanently at bay, but it, too, has to be deployed strategically to ensure that it gets to the regions where those at greatest risk receive it. With that, my team and I were tasked with creating what's called a hot map to aid in the most effective Mectizan distribution possible.

Because people contract river blindness from blackfly bites, our first order of business was working our way through the Sanaga River Basin in Central Cameroon, a body of water that plays host to a large number of blackflies, making it one of the most hyper-endemic regions of river blindness infection in the world.

Over the course of three weeks, we walked miles along the banks of the sprawling river. We saw men, women, and children already suffering from river blindness with tiny writhing worms swimming in their aqueous humor—a part of the eye that should be a basin of clear fluid that feeds vital optic organs, like the cornea and iris. Most of the people we encountered were shoeless, toes gnarled and knotted, their feet more thick pads of callous than flesh.

As we moved through the heavily populated villages that trace the water's edge, I began asking the people I met there what they needed most. Some said clean water. Many said agricultural products, which made perfect sense in a region where people farm to grow just enough food to feed their families. Medicine for other diseases, like malaria, often made the list. Others frequently spoke of having no access to education for their children and of wanting to be able to send them to school where they could learn and grow and have a chance at making a better life for themselves and their children. The more people I asked, the more the winding river running through each town became an unraveling scroll of infinite need. The longer the list became, the more impossible bringing any sort of real change began to feel. Then I met Baasa.

Baasa was a forty-two-year-old woman and a mother who, like so many women around the world, was holding her children's present in her hands and struggling to give them an unobstructed view of the future, with the stubborn challenges of subsistence blocking her in every direction.

"What do you need?" I asked her.

Without blinking Baasa replied, "Opportunity."

The instant she said it, it occurred to me that opportunity wasn't one thing—it was everything. Education is opportunity. Income is opportunity. Anything that offers people a shot at self-sufficiency, liberates them from mere survival, empowers them to do well for their loved ones and do the kind of good they have been uniquely created to do for their families, their communities, their countries, and the world is opportunity.

As we talked, I saw what had been there all along, but had taken many years and traveling many thousands of miles to become clear to me: Glasses were opportunity.

Having made a multiyear commitment to HKI, I continued my global public health work for nearly a decade more, but that conversation with Baasa had renewed my focus on glasses and their stealth power to meet a whole host of needs for millions (and what I would later learn was billions) of people in the developing world. Her voice and the word *opportunity* echoed as if from a high elevation everywhere I went.

I became fascinated by the relationship between public health and economic development and devoured information to shape my understanding of the intricate relationship between the two.

In the process, I happened upon the work of economist and historian David Landes. Landes's book, *The Wealth and Poverty of Nations*, was a guided tour of the link between health and economics that emerged on my trip to West Africa and had so captured my heart and my mind. As I followed Landes through the ages, time-traveling page by page from civilization to civilization, I learned why some societies had gotten rich, while others had not, and why. Then I turned to a page that made all the difference in the plan I was developing for making one.

Landes explained that Europe's economy had thrived for centuries, and therefore had made Europe a dominant world power, in large part because of the invention of eyeglasses. With the invention of the first pair of eyeglasses in thirteenth-century Pisa, other innovations flooded the market, like precision tools and gauges. The know-how required to make the lenses themselves also spilled over into the invention of the microscope and telescope.

Literacy also increased as glasses doubled the duration of a scribe's professional life and enabled more people to read; the production levels of skilled craftsmen, cobblers, and weavers also increased with glasses, keeping more people employed longer and towns and cities thriving right along with them.

It was a sign from the Middle Ages of a successful system of optical cause and effect that I believed could work just as effectively in the postmodern developing world. The far-reaching impact of one seemingly basic invention, its staggering effect on the worlds of commerce, academia, regional political stability, the arts, the strength of the social fabric, and individual quality of life convinced me all the more that nothing about a simple pair of glasses was simple in the least. From there my flywheel kept turning faster and faster.

In my office I began noticing that my patients who needed nonprescription readers tended to either wear the ten- or twenty-dollar prefabricated variety sold at pharmacies that weren't necessarily the best looking or the highest quality; or they wore super stylish high-quality readers sold in fancy optical shops with a $100 to $300 price tag to match. I did some research and learned that no middle ground in the market existed between the two. I wondered what it would be like to create a product to fill that vacuum in the US eyeglass market and use the profits to meet the need for glasses in the developing world.

In a year that idea grew into a for-profit company I cofounded called Scojo Vision that also had a not-for-profit counterpart called Scojo Foundation. The plan was to manufacture fashion forward, high quality Scojo Vision readers that would sell for twenty-five to sixty dollars, and then dedicate 5 percent of Scojo Vision's pretax profits to Scojo Foundation. Scojo Foundation would help women in the developing world start their own businesses selling brand-new reading glasses, also in a variety of styles, at an affordable price point (about two dollars a pair) in their own villages and surrounding towns.

While in the thick of getting Scojo Vision and Scojo Foundation off the ground, in particular looking for stores where we could sell Scojo Vision readers, a patient asked me to serve on the Board of Directors of a New York–based not-for-profit organization called Lighthouse International. Lighthouse provides community health and social services to people who are severely visually impaired or blind, offering a variety of programs and aid designed to help them function better in their daily lives. This includes sending professionals into people's homes to teach them independent living skills, like how to make their own meals and manage their own finances; how to develop outdoor skills, like walking on crowded city sidewalks and navigating the subway system; and how to work with people's employers to acquire the kinds of adaptive technologies, like computer hardware and software designed for those who are visually impaired, to help continue to maximize their professional talents and productivity.

One of my colleagues on the Lighthouse board was a man named Philip Miller, who at the time was the chairman and CEO of Saks Fifth Avenue. I shared the Scojo Vision/Scojo Foundation plan with Phil, and within months Scojo Vision readers were in Saks stores nationwide. Within another year we were also in Neiman Marcus, Bergdorf Goodman, and Bloomingdale's.

While sitting in a meeting one day with some buyers from Saks, poring over market research and talking about what shade of red would be the hottest color for Scojo Vision's spring line, my mind wandered. Scojo Vision had really taken off and Scojo Foundation was growing at a surprisingly quick pace and already making an impact. While I was pleased with Scojo Vision's success, growing the business was an all-consuming project, so much so that I was having trouble finding time to dedicate to the foundation, which, if I was being totally honest with myself, was where my heart and soul were.

I also had to be honest with myself about what was happening behind the scenes of our success. Although Scojo Vision was a thriving business, my business partnership was failing. It was becoming more and more apparent that our styles, philosophies, and the things that drove us were too different to keep making a go of it together.

I thought back to my mountaintop moment where my commitment to do something good with my life began. I thought about Raúl, Dr. V., Baasa, my parents, my patients, and so many others. I thought of Alaska, Boston, the Yucatán, Tamil Nadu, Maryland, the Andes, New York, Cameroon. Every person, every step, every experience had carried me to that place and that moment. In the twenty years that had passed, I knew I'd been doing good, but that the particular type of good I was meant to do was just beginning.

The red glasses meeting confirmed that my heart lay in the work of Scojo Foundation. Because this realization also came at the same time that my business partner and I knew for sure it was time to move on, together we decided to sell the company, keep the foundation, and change its name to VisionSpring.

Although it may seem tidy in the telling, nothing was smooth or linear about my path. And while I did choose every step, I would be leaving out a crucial part of the story if I were to say that I did all of the choosing alone. I firmly believe that when you keep pushing, keep searching, keep insisting in word and in deed that you are here to do something good, day after day and year after year, that if you put in the effort, the universe will conspire to help you land exactly where you are supposed to be.

Get Going

Let us, then, be up and doing,
With a heart for any fate;
Still achieving, still pursuing,
Learn to labor and to wait.
—HENRY WADSWORTH LONGFELLOW

Screenwriters often say that the easiest parts of a story to create are the beginning and the end. It's the middle that's the hardest.

For me, daring to matter was the easy and exhilarating beginning part of my life story. My story will end the same way as yours when the time comes for me to draw my last breath. It is the act of mattering itself that is part of my life's long and mysterious middle. And as you work to make your life matter, it will also be part of yours.

As I find myself still very happily in that long and mysterious middle of my unfolding life story, yet much closer to the end than when I began, I can say that finding the need that needed me most was harder than I ever thought it would be and took much longer than I imagined, but it was absolutely necessary in making the act of mattering possible every day.

This is my path. Yours will be different, and it should be because the need that needs you most is not the same as the one that needs me. It could take you twenty years to complete. It could take less. There will be times when you need to take a break and walk away to gather your energy and return with fresh eyes. No matter how the process plays out for you, know as you go that wanting to make a difference and being impatient to get started are great, but doing good well has no set time frame or clear benchmarks for success. It requires an openness to experiences that you may think are taking you off course. And even as you let go, you also have to stay present to recognize the chances for learning, growing, and developing that may be staring you right in the face.

As long as you keep trying, trusting that every step along the way is valuable in and of itself, rather than ascribing value only to what you think is a step forward in the feverish pursuit of your hunger to matter, I promise the world will conspire to help you. Just as the world guided me to glasses, it will guide you to the good that you will do best because you are you.

While your "so's" and observations about what inspires you, motivates you, and makes you come alive are vital to the process, take care to budget your reflection time. Although being thoughtful about what kind of good you want to do is critical to finding the need that needs you most, sometimes what you need most is to simply start doing. The easiest way to get going is to seize any and every opportunity already at hand.

For instance, does your employer have an in-house program dedicated to projects that make a difference in your community? Is there a place you've been thinking about volunteering, but haven't gotten around to learning more about? Is there a group you're already a part of that's hosting a one-day service event?

Whatever it is, dive in. Even if it doesn't seem big or exciting, even if it's a one-shot deal. Jump in anyway because waiting for the so-called perfect way to perfect the world is a surefire road to inaction. Don't hold yourself back because you think you have to know precisely how to move forward. While there is a way for you to do good best, there is no such thing as doing good poorly. When it comes to making a difference, you'll never regret doing something, but you will definitely regret doing nothing.

The other priceless thing about doing is that it begets doing. It puts you in the path of new people and new experiences, opens your eyes to things you might not ever have thought about or learned about or even known you cared about. Get excited about the good you can do right now, and your unique "how" will fall into place.

Remember all along the way that you have your own set of superpowers, and that what you're trying to do now is learn how to use them, channel them, and maximize their impact. Ask yourself what they are, and don't be modest. Allow yourself to think big and ride the high of knowing that you can leap tall buildings in a single bound.

Then bring yourself back to earth. Take note of the qualities you bring to even the simplest of day-to-day situations, as if you were interviewing yourself for a job. When you're in the grocery store, on the phone with a friend, at a soccer game, watching television. What do you tend to do best and like the most? What types of challenges do you enjoy taking on, even when, or despite the fact, they are difficult? Are you known among your friends, coworkers, or family members by nicknames or terms of endearment, like "the coach," "the planner," "the peacekeeper"? Ask yourself why. Is there a talent there, maybe something that comes easily to you that doesn't to others, that you can apply to the kind of difference you want to make?

Finding your right balance of self-evaluation, reflection, and action is a deeply personal process. As you go, try to be as patient with yourself as you pave your lifelong path to making your life matter as you are impatient to be a force for positive change.

You, and the world, will be better for it.

Take the Dare

As you work to zero in on the need that needs you most, be hyper aware of any injustice you encounter that ignites a fire in your belly so intense that the only way you can extinguish it is to act. Challenge yourself to examine the issue from all angles—don't stop at one giant problem. Tease the issue apart until you find the need within the need that you are uniquely suited to serve.

Bill Drayton, one of great pioneers of social entrepreneurship, calls this identifying your jujitsu move: what is the point of need where you can exert your energy that helps take down much bigger and more overwhelming problems.

For instance, poverty is a huge issue; income inequality is an enormous problem; lack of education is a vast issue area, too. My jujitsu move to try and take down these big overarching issues is glasses.

With that, I challenge you to begin finding your jujitsu move. Decide right now that for the next month you will spring into action mode. Do something, anything, that allows you to engage directly with the particular problem or injustice that you feel is calling you to service. This can mean everything from talking to the people who are affected by this need to reaching out to experts in this issue area; from identifying people who are already engaged in work in this issue area to finding one opportunity to get involved in bringing about the solution. Ask yourself as you go what is the need within the need that is particularly in need of you. What's your move?

Those who dream by night in the dusty recesses of their minds wake up in the day to find it was vanity, but the dreamers of the day are dangerous men, for they may act their dreams with open eyes, to make it possible.
—T. E. LAWRENCE

6 Dream in the Light

In everyone there are all sorts of good ideas, ready like tinder. But much of this tinder catches fire only when it meets some flame or spark from outside, from some other person.
—ALBERT SCHWEITZER

It seems like seeing requires nothing more than opening our eyes, but what we experience as instantaneous is the end result of a complex process.

Seeing begins when infinitesimally small particles of light hit the cornea, the eye's outermost layer, and then move further and further into its deepest, most delicate recesses, all the while filtering, focusing, and refining the information the light is trying to communicate.

The light's journey continues, triggering nerve impulses and pushing them through pathways leading to the occipital lobe, the brain's visual processing center, where the brain translates the visual information coming at your eyes into a picture that makes sense. As a result, without the brain as its partner, no matter how perfectly every surface, tissue, nerve, lining and lens of the eye functions, what we see has no context. Without the brain's help, it's all a meaningless jumble of light.

Just as the eyes must partner with the brain to make sense of the world around us, precious little can ever be complete or reach its fullest potential in isolation. This surely is the case with human beings. We crave connection and need it to thrive.

The basic need for connection is evidenced in a variety of studies that have been conducted in the last decade demonstrating that we are in the midst of a global "epidemic" of loneliness. People of all ages experience a sense of extreme isolation that can be both psychologically and physically harmful. As Paul Irving, chairman of the Milken Institute Center for the Future of Aging, writes in the *Wall Street Journal*, "Experts suggest that loneliness can increase the risk of premature death by 30 percent, making it as risky as obesity and as dangerous as smoking 15 cigarettes a day."

Yet we don't necessarily have to feel a sense of isolation on such a profound level to experience its ill effects. And while loneliness can come as a result of circumstances beyond our control, sometimes we are the architects of our own isolation without even being aware of it.

For many years, I created stark divisions between parts of myself and of my life that didn't have to exist at all. I carried the ambivalence I'd had about being an optometrist, and the dread I'd felt when I imagined spending my days in a dark, windowless exam room, right out of school and into my office as I began seeing patients.

I thought of my work in the practice, the job that generated the necessary income I needed to live, as my "lifestyle work"; while I viewed anything I was doing for the greater good (as I saw it) outside the practice as my "passion work."

When I was in the office, I was making a living. When I was in India or Africa or South America, I was making a life. The "lifestyle work" was the means; the "passion work" was the end. It was the path to mattering and to meaning, and my one true source of fulfillment.

By living this dichotomous and disjointed existence, although I had an overall sense of well-being and liked the life I was leading, at the same time I was robbing myself of a greater sense of connection.

Fortunately, I have learned through experience and through life-changing partnerships, both personal and professional, that making a difference is not something you do in a vacuum or on the side. It is a worldview and a way of life. It's working to be your whole self everywhere at all times, so that you can bring your whole self to everything that you do.

The more we integrate all the facets of our being, the more we bust through walls and make windows instead. We feel better, we function better, and we have the best shot at building the lives we dream of living.

While connection is good for our well-being and the quality of our lives in general, it is indispensable in the lifelong effort to make your life matter. Reaching out to others and letting people in leads to greater impact, often by leading you to ideas and insights you never would have had going it alone. When you're trying to do something big, key partnerships and collaborations make seemingly insurmountable tasks smaller. When you're feeling small, partnerships and collaborations give you strength.

There is a verse in Proverbs that essentially says that when you lose sight of your vision you lose your way. Great partners transform what can be a lonely pursuit, one that will at turns entice you into throwing in the towel, into a gateway to power and possibilities. With their support, the vision that lives in your mind's eye has the best chance of becoming a picture of real change you can see with your own eyes in the world.

Rolling the Stone from the Well

Think of the world you carry within you, and call this
thinking what you will; whether it be remembering your
own childhood or yearning toward your own future—only
be attentive to that which rises up in you and set it above
everything that you observe about you. What goes on in your
innermost being is worthy of your whole love.
—Rainer Maria Rilke

I once was invited to come talk about VisionSpring at Waynesburg University, a Christian college in Pennsylvania. After the lecture, I spoke briefly with an undergraduate student named

Chris, who was in the early days of discovering how to make his life matter, and already working on an interesting social venture with Costa Rican coffee farmers.

When I returned to New York, Chris sent me a really nice e-mail by way of follow-up. He talked more about being on the quest to discover the need that needed him most and said, "I don't know the exact details yet, but I'm planning to 'bloom where I'm planted,' as the saying goes."

I often think of the way that Chris described his path because blooming where you're planted requires discovering your roots. Much of why Chris had set out on his journey to matter had everything to do with his understanding of himself as a Christian and what that meant for the life he hoped to build. In that sense, Chris was growing out of a story much bigger than himself—of history, culture, and family.

Chris reminded me that before you can grow into yourself and reach out to others, you have to dig down first. You have to understand where you come from and know where your life and your vision for making a difference fit within the context of a story that began long before you. As you discover where you fit in the world's ongoing story, you must also find where your life fits into the larger story of your family and your people. You have to ask yourself what unfulfilled dream of your ancestors will you make a reality as you dream your own dreams of a better world. And you have to understand that you have to partner with your past to create your present and make a brighter future.

When I was a little older than Chris, I was far from as rooted as he was. Like many of the other kids I knew growing up in the shelter of our upper-middle-class suburb, I grew up in a nominally Jewish home. Synagogue for the "big" holidays (the Jewish New Year and the Day of Atonement), gifts and candles at Hanukkah, and a bar mitzvah on the checklist. I was raised to appreciate my religion, but not to be religious. Sometimes I felt at home in Judaism, and sometimes I felt like a stranger in its house.

For the most part, being Jewish was part of me because I was born Jewish. It was sort of like white noise—always on in the background, but not something I chose to listen to.

So when I earned a full scholarship to do one of my fourth-year optometry school rotations at Hadassah Ein Kerem Hospital in Israel, although I looked forward to visiting there for the first time in my life and certainly wanted to do some exploring, my excitement was mostly about the practical professional experience I would gain working in Jerusalem's only level one trauma center.

And gain that professional experience I did. What I hadn't anticipated was that the time I spent in Israel would also became a sojourn through my people's past that cemented my Jewish identity and prepared me for a life of service to all people.

The year 1987 marked one of the more complicated times in Israel's life. The day before my fellowship began, I'd driven a rental car to Jerusalem down the backbone of the West Bank, through Nablus, Ramallah and Bethlehem from northern Israel, where I'd spent three months working and trying to learn Hebrew on a kibbutz called Hazorea ("the sower").

The day my fellowship began, an Israeli army truck traveling through the West Bank on exactly the same road I'd been on not twenty-four hours earlier, spun out of control and careened into two cars carrying four Palestinian civilians. Every one of them was killed. That accident is said to have incited the first Intifada, during which stones and Molotov cocktails were popular weapons of choice. Those weapons were the reason why I spent the majority of my fellowship at Hadassah treating the resultant severe ocular trauma in Palestinians and Jewish Israelis alike.

It struck me, in particular, how the world of the hospital and the world outside were so dramatically different. Inside the hospital, doctors and patients, Palestinian and Israeli alike, were all just human beings who saw and treated one another as such, all while a battle raged outside fueled by hatred, demonization, and the dehumanization of the other. Every time I saw the difference, I wondered why it was so hard to make the world beyond the hospital doors match the world inside.

I brought my own personal conflicts with me to Jerusalem, too. Even as I was on the doorstep of completing my optometry degree, I continued wondering whether something else might be out there that would make me feel complete—something that would inspire more excitement.

Instantly fascinated by Jerusalem's history, I signed up for a free tour of the city's holiest sites on a day off. An American PhD history student named Sarah led the tour, which captured my attention and made me aware of how little I knew about Jerusalem, the Bible, and my ancestors. I needed to learn more, but for that I needed a guide.

My plan was to sign up for another tour Sarah was conducting the following week. But I didn't think it would be sufficient, so I asked her if she'd consider creating a three-month course to help me begin understanding Jerusalem's past and my own. I've no idea why a bright, busy student like Sarah thought it was worth the great effort she put in to designing a tailor-made curriculum for one person who had twenty dollars a week to spend on three hours of her valuable teaching time, but I'm eternally grateful that she did.

Sarah and I studied every Tuesday morning from 9:00 A.M. to noon. Our classroom was Jerusalem itself. Bible in hand as both history book and map, Sarah led me to different sites around the city, and, reading passages from the ancient text that corresponded with each location, told me the story of Jerusalem starting from 1000 BCE to the present day.

One of the biblical passages I studied with Sarah was that of Jacob (one of three patriarchs in Jewish tradition) and a family reunion following a period in his life of wandering and personal exile. Jacob encounters a large well with a stone equally as large covering it, preventing a nearby flock of sheep from drinking. The shepherd appears, and when the two men speak they realize they are related; the shepherd is Jacob's uncle. The feeling of connecting with family after his silent, solitary journey induces an astounding rush of adrenaline in Jacob, and with that strength he rolls the heavy stone from the mouth of the well.

Connecting with my heritage inspired a similar strength in me. For the first time in my life, I knew with utter clarity that I wanted to be a link in the three-thousand-year-old chain of Jewish history and tradition, and that I wanted the best of it to continue to live through the best of me.

Before I left Jerusalem, I visited the synagogue at Hadassah Ein Kerem to see the famous Chagall Windows. Born Moishe Segal to a Hasidic Jewish family in what is now Belarus, Marc Chagall spent two years in his Cote d'Azur studio crafting twelve eleven-by eight-foot stained-glass windows, one for each of the twelve tribes of Israel.

When the windows were installed in 1962, at the dedication ceremony Chagall said, "A stained glass window is a transparent partition between my heart and the heart of the world."

Jewish law requires that all synagogues have windows. Rabbi Abraham Isaac Kook, who immigrated to Palestine in 1904, elaborated on the precept, explaining that whenever we pray we must be aware of the outside world.

My six months in Israel introduced me to my roots. It also freed me to actively seek a spiritual framework in which and from which to live my life, and one whose values and teachings I can pass on to my children as they build lives of their own.

It also started me on a search for wisdom traditions and wise people, like Dr. V., of all backgrounds and faiths to open my mind and heart more expansively to the entire world. It invited me, maybe even commanded me, to explore what it means to be a true citizen of a universe whose workings are beyond all understanding, but whose mysterious code we must try to crack nonetheless.

My time in Israel opened a window between my heart and the heart of the world and made me aware that any people's highest purpose of peace, justice, dignity, and equality is an unanswered prayer until the world outside reflects it.

You don't have to travel to a distant land to dig deeper and explore where you've been planted. It can be as simple as filling in the blanks with statements, like:

I am the son/grandson/great-grandson of . . .
I am the daughter/granddaughter/great-granddaughter of . . .
I am the inheritor of . . .
I want to end the cycle of . . .
When I face a challenge or important decision, I hear the voice of . . .
I am the unfulfilled dream of . . .
I want to continue the work of . . .

As is the case in all traditions, memory and honoring those who have come before us figures prominently into ritual and practice. In Judaism, a special service called Yizkor takes place on certain holidays dedicated solely to remembrance. During this service prayers are said silently by each individual in remembrance of loved ones and communally for those who were persecuted and who perished for the crime of simply being who they were.

The common denominator in every one of these remembrance prayers is the stated commitment to do something to make a more just world that will do justice to the memory of the departed's life.

Something about this link between memory and action, between the call of the past and heeding the call to service, gets to the heart of how embracing our past lets us open our arms even wider to the future that awaits us and our efforts.

Partner Bravely

It looks like a solitary sport, but it takes a team.
—DIANA NYAD

Although delving deeper into my past opened a window between my heart and the heart of the world in a powerful and essential way, when I started working in the practice after graduating NECO, I kept the walls between my "lifestyle work" and my "passion work" firmly in place.

When my "passion work" led me to HKI and eventually turned into a decade of service with the organization, I spent those ten years living out of a suitcase abroad and a briefcase at home. Apart from some pictures of my travels here and there in the office, unless someone specifically asked about them I rarely spoke about the work I did beyond the walls of the practice.

By the last year of my commitment to HKI, I'd made more than thirty trips to Africa and had been doing far less of the sort of fieldwork that brought me into contact with people, like Baasa. Instead, I spent the majority of my time abroad trapped in conference rooms at the central offices of the African Program for Onchocerciasis Control (APOC) discussing public health policy issues for hours on end.

On one trip, I had just been given a seat on the first Technical Consultative Committee of the APOC. The committee was charged with reviewing and recommending funding for the best proposals submitted by African governments and their NGO partners in their efforts to fight river blindness.

I sat at the conference room table with people far more experienced and knowledgeable than I. Most were MDs and PhDs who had made combating river blindness their life's work.

Although I'd learned a ton from them and respected them greatly, I became frustrated listening to the discourse around the table. It was the midnineties, and the AIDS pandemic was pulsing out of control. Malaria and tuberculosis were resurgent as well, and I remember thinking that if the best doctors in the world kept talking only to one another in one room, while the brightest technocrats talked among themselves in another, we would never attract the kind of political will and financing necessary to fight these public health emergencies on all fronts. This was most especially the case when it came to meeting the eye care needs of the global poor, which hadn't received much attention to begin with.

To make significant, lasting change, I believed it was imperative to figure out a way to put critical health issues like these on the radar screens and to-do lists of African presidents, the finance minister, and minister of defense—people who had real power to allocate necessary resources to get the job done. We needed to be more strategic and demonstrate that these diseases were more than public health issues, but also compromised national security and crippled economic development. Only then would these issues get the kind of political and financial support they required and deserved.

Yet no matter how hard I pressed the doctors, I couldn't convince them that staying walled off in our little world wouldn't serve our cause best. The harder I pushed, the more content everyone was to stay right where they were.

After one of these marathon days of meetings, I returned to my hotel in Ouagadougou, a bustling capital city in the West African country of Burkina Faso. The accommodations were spare: a wooden chair, metal desk, and a cot. Even though I was exhausted, I couldn't sleep. Instead I paced the room, heart pounding, pupils the size of serving trays trying to come up with some compelling way to get these great minds to work together.

About an hour before my alarm was set to go off, I surrendered to sleep. Almost. My eyes closed like a garage door that gets stuck with about half a foot to go before it reaches the ground. Something clicked. I thought, I spend half my time in New York with the richest, most powerful people in the world, and the other half with the least powerful people in the poorest parts of the world. Instead of banging my head against a wall trying to break down the barriers between two narrow groups perfectly content with the status quo, why not close the chasm between the vast and variegated worlds of the powerful and the powerless and unite them to create sustainable impact instead?

Not long after my return from Ouagadougou, I was conducting a dilated fundus exam for a patient in my office—a fancy term for the part of a checkup when the doctor puts drops in your eyes, you sit and wait awhile for your pupils to dilate, and then you walk around in sunglasses for several hours after either looking like Jackie O. (if you came to your appointment prepared) or like you got lost on the way home from a 3D movie (you know who you are).

I was still so caught up on my recent experience in West Africa that I opened up about it, sharing my frustrations and my growing sense that cross-sector collective thinking and action was the only way forward. It's possible that my unusual candor may have had something to do with the fact that this particular patient was Madeleine Albright, who was the US ambassador to the United Nations at the time. I thought she might understand some of my feelings about the impasse.

She listened carefully and said, "You should take this to the Council on Foreign Relations."

Slightly embarrassed that I didn't know, I asked, "What is the Council on Foreign Relations?"

Secretary Albright gently explained that the Council on Foreign Relations (CFR) was one of the most influential foreign policy think tanks in the world, and pointed out that it was only eight blocks from my practice. She also told me that the CFR had something called a Term Membership Program. CFR term members are a diverse group of about one hundred young professionals of all types who spend five years learning about international affairs and US foreign policy. By the end of our conversation, Secretary Albright had offered to write a supporting letter for me to be nominated to participate in the program.

With Secretary Albright's help and encouragement, I went ahead and applied for CFR term membership, but I needed a primary nominator, someone who was a member of the Council. That person was Ambassador Don Easum.

Don was a highly regarded public servant who, among his many other achievements over the course of the more than three decades he spent at the US Department of State, also served as US Ambassador to Burkina Faso and Nigeria.

The first time I met Don he was wearing another hat as vice president of the River Blindness Foundation (RBF). He and the president of RBF, Bill Baldwin, were interviewing me by phone for a position there. After the call, I could tell that Don liked me, but that Bill could either take me or leave me (and was leaning hard toward the latter). Don prevailed and I got the job.

My first assignment was to meet Don and Bill at the Ethiopian Embassy in Washington, DC, to discuss river blindness control in that country. The day before I was supposed to take the train to

DC for the meeting, I was out for a late-night walk in New York when a taxi pulled up alongside me. I thought it odd as I wasn't trying to get a cab, just strolling along minding my own business. I picked up the pace a bit, but the cab kept inching forward.

"Jordy!" I heard and kept moving.

"Hey, Jordy," I heard again, "it's me, Trupper."

I turned to look, and the taxi driver was an old friend of mine from home whom I'd known since we were in fourth grade. I hadn't seen David Trupp in years, so we got to chatting. We'd been talking for a while when I told David I really needed to be getting home, that I had an early train to catch in the morning. But we agreed that we should get together another time so we could catch up properly.

We'd said our goodbyes, and just as David pulled away, he lurched to a quick stop and shouted, "Train to where?"

"What?" I said, over the traffic.

"Where are you headed in the morning?"

"DC."

"No problem," he said, "I'll take you."

It was a strange and generous offer for many reasons, not the least of which was that David was going to drive me off the meter. But he insisted, so I figured instead of making sincere overtures to catching up over a coffee that might not ever happen, why not.

True to his word, the next morning David was outside my apartment to pick me up. We talked the entire five hours with nary an awkward silence the whole way.

When we got to the embassy, we pulled up into this giant circular driveway. By chance, Don happened to be at the entrance with another gentleman standing next to him. As I stepped out of the dusty New York Yellow Cab taxi, Don said, "Jordan, welcome. Meet Bill Baldwin."

Bill just shook his head. He thought I'd paid to take a taxi all the way from New York for the meeting, which, when you're interviewing for a job with a not-for-profit, made me look like even more of a colossal idiot to Bill than he already thought I was.

While I don't know that Bill ever fully warmed to me, he did sign off on my hire with RBF, I suspect mostly because of Don. And based on that relationship, it was due in large part to Don's kind willingness to nominate me for the CFR term membership program that I was invited to join the 1998 class.

At the first meeting for new term members, Les Gelb, who was the CFR's president, was there to give us a charge. Les was the primary author of the Pentagon Papers, a Pulitzer Prize-winning journalist, had served as the editor of the *New York Times* op-ed page, wrote his doctoral dissertation with Henry Kissinger as his advisor, and was one of the world's most respected voices on foreign policy. He was hardly someone I would seek out for conversations, because I found talking to a person with that kind of résumé far too intimidating.

When Les approached the lectern to kick off the meeting, I settled into my chair for a long speech, most of which I felt certain would be too wonky for me to follow. Les proceeded to offer us some warm words of welcome, and then said he had something of critical import to tell us about the world. He took a dramatically long look around the room, made eye contact with every person, and proclaimed, "We screwed it up. You fix it." He also invited us to come to him directly if we had ideas about how to fix the world that the Council wasn't addressing. With that, the cocktail hour commenced.

During cocktails, I felt a bit like I had when I rolled up to the Ethiopian Embassy in a Yellow Cab. Nonetheless a lot of people had gambled on me to be in this room, so I summoned my courage and went over to introduce myself to Les.

As we talked, I shared with Les that I'd noticed that the CFR wasn't doing any health-related work, and I saw where I might be able to make a contribution. In addition to putting public health on the radar screen of every person in the class in every sphere and convincing them that they had a role to play in solving the biggest public health issues of our day, one of the arguments I hoped to make to advance the relevance and utility of my idea was to prove that public health was not only a health issue, a humanitarian issue, or an economic one, but a national security issue, too.

I could see that Les was curious, and he invited me to meet with him to continue the conversation.

A few weeks later, in Les's corner office, he looked at me and said, "So you think health is a national security issue?"

"Yes," I replied, conjuring my most emphatic voice.

"Prove it."

"If you hire me," I said, doubling down on my chutzpah, "I'll prove it."

When I walked out the door, Les had committed $2,000 so that I could hire a research assistant to build my case. Eight weeks and five iterations of an outline for detailing my argument later, Les hired me as the first adjunct senior fellow for Global Health Policy at CFR.

It was a big win. Global Health was now officially on the agenda of what is widely considered the preeminent think tank in the country. In the five years that followed, with the help of people like Ambassador Richard Holbrooke, Secretary of Health and Human Services Donna Shalala, world-renowned economist Jeffrey Sachs, and a veritable who's who of health and international affairs experts, we built a case for placing health more squarely on the foreign policy agenda. The work culminated in a white paper copublished by the CFR and the Milbank Memorial Fund entitled "Why Health is Important to U.S. Foreign Policy."

Although things worked out better than I ever could have imagined, the fact was that throughout that first welcome reception, during my conversation with Les, and more times than I can count in the years I spent as a term member thereafter, I'd often think, "I'm an eye doctor. What the hell am I doing here?" I didn't know the lingo, frequently had to look up words that were new to me (I recall "hegemony" being one of them). And in the age before smartphones and the magic Google machine, I periodically had to force myself to ask others in my program class to tell me more about geopolitical terms I wasn't familiar with. (I also vividly remember being especially clueless when "Maginot Line" was tossed about repeatedly during a discussion about World War II, while everyone else nodded their heads.) I still felt like the dumb one sitting in the back of the classroom, head down, hoping not to get called on by the teacher.

Rampant case of imposter syndrome notwithstanding, all the research I did to produce my findings, what it took to collect them, and the treasure trove of knowledge I was able to draw upon by being in rooms with the kinds of experts and thought leaders I would never had been in otherwise, made me a more agile thinker and, even more important, a much better listener.

My time at the CFR taught me how to draw on the strengths, skills, and insights of those who on the surface would appear to have no connection to, or investment in, public health whatsoever, yet without whom I couldn't have made any real progress in paving my path to making a difference.

What's more, I learned how to be strategic, catalytic, and how to grow networks—a skill set that has proven key in my efforts to be an effective leader. Being there was the beginning of understanding that the more minds and the more talent you engage to dream with you, the more powerful and promising the effort; and the more connections you create between presumably separate worlds, the easier it is to galvanize the strengths and energy of those who once might have said, "It's your problem" into forming a formidable team that claims your problem and calls it "ours."

If I hadn't opened up to Secretary Albright, I'm sure none of this would have happened. And I have no problem saying that without my time at the Council, I might never have founded Scojo Vision and Scojo Foundation or gotten the clarity I needed to know just how much I missed being in the field. Without people like Don and Les, I wouldn't have gained the experience and concrete knowledge I needed to get VisionSpring off the ground. Instead I would have been just like the professionals in Cameroon who frustrated me by being all too comfortable staying indefinitely within the same four walls.

I don't know when exactly my flywheel started spinning, but I do know for sure that it picked up real momentum when I invited others to start pushing with me. Although the process is not simple and still requires ceaseless pushing, these simple steps led me to the cherished partnerships that have fostered breakthroughs in my determination to make my life matter:

> Don't be afraid to share an idea that gets your heart pumping, no matter how half-baked it may be, no matter how much resistance it meets.
> Don't be afraid to ask for help. If your heart is in the right place, you'll find that people are not only happy to help, but that inviting someone into your effort to matter allows them to matter, too.
> Don't be afraid of being afraid. Fear is the gateway to better.
> Don't be afraid to look stupid. Stupidity is bravery in disguise.

Never dismiss or undervalue one part of your life and glorify another. A meaningful life is a connected one, and while you may not yet have a clear path for making your unique kind of difference, you do have the power to create and foster the connections that will help you find it.

If you are the architect of the wall standing between you and the positive change you want to make, get out your sledgehammer and start swinging.

Partner Gladly

I would rather walk alone with a friend in the dark than walk alone in the light.
—HELEN KELLER

There's a great scene in the 1975 movie *Return of the Pink Panther* in which the reliably bumbling Inspector Clouseau (a role made famous by Peter Sellers) allows a bank heist to go on right behind him because he has decided to interrogate an organ grinder.

Clouseau asks the organ grinder, who has a chimpanzee sidekick on his shoulder, whether he has paid for the proper permits to perform on the street.

The organ grinder replies, "I am a musician and the monkey

is a businessman. He doesn't tell me what to play, and I don't tell him what to do with his money."

About four years into VisionSpring's life, I felt like I was doing the work of both the organ grinder and the chimp but doing neither job particularly well. We were growing at a good clip, which was great, but as a result of our growth we also were at a major inflection point where having one person acting as the CEO, chairman of the board, and chief fund-raiser wasn't going to cut it for much longer. This was especially the case when it came to business and market development.

I called up my friend Reade Fahs and shared my predicament. Reade is CEO and President of National Vision, one of the world's leading optical chains with more than one thousand stores across the United States. Before his tenure at National Vision, Reade spent a decade with Lenscrafters doing advertising, marketing, and new product development. I reached out to him because he really gets the market and has a depth of knowledge and experience unsurpassed by many.

"Reade," I said, "I feel like I'm alone in a rowboat with a hole in it in the middle of the Pacific Ocean."

Without hesitation he replied, "I'll get in with you."

Shortly thereafter, Reade jumped in indeed. He became VisionSpring's chairman of the board and a key driver of VisionSpring's success.

One of Reade's greatest contributions to VisionSpring lay in his own talent for dreaming in the light. From the moment he became chairman, he set a collaborative culture inside the boardroom and beyond that turned everyone—board member, colleague, donor, and key stakeholder alike—into a group of friends sharing a big bold mission. And even as he broke down barriers to create a sense of community, he also set clear boundaries to help everyone understand the best and most effective ways for them to channel their ideas and expertise.

For all these reasons and more, Reade continues to be my right hand and steadfast partner to this day.

We spend most of our lives in our own little rowboats. When

the waters are calm and the sun is shining, it's not hard to get folks to come along for the ride. But when the weather fouls, your vessel gets tossed, and you're starting to take on water, it's the rare person who volunteers to join you.

Partner Consciously

Rabbi Yosei said: In all my days I did not call my wife my wife . . . I called my wife my home.
—BABYLONIAN TALMUD, TRACTATE SHABBAT 118B

Twenty-five years ago, a patient walked into my office for an exam with one of my partners. She was in the contact lens insertion and removal room and asked the technician about the photographs on the wall of places around the world. When I walked in, the technician turned to Erica and said, "This is Dr. Kassalow. He's the photographer." Erica and I exchanged greetings and had a cordial chat.

Some months later, Erica was back in the office and, remembering my interest in the developing world, invited me to attend an opera she was singing in with the Greenwich Village Opera Company. The proceeds would go to support educational programs in El Salvador. I figured if I took Erica up on the invitation, then she might say yes if I invited her to dinner.

Fortunately, she accepted. When I picked her up, Erica came out wearing pearls and a fur coat. I thought she might have been thinking that I was some rich New York doctor who golfed in his spare time, which made me a little nervous. It turned out to be the best date of my entire life. Until the following week, when our second date was even better.

As we walked through Greenwich Village I was engrossed in some meandering paean to India, saying I could be perfectly happy living there in a cave for the rest of my days. What I said wasn't entirely untrue, but truth be told I also wanted to see how she would react. Would talk of an ascetic existence in a developing country scare her off?

Erica was completely unfazed. Instead she asked me to tell her more about what I loved about India and why I dreamed of living there. As we talked more, I also learned that the fur and pearls belonged to her mom. They were gifts from Erica's dad, whom she was especially close to. He died when Erica was just nineteen years old.

Erica dazzled me with her smarts and her strength, her honesty and her curiosity. When I talked about my commitment to making my life matter, she understood and accepted that unless I was doing something to heal the world, I couldn't fully be myself and I couldn't be happy. She didn't see what I cared about as something I would eventually grow out of, but instead respected it and wanted to grow with me. We've been sharing the same rowboat, in ideal conditions and rough ones, without hesitation, ever since.

Viewing the world not only through my eyes, but also placing my trust in what I knew would make me a better man by seeing it through Erica's, marked the beginning of a deeply personal transformation that also has made me a more open person.

The openness Erica inspired in me has a great deal to do with transparency, something that has made our partnership an enduring and successful one. From the beginning, we had open and honest conversations about the things that mattered to us most, about what we valued: the nonnegotiables, the nice-to-haves, and the totally intolerable. These conversations allowed us both to know for sure whether we wanted to take a leap of faith in walking through life together, and they also caused us both to be more deliberate in communicating our real feelings and priorities to each other.

What that means for us today is that, for better or worse, we rarely have to deal with brewing hostilities that build up over time and then eventually blow up in a tense moment. Given the kind of schedule I keep and the big sacrifices Erica makes to support me in working to make a difference, getting frustrations on the table rather than holding back is of the utmost importance.

For instance, travel has been an integral part of my work, and in order to do the amount of travel that work entails, plus meet my obligations to my practice, I use all but two weeks of my vacation time for VisionSpring and VisionSpring related trips. Because my work takes me all over the world, it doubles as my adventure, so my idea of a vacation is to stick close to home. Staying somewhere close to New York, like in the Connecticut countryside, for instance, is ideal.

Erica, on the other hand, is the one who is at home with our kids and working in her psychotherapy practice when I'm abroad. As a result, her idea of vacation is about having an adventure that takes her out of the familiar, far from work and far from home.

Erica is completely open with me about how much it bothers her that I don't get excited about using my limited vacation time for family adventures, and sometimes she takes it upon herself to do the planning and make those family adventures happen—with or without me. Although this admittedly is an ongoing source of conflict between us, because it's out there, while we may sometimes struggle to get to a comfortable place of compromise over the details, the issue is not something that festers and eats away at our bond. It's a difference, but not a deal breaker.

This ability to have conflict and stay closely connected also gets back to being aligned in our values. This is one of our guiding lights. This doesn't mean that we value the exact same things, but we began with and continue to have a matching overall value system that makes us true allies in sacrificing for, and dedicating ourselves to, the same things: a mutually agreed upon hierarchy of financial priorities; family; and individual fulfillment in our chosen paths. And because we are aligned in this way, when the life we want to lead gets reality tested, when the struggles we have accepted in theory become real, when we experience anger, frustration, or regret, the things we value most together always guide us home to the foundation of us.

When Erica and I were thinking about having a third child and trying to determine whether we could afford it, one of the things Erica agreed to was that we would forego taking any vacations (regardless of location) for several years.

In addition, because Erica and I had decided individually, and then as a couple, that Judaism would be a significant part of our lives and of our family's life, we made it a team project to find a synagogue community not just so our kids would have a place to learn about Judaism, but also so that we could live Judaism together.

This didn't begin with sending our kids to Hebrew school, but with me and Erica finding a rabbi we felt connected to and with whom we could be completely honest about our theological struggles, ask questions, and from whom we could learn and grow in our understanding of inherited Jewish rituals and traditions.

We were fortunate to find that community at the Stephen Wise Free Synagogue and that rabbi in Rabbi Ammiel Hirsch.

Erica sometimes joins our cantor in leading the community in song during the Jewish High Holidays. We also make it a point to the best of our ability to attend Friday night Sabbath worship together. Although it's getting more and more difficult to do as an entire family with Bryce away at college and with Jonas and Sofia progressing into their teenage years, Erica and I still make sure to be there, and sometimes make a date night out of it by having dinner together after services. It's one of the ways we make sure that time to be with each other, enjoy each other, and check in doesn't fall to the bottom of our long list of priorities.

Erica has taught me that a matching values system is so critical because while we're always changing, really should be changing, sometimes in radical ways and sometimes in more subtle ones, the overarching aspects of our values systems don't. Over the course of a long partnership, jobs may come and go, career interests may change, and priorities may shift. But if you can adapt, keep an open line of communication, remain willing to compromise, be clear with yourself and your partner about what you can accept without resentment; and if you also can maintain the awareness that in a partnership no one grows in isolation—that your individual changes don't occur in a bubble or solely affect you—you can stay true to a core value, like supporting whatever will support your partner's overall sense of satisfaction and well-being.

This gets to the heart and soul of a lifelong love: admiration. Erica often says that just as the body is 60 percent water, love is at least (if not more) 60 percent admiration. Admiration is the glue in the great times and in the toughest ones. You can be pissed at your partner; you can feel distant from your partner; but if you can still look at your partner and say that you admire that person, then the sacrifices don't feel as hard and the conflicts don't seem as difficult to resolve. Because if you can remember how much of the love you feel for your partner stems from what you admire about them most, you won't want to do anything that will stop them from being that person. If you can nurture the admiration, you will remain each other's home in the world, as you change and as you work for change.

Partner for Life

All real living is meeting.
—MARTIN BUBER

For having been so ambivalent about my optometry work, so invested in keeping my practice separate, seeing it as a means to an end rather than something endowed with its own meaning, I am astounded by the way that every major turning point in my life leads back to it, and how almost everything that imbues my life with meaning is rooted in it.

This starts with my business partner, Barry, and my other business partner, Sue Resnick, who has been with the practice for more years than I. I rely on Barry and Sue to make it possible for me to continue pursuing the path I have chosen beyond our office door. They have put a tremendous amount of faith in me by allowing me the freedom to structure my time so that I can work to make a difference, and also by trusting that my work to make a difference won't interfere with my ability to be a good partner to them and a good steward of our practice. Without their belief in me and their unwavering support of this path I have taken, it would be impossible for me to make the living that enables me to both take care of my family and work for positive change in the world.

My patients, too, have been and remain invaluable partners.

I have patients who surprise me with totally unsolicited—some large and some small—checks for VisionSpring when they come for their routine eye exams because they like being part of something bigger than themselves.

I have also had patients who have become major supporters of my work in public health and in growing VisionSpring, including an amazing woman named Sally Ganz.

I met Sally in the midnineties. She was a new patient, but it felt like we'd known each other for years. Just as Erica had done, Sally also noticed the photos in my office, although the one she focused on in particular was of Africa. Sally commented that she had recently visited there, and that the continent had moved her more than any place she'd ever been.

Our conversation was so interesting, before I knew it I was running behind schedule, but we agreed it would be nice to talk some more. Sally was quick to follow up with an invitation to her home.

When I arrived it was as if I had entered a museum. It turned out that Sally, who was in her eighties, and her late husband, Victor, had been great lovers of art and had been collecting together for fifty years. No connoisseur of art myself, I had no clue that I was surrounded by works by Robert Rauschenberg and Jasper Johns.

On the way to what Sally called "The Red Room," we passed a Pablo Picasso painting called "Le Rêve" ("The Dream"). The Red Room itself was home to four Picassos from a series of fifteen called "Women of Algiers." More than a bit intimidated by my surroundings, I recall Sally saying, "I don't live around the paintings; the paintings live around me."

Both Sally and Victor came from humble beginnings, and they didn't buy art to become collectors. They simply saw things they loved and bought them when they could manage it.

Sally quickly became a supporter of HKI. When her grandson Anthony was about to graduate from college with aspirations to pursue an MBA and a career in finance, she asked if I could find a place for him at HKI "before the banks got to him." Anthony worked with HKI for several years before moving on to get that MBA, and while he now works in the for-profit sector, he serves on HKI's Board of Trustees. And when Scojo Foundation first got off the ground, Sally's granddaughter Lily was our first employee.

Six months after Sally died, the family decided to put Sally and Victor's entire collection up for auction at Christie's. (Le Rêve, which Victor originally purchased for $7,000, sold for more than $48 million.) Around the time of the auction, Christie's published a beautiful coffee table book featuring their entire collection, which at the time sold for $100 a pop. The family made sure that 100 percent of the proceeds went to support HKI's river blindness work.

And then of course, without the practice I never would have met Erica, my most important partner in life.

Only good things have come from opening up and reaching out. Even when partnerships have been episodic and right only for a particular chapter but not for the long haul, I have also grown from connecting, learned from connecting, and have become a better person, doctor, change agent, husband, father, and friend for it.

Although I once divided my life and my days into "lifestyle work" and "passion work," now I see everything I do as my life's work: private practice, VisionSpring, marriage, children. That's because if you want to dedicate some of your life to making a fragmented world whole, you can't live a fragmented existence while doing it.

In that same e-mail from Chris following the Waynesburg University visit that left such an impression on me, he wished me well on an upcoming trip to India I had discussed in my lecture and signed the message, "Bendiciones." Chris told me that while the word literally means "blessings," in Christian communities in Costa Rica it is a both a word of greeting and a word of parting.

Similarly the Hebrew word *shalom*, which literally means "peace," also is used when saying hello and saying goodbye. The root letters in "shalom" mean "whole," and I believe that every meeting, every point of connection with another person in every realm of our existence holds the potential for wholeness—in our-selves, in others, and in the how and the why of whatever our chosen paths may be in fixing a broken world. Wherever we discover them, wherever they discover us, the best partnerships become part of us; they make us who we are and inform everything we do. In that there is no separation. Boundaries, yes. But borders, no. Not if we will it so.

Your path to making a difference, whether you're at the beginning or somewhere in the midst, must be paved with partnerships for true impact and momentum. So take the time to ask yourself now:

> Where are the points of connection between what I currently see as two separate efforts—what I do to earn money, and what I do out of the commitment I have made, or want to make, to making a difference in the world?
> How can I begin putting these separate worlds in dialogue with each other?
> Whose support can I enlist in doing it?
> Who are the people I encounter every day, or have encountered in the past, who might be interested in what I'm doing or hope to do to make a difference? Who might be eager to help if I just asked?

In addition to asking yourself these questions, start telling as many people as you can about what you care about, what you're working on or aiming to do in making your life matter. Make it an exercise in what you might feel is oversharing. How do people respond? Who is the most interested? Who wants to know more? Who is ready with ideas, and of those ideas which ones do you think are great ones?

On the order of ideas, don't just look for great partners—be one. Listen to what others' interests are, their concerns, what they value most highly. How can you help them? How can you support them on their path? Are there places where your paths overlap? Where can you walk together?

Also take stock of partnerships of all kinds that have had, or are having, a positive impact on you—personal and professional, classmates, teachers and mentors who inspire you. Why are those relationships important? Why are they successful? In relationships of any significance, what are your nonnegotiables, nice-to-haves, and intolerables? Make a list. You may find, as I have, that your list also transcends the many spaces in which you live your life. As you develop yours, can you refocus your attention to certain aspects in partnerships of significance that you have neglected in order to strengthen the bonds you already share? As you form new partnerships of all kinds, and also in existing ones if you're coming to the desire to make a difference later in life, how can you be the most transparent about why making your life matter is a nonnegotiable commitment? Can you communicate the sacrifices you are willing to make to uphold that commitment? Can your partner accept those sacrifices, even in tough times, without resentment? Does your partner understand what it really means for them to join you in your rowboat?

To help you get started, these are the key ingredients and the common denominators in all the successful partnerships that have helped me make a difference, and that continue helping me make my life matter:

Trust
Mutual respect
Matching value system
Shared goals
Complementary strengths
Listening and open communication
Compromise
Acceptance
Admiration
Ability to share the lead
Looking out for one another's best interests
Growing together

Ability to surface difficult feelings and topics
Shared financial philosophies

Just as your path to making a difference will be different from mine, so will your list. What's on it is your choice and your business. Whether written, typed, or in your head, as you work to make your life matter, do make a point of knowing what matters to you in the partnerships that will change your life and will help you be a change-maker for life.

Take the Dare

If there was ever a time to overshare, it's now. With a purpose, that is.

Your challenge is to tell as many people as you can what you care about and what you're working on to make your life matter. Your accompanying challenge is then to listen to what they have to say. They may have an insight, they may know someone who is working on a similar problem. They may have heard of an initiative you can become a part of to strengthen your efforts. They may want to help. Be open to the good that can come from dreaming in the light about the positive change in the world you not only want to see, but that you want to create. As you share that dream, keep in mind that your goal is not to argue or debate the problem, but to cultivate partnerships to help you do your chosen part to heal it.

I also encourage you to think seriously about your most important partnerships—current and future. What makes your most significant partnerships work? What are your non-negotiables, must-haves, and intolerables? How do these ingredients enhance and support your commitment to making a difference? Which elements conflict with that goal? How can you better communicate their importance? How can you be a better partner to others, and similarly support them in their desire to make the world a better place?

Rabbi Yitzhak said: If a person says to you: I have labored and not found success, do not believe him. Similarly, if he says to you: I have not labored but nevertheless I have found success, do not believe him. If, however, he says to you: I have labored and I have found success, believe him.

—BABYLONIAN TALMUD, TRACTATE MEGILLAH 6B

7 Put the Change in Change-Maker

When we are no longer able to change a situation, we are challenged to change ourselves.
—Viktor Frankl

At some point or another, we've all played "Rock, Paper, Scissors." The outcomes are simple: Rock breaks scissors, scissors cut paper, paper covers rock, and that's that. But I think one important element in the game is missing: water.

In the spirit of the teaching of the ancient Chinese poet and philosopher Lao Tzu, "Water is fluid, soft, and yielding. But water will wear away rock, which is rigid and cannot yield. As a rule, whatever is fluid, soft, and yielding will overcome whatever is rigid and hard. This is another paradox: what is soft is strong." When you go toe to toe with a stubborn world that both resists change and invites it, and you work to make making a difference an integral part of your busy and demanding life, water covers rock every time.

Water covers rock every time because deep, lasting change is a process. And in that process, fluidity and flexibility are oftentimes much stronger than sheer might.

In the last twenty years, the word *disrupt* has become an increasingly popular part of the vernacular. When people think of disruption they think of big breakthroughs and radical change, when in fact disruption is more of a gathering storm than a tsunami.

In 1995 Harvard business professor Clayton Christensen literally wrote the book, called *The Innovator's Dilemma*, on disruption. In it, Christensen describes "disruption" as a process in which a small business with comparatively scarce resources challenges a vanguard company by serving a market the big guys have ignored. While the big guys keep getting better at serving their existing consumer base, the little guys start serving the overlooked consumers, until eventually they do it so well (and usually for less money or more bang for the consumer buck) that they lure the big guy's consumer base away as well. Then, and only then, according to Christensen's definition, has disruption occurred.

Three years ago, Christensen, his Harvard faculty colleagues Rory McDonald and Michael Raynor, co-authors of *The Innovator's Solution*, penned an article together in the *Harvard Business Review* aimed at reintroducing the original definition and meaning of disruption. With that objective in mind, they do an excellent job of offering a concrete example of what a bona fide disruptor is, but also highlight how long it can take to achieve successful disruption, by sharing the David and Goliath story of Netflix and Blockbuster.

Christensen, McDonald, and Raynor explain that at the time of Netflix's inception in 1997, Netflix didn't go after Blockbuster's customer base. Blockbuster's people were impulse movie renters who liked the convenience of walking into a store and walking out minutes later (most likely with a new release). Instead Netflix attracted tech-savvy customers who already had moved from VHS to DVD, were comfortable shopping online, and didn't mind waiting a few days for their selections (mostly of older films) to come in the mail. Because Netflix appealed to a consumer base that Blockbuster neither needed nor cared about, for a while Blockbuster could continue on its merry way.

But when the technological tide turned and gave Netflix, already online rather than in strip malls, the ability to stream video, Blockbuster's fortunes changed. For just a little bit of money, customers could watch as much content as they wanted whenever they wanted. By the time Blockbuster bothered to look and see whether Netflix was on its tail, it had little choice but to put its feet up and start binge watching with the rest of the world.

Today Netflix is a $140 billion company and Blockbuster's "be kind rewind" video return catchphrase is the stuff of memes and retro novelty T-shirts.

Not-for-profit social enterprises, like VisionSpring, start out like Netflix in that they also identify a consumer base that the Blockbusters of the world have ignored. The way VisionSpring has taken on the challenge is via what Christensen would call a "new market foothold"—turning people who have never bought your product before into consumers. VisionSpring has achieved this by seeing what pioneering business strategist C. K. Prahalad called the "invisible opportunity."

Up until his death in 2010, Prahalad was a beloved management professor at the University of Michigan's Ross School of Business. He remains one of the founding fathers of the social enterprise model.

Born in the south Indian city of Coimbatore (now Kovai) in 1941, Prahalad moved to the United States in the 1970s to earn a PhD in management at Harvard Business School, and returned to India degree in hand in 1975, just as Prime Minister Indira Gandhi cloaked the declaration of emergency rule in the guise of protecting India's security. Her measures included appalling civil rights violations, such as kidnapping men from poor neighborhoods and forcibly sterilizing them; jailing her opposition; and taking control of what had been the free press.

Prahalad's father, who had been a judge, labor rights attorney, and expert in Hindu philosophy, was so devastated at the sight of what was happening to the country he loved and even more devastated by his inability to combat it that he moved the family to the United States, including C. K., who began his tenure at Michigan.

Still invested in the fate of his country of birth, Prahalad looked on in the midnineties as the world began turning its attention to Indian consumers as a lucrative market. However, foreign businesses focused primarily on the middle-class and upper-class consumer. This inspired Prahalad to combine his love for India and his formidable business strategy skills to convince companies to turn their attention to a historically untapped market called the

Base of the Pyramid (BoP). The people who comprise the BoP market economy are some of the poorest in the world, making an average of four dollars a day. Prahalad argued that if companies turned their attention to the billions of people at the BoP, they could turn those people into consumers, turn untold profits, and combat poverty at the same time.

Prahalad's vision for how a radically altered market economy could fundamentally turn the tide of extreme poverty opened the doors to brilliant social entrepreneurs who had discovered the need that needed them most and in turn, developed creative strategies to make a difference.

In 1997 Iqbal Quadir created Grameenphone, the first affordable mobile phone service provider to the BoP market consumer in rural Bangladesh. Quadir grew up in rural Bangladesh, and as a boy he once walked for half a day to another village in order to see a doctor. When he arrived, the doctor wasn't there. Had his parents been able to call first, Quadir would have known. This was half a day that Quadir missed in school. If this had happened to Quadir's mother or father, they would have missed half a day of work, time that subsistence farmers and other BoP consumers can't afford to lose.

Because of the spotlight that Grameenphone shone on the spending power of the BoP consumer, Bangladesh is now home to dozens of mobile service providers. Grameenphone also opened the door to the invention and expansion of mobile banking technology for the BoP consumer, which has proven to combat poverty not only by helping Bangladeshis save money, but also by creating dependable networks for them to receive funds (and receive them without having to miss work to go to brick-and-mortar establishments far from home to get them). This technology is of critical import today when some 300,000 Bangladeshis work abroad and send money home to support an average of thirty-seven other family members.

Just as Quadir created Grameenphone to introduce global mobile technology to an underserved consumer base, I founded VisionSpring to do the same with eyeglasses. The optical industry historically has focused all of its attention on you and me—the one billon consumers in the world at the top of the market economy pyramid who can afford to spend as much as $400 (and some even more) on a pair of glasses. As a result, we have countless options when it comes to buying prescription glasses that fit our specific vision needs, our budgets, and personal style—three things that ensure that we will buy glasses, and that we will wear the glasses we buy.

Because the one billion people in the developing world whose livelihoods, ability to get an education, and safety hinge on the simple need for glasses are the same people who have been invisible to the global optical industry that deems them too poor to be a potential revenue source, VisionSpring focuses all of our attention on the BoP consumer by selling high quality glasses that fit their specific vision needs, budgets, and personal style.

Our hope is that by demonstrating the value of glasses to the BoP market customer, over time the customers themselves will in turn show the rest of the optical industry what a lucrative consumer base they represent. Because our biggest competitor is not the industry itself, but rather the issue of people not having access to glasses. What success looks like to us then is actually strengthening other companies' presence and position in the gaps in the markets we exist to serve by first getting them to recognize the opportunity and then crowding them in to take over in that marketplace. In a perfect world, we want them to put us out of business by figuring out how to profitably serve that marketplace, and do it better than we do it, because they always will have more resources and better supply chains. In fact, we have already seen this phenomenon starting to occur.

When I first started VisionSpring, we were speaking to a man named Claude Darnault. At the time Darnault was the director of Corporate Sustainabilty at Essilor, the world's largest lens manufacturer. Given his interest in future markets, I introduced him to Prahalad's book. Shortly thereafter, Essilor's CEO invited Prahalad to come and consult with them in their corporate headquarters in Paris.

Prahalad's work with Essilor eventually led to the company creating a robust strategy to serve the BoP market—so robust that

Essilor now has dedicated an entire division solely to the BoP market. Essilor's 2.5 New Vision Generation Division is a for-profit unit of their company whose mandate is to create 50 million new eyeglass users a year in places like India, Indonesia, and Brazil.

The capital interests of incumbent eyewear companies, like Essilor, will only strengthen and broaden VisionSpring's impact in our efforts to meet the unmet need for glasses in the developing world. Essilor's participation will aid us in eliminating a public health crisis, lifting a billion people out of poverty by helping them stay employed, and replacing the more than $200 billion the global economy currently loses each year as a result of uncorrected vision in developing nations.

In addition, getting glasses on the faces of more children who need them today helps prevent future generations from living in poverty tomorrow. By giving kids access to the indispensable tool they need to stay in school, they will grow up to join the labor force, become employers, teachers, medical professionals, and leaders who can better their own lives, those of their families, and make the difference they were created to make in their own communities, countries, and the world.

VisionSpring has been in existence for just about as long as it took Netflix to effect successful disruption. This, however, is where the similarities end. VisionSpring's definition of successful disruption is when our attempt to correct a market failure results in the one billion people in the developing world who need glasses having glasses, and when they have enough regular access to eyeglasses and eye care that the number of people who need glasses stays at zero. We've reached nearly six million people to date. Needless to say, reaching our goal will take far longer than it takes any for-profit business to achieve its own, and is one in which capturing market share is just the tip of the iceberg.

One of the lessons I've learned from taking the not-for-profit social enterprise route is a lesson for anyone who wants to make real, sustainable, lasting change. You have to be prepared going in for slow progress and what may seem like minimal results from maximum effort. But the effort not only is necessary if we're ever to solve big problems. It also yields great returns in the satisfaction you'll get when you focus on how essential you are to the fight, when you approach the work as one who is part of a great mystery you're trying to solve, clue by clue.

See yourself as one on a steady search for the invisible opportunity that will take your work, and that of others, a little bit—and maybe even a lot—further to creating positive, enduring change.

When Bad Ideas Happen to Good People

Success is never final. Failure is never fatal. It is the courage to continue that counts.
—SIR WINSTON CHURCHILL

Back in school when I started volunteering, although each VOSH trip made a difference during the five or six days in the towns and villages where we set up clinics, we rarely returned to the same place in any systematic way and, therefore, didn't have a strategy for creating sustainable change in these communities over time. Even though we made a difference during our missions, we left the people whose lives we touched without the ability to *maintain* their eye care needs. Who were they going to follow up with after we'd gone?

In addition, because the missions also required coordinating the already packed schedules of volunteer American eye care professionals and flying them over at great expense, the thousands of dollars we had to raise for every trip was a poor strategy for long-term impact and a low-impact use of our collective energy.

The glasses donations approach also proved ineffective. As it turned out, recycling and giving away donated glasses for free wasn't free, wasn't solving the problem, and was perpetuating a cycle of dependence. Between the amount of human and financial capital required to collect the glasses from their original owners, check and discard the ones that were too damaged, had highly unusual prescriptions, or had far too much wear and tear on them to put to good use, clean and sort the pairs that were of a quality we could take with us, transport them to each eye clinic location, and properly distribute them once we got on the ground, one pair of glasses cost the charitable organizations behind our missions, like VOSH and the Lions Club, $20.49 per pair to give away for free.

Even if philanthropic and volunteer resources were unlimited, which they aren't, even if you could spend $1.5 billion to put glasses in the hands of every single person in the developing world who needs them in one fell swoop, you still wouldn't eliminate the need, because donated glasses—even in the best possible shape—have limited longevity. Where do people who needed glasses go when the donated glasses they received for free broke? Where were they going to go to replace their free glasses when their prescriptions changed? And what about those who didn't need glasses at the time of our visits, or who did need them but couldn't get to the clinic or even know about the clinic because it was too far away from their homes? How many more donated frames would have to be collected, sorted, transported, and distributed to keep pace with these inevitabilities in years to come?

In addition, a different form of failure accompanied donated freebies. Because we had to work with whatever we had in the crates on our missions, although we might have been able to find a pair of used frames that fit a child's prescription, for instance, the lenses might have come in adult-sized frames. Similarly, we might have had the right lenses for a woman's prescription, yet set in a frame designed for a man. Or a pair of frames in a style so outdated and unattractive that even if they did the job from a clinical standpoint, they were simply too embarrassing to wear (as was the case with Noka).

Think about how glasses figure into your own life for a moment: Would your child wear a pair of glasses that kept falling off on the playground or that had to be secured in some jury-rigged manner? Would you be comfortable wearing a pair of glasses in a style that you associated with a gender other than the gender you identify with? Would you wear a pair of glasses that made you feel self-conscious or unattractive or that made you the target of jokes and sideways glances? The same factors that might keep you from wearing your glasses keep the people who need them in the developing world from wearing them, too. Having glasses you don't wear is like having no glasses at all.

Because I knew from long experience that something in the approach had to change, I arrived at the social enterprise model. My idea was simple: correct the market failure, then train an army of local people on the ground, like so many I'd encountered on the volunteer missions and in the public health work I'd done in the past, to assist with distribution, and get the glasses on the faces. Problem solved.

I loved my idea and I was sure it would work if I could get VisionSpring off the ground. I thought bringing affordable, stylish, high quality glasses was going to be huge, like cell phones, and everyone would want them. I was sure trying to keep up with demand would be like riding a wild horse.

Yet barely six months into VisionSpring's young life, we were losing money at such a fantastic rate that success in our founding mission plummeted to the bottom of our to-do list. Instead, every ounce of our time and focus went to combating obstacles to VisionSpring's survival that I had never anticipated.

That wild horse I was sure we'd be riding, for instance, turned out to be a mule. Our greatest obstacle to demand wasn't keeping up with it; it was finding it. Although I'd seen enormous need for glasses in the developing world, I'd never stopped to consider whether the people who needed them would see the need, too.

Of the hundreds of questions I'd never thought to ask myself, one was why would people who made between one dollar and four dollars a day choose to spend their hard-earned, highly limited resources to correct a problem that didn't cause them any pain. And how would someone who'd never had his eyes tested in his entire life necessarily know he needed glasses? When the physiological need is latent, sometimes you have to show people the difference between how they see now and how they could instantly see better. It's just like when you visit your optometrist and look at the eye chart through a phoropter (aka that weird apparatus that makes you look like C-3PO) while the doctor tries different lenses, saying, "Which is better, one or two?" Sometimes you don't realize how poorly you've been seeing until you see the evidence. It's hard to value vision when you don't know how valuable and life-changing seeing well is.

In addition to not realizing that people in the developing world might not automatically value vision the way that we do, I'd also overlooked the cultural obstacles that might stand in the way of success.

In India, three-quarters of girls of marriageable age believe their marriage prospects will decline if they wear glasses. What is the likelihood that she will wear the glasses even if she has them? Moreover, what is the likelihood that her parents will value vision so highly that they will allocate their scarce resources to purchasing glasses, even as they consider that they may also be risking their ability to find their daughter a suitable match by doing so?

In some other countries in the developing world, people believe that wearing glasses will make their eyes worse. In others, people believe that wearing glasses makes you look conceited. In Cambodia, for instance, Pol Pot killed the intellectual class, and the best way for him and his henchmen to root out the intellectuals was to see if they were wearing glasses. Images of huge piles of eyeglasses still haunt Cambodians' minds today.

With all these factors that had never come to mind at the outset, VisionSpring had much more to do than correct a market failure. We had to create the market itself.

One of the biggest challenges we faced as we tried to keep VisionSpring afloat long enough for us to find solutions was lack of data. Scrambling to keep funders engaged, I would get the same questions: How do you know that glasses really help productivity? Do glasses actually help people earn more money? Can you show us the research?

Unfortunately I didn't have any research to show because we hadn't done any, and to our surprise, neither had anyone else. My research was based on what I'd seen with my own eyes for decades in the field. In fact, one of the questions I loved asking people to consider when I spoke with them about VisionSpring and the power of glasses was, "What else can you buy for a dollar that can double someone's working life?" I believed what I knew was enough, and because I was impatient to get from observing the problem to doing something to change it, my stock answer when people asked me for the data often came off sounding flippant.

After the volley of questions, I usually would respond by telling funders that they could either give us a bunch of money to sit around and waste time doing a study or they could get everyone in their office to go a day without wearing their glasses, and then ask them how productive they had been.

Needless to say, my "because I say so" approach wasn't making what were perfectly reasonable questions go away, and ignoring them wasn't doing VisionSpring any favors.

My stance wasn't doing the VisionSpring staff any favors, either. They were a small group of bright, passionate recent college graduates as hungry to make a difference as I was at their age, and they were making major financial sacrifices to work at VisionSpring for next to nothing. Yet for everything they had in energy and enthusiasm, they had little experience in social enterprise, business, or fund-raising. And because we were a tiny start-up, regardless of our titles on paper, every one of us was wearing multiple hats as fund-raisers, awareness builders, and evangelists on the front lines.

Because I thought that my impassioned, well-reasoned, yet unproven assertions about the power of glasses would be enough, I sent the team into conference rooms and phone conversations with people who had the financial resources to help VisionSpring stay alive and thrive poorly equipped to offer the data that would convince funders awash in a sea of requests for money why they should invest in VisionSpring. They were doing their already difficult jobs, but my failing to do mine was making theirs impossible.

It was my job to convince private sector investors, foundations, public health officials, and governments why VisionSpring deserved their limited financial resources, their time, and their focus. It was my job to offer a precise, clear sense of exactly where their money would go, how we would spend it, and what the end results would be. And it was my job to arm the VisionSpring staff with the tools to do the same. The evidence was clear that regardless of whether I thought it was necessary, we needed a serious study to demonstrate the direct link between vision, productivity, and income if we wanted to live to fight another day.

Park Your Ego

Every person should have two pockets: One pocket for a piece of paper that reads, "I am but dust and ashes"; the other pocket for a piece of paper that says, "For my sake the world was created."
—RABBI SIMCHA BUNIM OF PESHISCHA

It took roughly four years of white-knuckling it, funding-wise and business-wise, to keep VisionSpring going until we received a grant from the Mulago Foundation to partner with Professor Ted London and the Ross School of Business to conduct an independent academic study examining the link between productivity and glasses. Had it not been for this study, the results it yielded, and everything else it told us that we already knew, and most importantly everything it showed us that we didn't, VisionSpring wouldn't exist today.

First and foremost, the study yielded the hard data that our potential funders wanted and that our team needed: glasses did increase productivity by 35 percent, and they did increase earning power by as much as 20 percent.

The study also yielded invaluable information about the barriers we'd encountered in certain areas, such as awareness, accessibility, latent demand, and cultural context. These key findings helped us develop and implement new strategies that have significantly strengthened our impact, including showing us why our distribution channels were either limited or in some cases failing.

One of those failures was that building our own sales forces from scratch via our Vision Entrepreneur (VE) program in every market was proving to be prohibitively expensive. With a clear picture in front of us, we developed new ideas, one of which was seeing if we could we find other organizations that already had distribution networks of people in the field selling products rather than starting from scratch building a local sales force on our own.

One of those organizations was BRAC, which emerged in the early 1970s as the Bangladesh Rural Advancement Committee, a temporary effort to provide assistance to refugees in the wake of the Bangladesh Liberation War. Now known simply as BRAC, it is the world's largest NGO. Based in Bangladesh, BRAC is dedicated to alleviating poverty by empowering the poor.

I met Mushtaque Chowdhury, a BRAC executive, in 2008 and learned more about its Shasthya Shebika (SS) program. The SSs were local women whom BRAC had trained to carry what BRAC called "mini pharmacies on foot"—baskets filled with basic health products, including sanitary napkins, soap, condoms, oral rehydration salts, iron pills, and clean birthing kits. It was a network eighty thousand women strong.

Each SS had her own territory of one village and went door to door to selling these products, earning a 10 to 15 percent commission on every product they sold.

One of VisionSpring's biggest problems wasn't only that our Vision Entrepreneurs (VE) were as of yet too few in number, but also that we were sending them into the field with just one product to sell. As we already knew, selling one pair of glasses already was a challenge to begin with. And if a VE did make a sale, she was selling a product that the average consumer doesn't tend to need to buy again right away. It could be years before the same person purchased another pair of glasses from the same VE.

With the facts and the external feedback from additional studies and surveys that followed after Michigan, combined with our intuition and direct experience, I wondered what would happen if we were to add our simplest product, nonprescription readers, to the SSs' baskets. I pitched the idea to Mushtaque, who agreed to a trial with fifty SSs.

The deal was that we would sell the reading glasses to BRAC for a small amount above cost, BRAC would then sell the glasses to the SSs with a small markup, and they in turn would sell them to their customers at another small markup.

Fortunately the initial results were positive enough that the program soon expanded to approximately five hundred SSs. It helped that BRAC served some of the most remote rural areas with villages with as few as one hundred families, which were the exact sort of territories we'd had the most difficult time serving. Each SS sells to customers from her own village, understands how to address cultural concerns, and has already sold products that had proved helpful to the customer. Because of the overall foundation of trust the SS had with the customer, she was able to successfully raise customer awareness about the value of vision. Putting the readers in the SSs' baskets made all the difference. With the SSs know-how combined with BRAC's highly developed infrastructure, seven years into the life of the business we started seeing the kind of impact I'd imagined we'd see overnight when I founded VisionSpring.

In February 2017, Ella, Reade, former VisionSpring CEO and board member Kevin Hassey, and I flew to Dhaka to mark VisionSpring's and BRAC's distribution of our one-millionth pair of eyeglasses in Bangladesh. Yet more than a celebration of VisionSpring's success or the success of our NGO partners in the region, the event celebrated the thirty thousand Shasthya Shebikas who had done the heavy lifting, one house, one field, and one village at a time.

During the visit, our team had the privilege of sitting down with ten of the top SSs, many of whom had never been to Bangladesh's capital city, home to seven million people. With the help of a translator, we talked about the need for eye care and glasses, and they shared how meeting that need has changed them and become their passion. They told stories about their experiences with their customers and why they love what they do.

Prior to that conversation, I looked on as each SS took the stage at a formal ceremony to receive special recognition for their outstanding efforts and exceptional entrepreneurial talents. And I marveled at a world where it's possible for a Jewish boy from Scarsdale and a group of Muslim women from small rural villages in South Asia to connect through the same values and ideals, united by the desire to make a difference in the world and working to help millions of people see.

Although the success we celebrated grew from that initial study I'd resisted so stubbornly, it wasn't the study alone that saved VisionSpring and helped it grow. It was dozens of changes, including knowing when I had to change, too.

From VisionSpring's earliest days I took the stance that the work wasn't about me, but rather about solving a problem that was creating and perpetuating injustice in the world. And it wasn't artifice. I believed it then and I believe it wholeheartedly now. But when my first big idea was failing, it was a little harder letting it go than I imagined it would be. When the work is a part of you, which it must be on some level in order to be a real part of your life, knowing when to take yourself out of the equation can be a bit more challenging than you think.

Having strong ideas and convictions of how to best solve the problem is necessary, but when your ideas aren't working in the real world, knowing how and when to listen objectively and analyze the facts in front of you is even more necessary. In my work, I'm unusually fortunate that the market is a ruthless truth teller. The glasses are either selling or they aren't. The glasses are getting on the faces of the people who need them or they aren't. Either the local women being trained to get those glasses on the faces of the people who need them are earning a better living in the process or they aren't. When everything tells you that the problem you care most about solving is going unsolved, when you really care, the last thing you want to be is another problem that needs fixing. In those moments, and some will be harder than others, you have to park your ego to put things back in drive.

It isn't that ego has no place in making a difference; it's about determining when it belongs and when it doesn't. To think you have the power to change anything in this world takes ego, but changing the world also requires that you remember you don't have all the answers or hold all the power. To believe you can make a difference in a problem because of who you are and the talents you possess make you the best person for the job takes ego, but to be the best person for the job also takes knowing when someone or something else knows better so that solving the problem remains the focus—not you.

Every change-maker's story grows from that person's own story, so while the change she wants to make is for the greater good, it also is tethered to something deeply personal. The personal investment is both the change-maker's strength and the change-maker's weakness. When your being is connected to your vision for how the world could be, but isn't yet, your heart is a mighty engine. But when you have to be right about the way that change comes into being, your heart can also be the impediment.

And so it is that in your life as a change-maker, you will face moments when you'll have to know that parking your ego is part of the solution. You'll have to learn when to separate your personal feelings from incontrovertible facts and embrace ideas based on where they take you, not on whether they come from you.

Whether you're already working to make a difference or are thinking seriously about how to start, one of the best ways to go from being a change seeker to a change-maker is to get good at changing. In any setting, at any time, you have opportunity to grow into a person who makes a difference by challenging yourself to be different, too.

As you dedicate yourself more consciously to making a difference, get into the habit of giving yourself pop quizzes whenever you find yourself struggling with a situation. Ask yourself:

What am I afraid of?
What's at stake?
How am I part of what's wrong?
How am I part of what's right?
What is the outcome I desire most?
What is the outcome that would be the best?
If the outcomes are aligned, how can I help ensure a successful end result?
If the outcomes are in conflict, what stands between them?
If I could change anything about this situation, I would . . .

If I could change anything about myself that would help
this situation, I would . . .

Am I getting in my own way? If yes, what stands between
me and the better me?

Quitters Never Lose

Bad is the plan that can never be changed.
—PUBLILIUS SYRUS

I've never seen a motivational office poster that says, "Quitting
is the key to success!" or "Never give up (unless it makes sense)!"
And I'm confident no coach in the history of a fiery halftime
locker room speech when the team's chips are down has ever said,
"Now let's get out there and quit!"

Yet whether you're on your way to finding the need that needs
you most or you're in the midst of discovering where you can have
the greatest impact in your efforts to do good, one way to achieve
your goal is to quit.

Your time is precious and your energy is valuable, as are your
strengths, talents, and abilities. With that, one of the biggest questions you must ask as you work to make a difference is whether
your investment of self is yielding the greatest impact. If the answer is no, you have to ask yourself if it's time to quit.

To be clear, what you're quitting is not the commitment you've
made to yourself and the world to make your life matter. What
you may need to quit is where and how you're directing your efforts. You're quitting a place, not the pursuit. A method, not the
mission. You're quitting with a purpose.

You may be surprised to know that the universe we share is the
product of purposeful quitting—at least in the ancient rabbinic
imagination. The first words of the Book of Genesis as we're accustomed to reading them in most every critical translation of the
Bible are, "In the beginning. . . ." In the Hebrew, however, the
word for "in the beginning" is *bereishit,* and a more accurate translation of *bereishit* is something like "in the midst of beginning."
From this, some of the ancients effectively conjured a prequel to

the Bible's creation tale. The rabbis imagined that our world is not God's first draft, but rather that God spent eons creating worlds. With each attempt, God would do the work, look around, and say, "This is good, but I can do better." Then God would destroy the draft and start over. Eventually God created the world we live in now, looked around, and said, "This is very good." How did God know when to stop starting and start building?

Setting out on your path to change the world is a bit like setting out to create it. You're starting a big project, an arguably impossible one, from scratch. The stakes are high. Where do you begin? How do you know if you're doing it right?

I hear from many people that when they first get their feet wet in the change-making space that they don't feel like they're doing much. For instance, you decide you're going to volunteer at a local organization where you'll be helping grade-school kids with their homework for a three-hour period one afternoon a week. You arrive on your first day full of energy and enthusiasm and ready to change lives. Instead you spend the first day in orientation. The following week you spend your time making photocopies and sorting supplies. The week after that, you finally get a chance to do the work you thought you'd be doing, but on that particular day more volunteers are there than students. You wait for more students to arrive, but it's a slow day and no one else shows. You look to do something else, but there isn't even enough office work to go around. This isn't what you had in mind. Do you quit?

Only you can make the decision as to when and if you need to pull up stakes at one place and move on to another, but don't do anything until you've explored why you want to quit. In fact, don't just ask yourself, interrogate yourself—make the process rigorous, and push yourself to make a strong case for why now is the time to move on.

For instance, if your answer to why you want to quit is that you don't feel valued, ask, "What have you demonstrated to make you worthy of being valued?" If you're looking to be valued just because you're showing up, it's not time to quit.

If your answer is that the work isn't fulfilling, ask yourself why.

If you've just begun and feel like what you're doing is entry level, not hands-on enough in your estimation, it's not time to quit.

As with any job, you have to start somewhere and learn the ropes. You also have to work with people who are more senior than you, who have been there longer, and therefore have easier access to the opportunities you would like to have. The best thing to do is to hang in, continue doing what you're asked, and also observe what other opportunities there are to do things you think will be more meaningful to you. Get to know the people who are doing those things, ask them about their experiences and what it was like when they first started volunteering their time.

After you've spent time observing and learning from others, ask how you can train to do the work that inspires you. If you see an opening to do something that doesn't already exist, a way to make things more efficient, or a way to partner with another volunteer, don't just say you want to "do more" or "do something else." Share your plan and ask for exactly what you need to execute it. If you haven't yet tried this, it's not time to quit. If you've identified inefficiencies that you can help change to make the experience better, but you haven't shared them or offered to be part of the solution, it's not time to quit. If you've tried it all to what you deem is the best of your abilities, and you're still feeling stuck and not energized in some way, well then, it's time to move on.

In addition, challenge yourself on what it means to be fulfilled in your work to make a difference. Remind yourself that change is a process, and rather than expect instant gratification, accept that most days the gratification you'll feel is from knowing that you are doing what you've set out to do: be part of the process. You will not have a life-altering moment that validates your existence on a daily basis. Those moments come by chance, and they only come when you stay in one place long enough for them to find you. If you've been putting in the time somewhere for months (not days or weeks), and when you evaluate the experience, your overall feeling is that the time you put in feeds you, it's not time to quit.

When you find yourself wondering whether it's time to quit

and your answer to why is that you're tired, ask yourself whether you find the work itself draining or if you're actually showing up for work already drained. Are you using the rest of your time in a way that sets you up for success in the work you're doing to make a difference? Consciously log exactly what you spend your time doing for two full weeks (weekdays and weekends). Include everything and then review. Is there some way you can reallocate your time so that you have more energy overall? Do you need to cut out some things that either are time wasters or that have a net neutral effect on your well-being so that you aren't expecting more out of your making-a-difference work than you have the capacity to put in? If you haven't asked yourselves these questions, it's not time to quit.

If you really are drained or if you are in a place where something or someone else needs you more, take a break. Any major undertaking has built-in vacations. Making a difference is one of them, and to ensure your impact over the long haul, you have to know when to take a step back for the sake of jumping back in. If this is what you need, have a plan. If you're dedicating time someplace and you want to keep putting in the hours there, treat your break as you would a vacation in a remunerative job. Establish how many days you'll be gone. If you have begun a project, make sure you have spoken to others about how the work will continue without you and how you plan to help when you return. If once you've taken a breath you return and still feel like you could be having a greater impact elsewhere, it's time to quit.

Although your path is your own creation, you don't have to walk alone, including when you're determining whether it's time to quit what you're doing to make a difference now, in order to do more in a more efficient and meaningful way.

In her article, "Sometimes You Have to Quit to Get Ahead," *New York Times* reporter Stephanie Lee reminds us that we are surrounded by people who have been where we are and found a smart way forward, and who encourage us to seek them out in these pivotal moments and ask, "What was it like for them? What did *they* have to give up to find their own success? After all, there's an opportunity cost to everything. No matter your goal, you have to pay in money, pain, relationships, effort or time. And these costs aren't always obvious."

If you find that your path to making a difference is starting to resemble the creation prequel, and that you're spending most of your time doing more starting over than you are building, it's probably time to quit something. Just make sure that you aren't quitting because what you're doing is hard in the near term. Quit because it's right for your vision for making a difference, and because quitting will move you closer to *very* good.

From A to Z

You are a bundle of mysteries. Finding and conquering yourself is a lifetime task. There are unplumbed depths in you full of the rich ore of personal discovery.
—WILFERD PETERSON

The Talmudic rabbinic character Rabbi Akiva is as famous for his command of Jewish texts and his ability to imbue them with meaning and relevance as he is for the late stage in his life when he first began his studies. The legend, an apocryphal one to be sure, is that Akiva, who didn't even know the alphabet, began his education at the age of forty, studied for another forty years, and only then started teaching.

In Rabbi Akiva's case, the story goes that he'd never even thought about studying or being a scholar until one day he stood at the mouth of a deep well. He'd been to the same well many times before, but today this commonplace thing became an object of fascination.

"Who hollowed out this stone?" he asked someone standing nearby.

"It was the water falling on it constantly, day after day," the bystander replied.

Akiva kept staring at the well, thinking that if something as soft as water could hollow out something as hard as stone, then surely new things still could penetrate his heart and mind, which are only flesh and blood.

With that, he walked straight to the schoolhouse where his son was in class learning the alphabet. Akiva sat down beside him, and both began writing the letters in the child's notebook.

Starting anything new can be difficult for anyone of any age. Taking on new challenges later in life can be all the more so: taking up an instrument, learning a language, going back to school; moving across the country, finding a new job, pursuing an entirely new career. While certain obstacles beyond our control may stand in our way, like finances or the conditions of the job market, regardless of how or when we start from square one, our success has more to do with how much we're willing to do to make a big change happen than it does with how old we are when we decide the moment is now.

Part of that willingness hinges on how much you're willing to change yourself. Because however difficult it may be to disrupt a market, public policy, technology, philanthropy, poverty, or injustice, a successful disruptor isn't the person with the best ideas, the loudest voice, or even the clearest vision. It's the person who isn't afraid to disrupt his own personal status quo.

Take the Dare

Because personal change is a dynamic and never-ending process, chances are there is something happening in your life right now in which your inflexibility is an impediment to progress. What is one thing you can do in this situation to be more like water and less like rock? How can you replace rigidity with fluidity? I have found that it's helpful to consider this on a regular basis because flexibility in one area of our lives enables us to practice openness to new ideas and progress on the road to the dynamic process of creating real and sustainable change when facing complex social needs. You will always be better equipped to change the world if you have the ability to change yourself.

Man worries about the loss of his money, but fails to worry about the loss of his time. His money does not really help him, whereas his time is lost irretrievably.
—RABBI ISAAC BEN MOSES ARAMA

8 Practice Dying

Even a short time frame is extremely precious. When such time is spent constructively, it can double and triple its value, since it represents the entrance fee to a world of permanence.
—RABBI ISAAC BEN MOSES ARAMA

A few years ago, I was sitting in the windowsill of my apartment. A heavy snow was falling, and a rare quiet had settled both indoors and out. A thick blanket of snow covered the empty pavement, giving the heavy snowflakes a soft, safe place to land. Their peaceful, hypnotic descent sent a hush through the usual noise in my head. I began counting the flakes, and before I knew it I was counting my blessings: My parents are alive. My marriage is wonderful. My kids are thriving. Work is good. All is well. The puzzle of my life is complete.

Twelve months later, I stared out the car window on the way to a Michigan hospital where my mom lay dying. As I whizzed past the American flags and festive regalia gracing houses and storefronts in anticipation of the Fourth of July holiday, I again felt like the world on my side of the glass was in black and white, while the world outside was in living color.

Standing at my mother's bedside, I looked at her and wondered how it was possible for everything to have changed so quickly. One day she had been my mom as I'd always known her: a vibrant force, and likely the one most responsible for giving me my entrepreneurial drive, open spirit, and hunger for adventure. Next thing I knew, she had taken a nasty fall and was in the hospital with a broken hip. Five months later, despite her best efforts, her body couldn't take what the long and challenging recovery demanded.

When my mom drew her last breaths, all the love she created in her lifetime surrounded her. My father—her husband of sixty-one years—my sisters, and I were beside her as her body exited the world and her soul returned to the place where all souls live forever. She died with dignity—what the rabbis of old call a *mitah yafah*, a beautiful death.

Whenever I reflect upon my mom's last moments, I think of a Talmudic tale in which a student named Rava asks that his much beloved teacher, Rav Nachman, return to him in a dream after he dies to let him know that he is okay.

Following Rav Nachman's death, he appears to Rava in a dream as promised. Rava asks, "Did you have pain in death?"

Rav Nachman replies, "It was as gentle as removing a strand of hair from a saucer of milk."

Having been with my mom at the end, I believe that if she were to visit me in a dream, she would tell me that her departure from this life had been just as gentle. And while I would give anything for even one more day with her, the feelings of grief and profound loss I still experience are tempered with the knowledge that she is at peace.

Shortly after my mom died, the memory of being there as she took her last breath still fresh, I began counting my own breaths. As I inhaled and exhaled, I wondered how many breaths I had left and how I would make them count.

During this period of mourning, faced with my own mortality in a more immediate way than ever before, I heard a podcast called "On Being" with Krista Tippett. Tippett's guest was Joan Halifax, a Zen abbot and medical anthropologist, who often is at the bedside of the dying. Being in such close proximity to those whose death is imminent and also to death itself has offered her a perspective that few of us have.

As Halifax shared from her long experience, "The potential within the dying process to refine one's priorities, to enter into relationality that has been turned away from and also to find meaning—to make meaning of one's life—is really extraordinary."

While I can't know for sure, I hope this is the experience of dying that my mother had. Sadly, not everyone has the same chance to prepare as she did: to say their goodbyes, have the time to reflect upon their lives, share stories and memories, and tell their loved ones what they have meant to them. But for those who do, death can be just as much of a gift as life.

Yet calling death a gift may cause us to shift uncomfortably in our seats, trigger an immediate shake of our heads to dislodge the thought of death from our minds. After all, we spend most of our lives trying to cheat death, vanquish it, keep it at bay. Fifty is the new forty; seventy is the new sixty. Paleo. Keto. Standing desks. More coffee. No coffee. Fewer reps with heavy weights. More reps with lighter weights. Sleep hygiene. These methods all are part of our attempt to take care of our bodies and minds (or think about it and wish we could do better) in order to keep ourselves in the game of life for as long as possible. Ultimately, however, as adversaries we are death's unworthy opponents. No matter how fit we are, careful we are, smart we are, if we're out to defeat death, eventually we're guaranteed to lose.

Surely trying to give ourselves as much time as we can remains a worthy endeavor. We don't hesitate to say that life is a gift, and however crazy it may be to think that we exercise total control over how much of it we have, it would be just as peculiar not to try our best to protect this gift for as long as we want to—to imbue it with as much joy and meaning as humanly (the key word being humanly) possible.

Still, even as we work to sustain our lives, little of life as we know it helps prepare us for the end. We live in a time and in places where our direct contact with death and the dying is mostly mediated by professionals. Unless or until we are at the bedside of a family member or close friend when he or she dies, we have no frame of reference for what those final moments look like. More often than not, it is physicians, nurses, and sometimes hospital chaplains who are the ones to bear witness to people's deaths.

Upon death, funeral directors, funeral home staff, and clergy people have most, if not all, contact with the dead prior to burial, while our contact with our departed loved ones is comparatively brief, if not entirely nonexistent. (Of course, this varies based on cultural and religious practices, but even in cases where wakes or open caskets are the norm, the person who is to be put to rest has been embalmed, with makeup applied and hair done, dressed in clothes he or she may have once worn in order to look as lifelike as possible.)

As author and surgeon Atul Gawande writes in his book, *Being Mortal*, much of this distance is an outgrowth of the fact that "as recently as 1945, most deaths occurred in the home. By the 1980s, just 17 percent did." The less direct contact we have with death, the more death becomes something that lives outside of life rather than a natural part of it—something we consider only when death is imminent or when we are forced to look at it in a way that is not purely conceptual.

Yet life and death needn't be at odds. Viewed as part of life, death can be but one of the many powers we possess to add focus to who we aspire to become, how we want to lead our lives, and what we do with our days. Or as the psalmist says, "Number your days so that you may acquire a heart of wisdom" (Psalm 90:12).

The eleventh-century Spanish poet, theologian, and biblical commentator Abraham Ibn Ezra offers additional perspective on what exactly it means to "number our days." He suggests that the verse is not simply a statement, but a prayer, in which we say, "Give us a heart that knows how to count our days on this earth, so that we may use them wisely."

While this interpretation brings more clarity to what the psalm may be trying to impart, the closest I have ever come to understanding the verse fully is in the words of contemporary American poet Marie Howe.

In the "On Being" episode that had me so riveted, one of Howe's poems, "The Last Time," was recited between segments. Howe composed "The Last Time" based on a conversation she had with her twenty-eight-year-old younger brother, Johnny, before he died from an AIDS-related illness in 1989.

In Howe's poem, she and Johnny sit across from each other in a nice restaurant, both of them knowing it could well be the last dinner they shared. Johnny reaches across the table and takes her hands in his, telling her that he wants her to know that he is soon to die. This pronouncement sadly comes as no surprise to her. He presses his sister nonetheless, saying he's surprised that she does not know—not that he is dying, but that she's dying, too.

If asked, we all would say that we know we're going to die, but I'm less certain we would say that we know we are dying—that every day, even as we are living we also are in the process of dying. Of course, some of us are theoretically closer to death based on our ages, some theoretically farther away, nearer to the beginning of our lives than we are to the end (assuming age is the only factor, which it isn't). And even if we were to acknowledge that, yes, we are dying, as is the case with many things, what our head knows and what our heart understands can be two different things entirely. We can know something intellectually, but until we *feel* what we know, the knowledge that we possess is just information. When it reaches the heart and becomes part of the choices we make, the actions we take, and the things that we do, the information becomes wisdom.

To possess a wise heart, one that understands the fundamentally impenetrable calculus of mortality, we must face the fact that we are dying. That we will die. And the time to do this is long before death is imminent.

Halifax's words helped me with my grief by making me see that embracing mortality has its own strange magic. Death's reality shakes us awake like nothing else can, compelling us to seize the opportunities that arrive each day to live more intentionally and love more fully—not with a sense of panic but with a sense of sacred urgency. Not to obsess over our mortality, but to realize that while everything we do holds the potential for having an impact now, it also contains the promise of the only thing that can grant us anything close to immortality: our legacy.

As aspiring change-makers and change-makers-in-progress, developing a wise heart and counting our days is all the more vital to the commitment we have taken upon ourselves to make our lives matter, because making a difference is hard.

When you take on complex problems that have compounded over decades if not generations, you won't always be able to measure your impact in the here and now. And when you do see incremental successes, they will be just that: incremental. Even the momentary high of an incremental success will vanish into the long shadow the big problem casts as your gaze returns to the enormity of the task at hand.

As a change-maker for life you will invariably go through periods when you will second-guess yourself and your choice to work for positive change in a real, sustained, and thoughtful fashion. You will wonder if your efforts are making a dent, and you will question whether the sacrifices, added pressures, and frustrations (whether your own, those of the people who are supporting you along your path, or all of the above) are worth it.

In moments like these, if we take a beat to see how what we do in our lifetime can change lives long after we're gone in ways we cannot control or imagine, we can measure success in a way that supports us in recovering our strength, reinvigorating our resolve, redoubling our efforts, and continuing to invest in our transformative power.

When I take this bigger big picture view, I see a lifelong change-maker's impact as something akin to compound interest. Let's say I put $500 in a savings account with an online banking company, and every month I invest $50 in that account. If I never touch the principal and allow all the interest to remain in the account for fifty years, with a 1.75 percent interest rate I will have accrued almost $50,000.

When you commit to helping bring about positive change for the long haul, daring to matter is your initial investment—it's an investment in yourself and of yourself to dedicate some portion of your precious life to the life of the world. As you work toward that goal, taking the action you have chosen to take over the course of months, and then years, your impact compounds. At the end of your life, what you will have accumulated and what you will bequeath is that better world that you dreamed of leaving behind.

Even if you don't live to see the full fruits of your labors, future generations will. The tomorrows of your children, your children's children, people you'll never meet, and people who have yet to be born are counting on what you do today. And by showing the people you have loved and who have loved you, by demonstrating what it means to make your life matter to all those who have encountered you in their lifetime, your example will be their inheritance. What your example inspires them to do with their precious lives also will be your lasting gift to the world.

As my rabbi once said in a moving High Holy Day sermon, "We are not alone. We are in the bloodstream of human existence. . . . I am part of all that I have met. I am inside the flow of time, a participant, a player, not a passerby."

Confronting our mortality is scary, but we needn't wait until death is imminent to think about the legacy we want to leave behind. By imagining what we hope people will think of when they hear our name, envisioning what the world will look like long after our names have been lost to time but our work still courses through humanity's bloodstream, we make friends with our mortality. We make death our partner in life.

Children Will Listen

One day, a man named Honi was walking along the way when he spotted a man about to plant a carob tree. Honi said to him, "How many years until it will bear fruit?" The man answered, "Seventy years." Honi asked, "How can you be so sure you'll be alive in seventy years?" The man answered, "I found this world complete with carob trees that my ancestors planted. So too I will plant some for my children." Honi sat down to rest, and slept for seventy years. When he awakened he saw the same man harvesting the carob tree. Honi said, "Are you the one who planted this?" He answered, "No, I am his son's son."
—Babylonian Talmud, Tractate Taanit 23a

In 2009 VisionSpring sold 100,000 glasses in the course of one year—a benchmark we never imagined possible. Right around the same time, I took my son Bryce to a Yankee game to celebrate his tenth birthday. The stadium was packed as the Yanks faced off with their archrival Boston Red Sox, and every fan in attendance was treated to a game for the ages as nine thrilling innings turned into an even more spectacular fifteen. We didn't leave the ballpark until one thirty in the morning when A-Rod's crushing home run ended the 0–0 deadlock.

At one point during the game, I remember looking around the stands, taking in the view of the vast sea of people. As I did I thought, wow, we helped two Yankee Stadium's worth of people this year. It made an already amazing night even better.

Yet on the subway home, still riding high on a terrific night out with my son that I knew we'd always remember, another thought popped into my head: in one year we'd only helped two Yankee Stadium's worth of people. It was barely a drop in the bucket of the billion who needed to be reached.

The thought dogged me wherever I went, including to my first Crown Fellowship seminar, part of a two-year servant leadership program, at Colorado's Aspen Institute. While there, the beauty of my surroundings reminded me of the connection I'd once had with the natural world—how alive, at home, and at peace I used to feel in the outdoors.

Happy memories of the trip I'd taken in the Brooks Range with Rob and Mike came to mind, as I recalled the way that nature had once been my holy of holies. Twenty years had passed in a blink since then, and other priorities, including my family, wife, the practice, and VisionSpring had made mountaineering and months spent hiking and living in tents a thing of the past. I knew I couldn't get those early days back, but in Colorado a sense of longing for them grabbed me by the shoulders, shook me, and wouldn't let go nonetheless.

A week later, I returned to New York determined to find a way to get back to nature, which eventually came in the form of a little rental property in Connecticut where Erica, the kids, and I could spend summer weekends escaping the New York City chaos.

Our first weekend there, I took full advantage of the fact that the house was beautifully tucked away in the woods, and I could walk into the wilderness for seven straight miles without seeing a road. The seclusion pulled me in, and I wound up going a bit overboard, bushwhacking my way like a madman through those woods. Every step pulled me back to the land with a force beyond my understanding. I cherished every minute.

The longer I was out there, the more time I had to get reacquainted with the weightlessness of the wilderness. Even when I'd trekked with seventy pounds of gear on my back in my younger days, I always felt lighter than I did anywhere else, like the laws of gravity didn't apply in the trees and on the mountains.

The doubts I had about whether VisionSpring could ever be successful enough to make a real difference didn't fall away, but instead gave way to thoughts of a simpler life. What if I were to step aside, let others come in and take over, feel good about where I'd taken things, and focus solely on my practice? How nice it would be to have fewer worries and more time—for Erica and the kids, for the practice, for me.

Giving up VisionSpring would allow me to slow down, travel less, and lead a "normal" life. I imagined what it would be like to come home at the end of the day in time for dinner with no additional work to do at night, put my suitcases in the storage closet, and for me and Erica to spend less time juggling calendars and time zones and more time just being together.

If I were to focus entirely on my practice, we'd also have more financial breathing room, more disposable income to take the kids on the sorts of adventures I'd loved so much in my youth—to share, as my parents did with me and my sisters, the joy of discovering as yet unexplored parts of the world, meeting new people, experiencing different languages and cultures, seeing landscapes that no screen saver or YouTube video could do justice. The more I considered these possibilities, the greener the grass on the other side of the fence grew.

Those Connecticut weekends held a combination of relaxation and rumination as I continued seriously considering changing course. Sitting out on the lawn one day with Bryce, we looked on in silence as our dog Griffey raced around trying to make sense of the strange absence of pavement and embracing the foreign concept that trees exist in places other than Central Park. Bryce broke the silence.

"Seems like you've been thinking a lot. What's on your mind?" he asked.

I looked over at my son, wondered when he had gotten so grown up, and shared the gist. I told him that if I quit VisionSpring, I'd be more like his friends' parents—home more often and able to provide him, his brother, and sister with more stuff.

Bryce looked me square in the eyes and said, "Who cares about the stuff, Dad? You can't quit. VisionSpring is your legacy work."

I couldn't remember having ever used the word *legacy* around Bryce before in any context and was blown away by his wisdom. It was the first time I realized that Bryce was actively observing what I did and why I did it.

Just as Bryce knew that Erica helped people in her way, he also saw that I helped people in mine, and understood that this was part of who we were. Every day of his life, we were teaching him what we cared about, not by talking or telling, but by doing. I realized that quitting VisionSpring and giving up trying to make a difference in an integral part of my life would have repercussions in my own backyard.

Back in the city a month later, we returned to the regular rhythm of real life. I still wavered about VisionSpring, but every time I breathed a sigh of relief at the thought of letting it go, I remembered Bryce's words, which took my breath away.

While hailing a cab one day, I got a monster headache and was drenched in sweat. When a taxi pulled up, I almost fainted trying to slide into the backseat. A visit to the doctor shortly thereafter revealed that on that wonderful day in the great Connecticut outdoors when I got a renewed sense of oneness with the land, I also got Lyme disease.

With the help of strong antibiotics, I returned to my old self. Reflecting on how I got there, however, it became clear to me that giving up hiking and mountaineering had zero consequences. I could miss it and occasionally wax nostalgic for the good old days, but it would never miss me. Whereas if I truly believed that I had been put on this earth to do something more than take from it, the stakes were higher. If I gave up on the work for change that I had chosen, and that had chosen me, I would fail to give my son quite possibly the only thing—apart from security, love, and the best possible start in life we could offer—that would survive me and mean more than any material goods we could buy: a legacy of doing good. If I gave up VisionSpring, I would be doing it because it was easier and safer for me—not for Erica, not for Bryce, Jonas, or Sofia. Bryce had told me as much himself.

I imagined looking Bryce in the eye the way he had looked at me, and telling him that I'd walked away from VisionSpring, walked back my commitment to serving a purpose in my life greater than myself. How would he see me? What lesson would he take away from my decision?

In an *Entrepreneur* magazine article called "7 Tips to Building a Business While Working a Day Job," executive coach and clinical social worker Grace Bluerock says that one step is committing yourself to your dream. She explains that in order to take a major decision to the next level, you also have to tell other people about it. It certainly resonated with me, as I had benefited mightily from sharing my dreams with others. I had learned that saying what you care about out loud makes you more accountable, makes your goals and aspirations more real, invites others to become invested in your investment, and makes it much harder to walk away without at least having some explaining to do. We need witnesses in order for something to be real.

This is the case in Jewish law. A wedding contract (*ketubah* in Hebrew), for instance, must have two witnesses who are unrelated to the partners who are to be joined in marriage; the ceremony itself must take place in the presence of minyan.

Yet this wasn't always the case. There was a time when two people becoming married was a purely private event. In that era (a decidedly nonegalitarian and heteronormative one), a man could "acquire" a woman as his wife (although not without her consent, as stipulated in the Talmud) in any one of three ways: by giving her a material object, usually a ring, of some minimum established value; by giving her a contract; or by sexual intercourse. Following any of these, a couple could simply announce to others that they were married.

This private approach proved problematic for a variety of reasons over time, including that committing one's life to another in private lacked the same gravitas that it does when the commitment is made openly and rendered valid and binding in the eyes of others. As a result, these commitments often were taken lightly and even denied by husbands when it was no longer convenient or of interest to be in a relationship.

Whether it's an intended lifetime commitment to another human being, a serious professional undertaking, or a desire to make a significant change in your life, while taking anything that means something to you from a quiet promise to a public declaration is a first step, going from trying to doing is what speaks the loudest and says the most. This is all the more so when what you have declared you will do is tested.

When we know that people are listening, we are careful with our words, but when we know that people are watching, we are more thoughtful about how we act. When people are watching, we are more apt to do things differently. At the end of the day, while words count and have a power all their own to hurt and heal, inspire and diminish, words do not provide shelter from storms or fill empty bellies. Words don't plant fields or harvest them. And while legacies may be born of words, they are built through action upon action.

As Roy Scranton, author of *We're Doomed. Now What?*, writes, "I can't protect my daughter from the future and I can't even promise her a better life. All I can do is teach her: teach her how to care, how to be kind and how to live within the limits of nature's grace. I can teach her to be tough and resilient, adaptable and prudent, because she's going to have to struggle for what she needs. But I also need to teach her to fight for what's right, because none of us is in this alone."

Scranton, too, must know we don't have the luxury of giving up because our children are watching. Their futures ride on what we do today and how we do it.

Whether you help change the lives of thousands or hundreds or dozens, you will never have a greater opportunity to make the difference you want to make in the world than you will by consistently modeling that commitment to the people who are the closest to you in the world. The path to change is through them, what they take from your example, and how to build upon it as they, too, discover what they have been put here to do.

Think about this when you doubt yourself, when it would be much easier to take a path that doesn't require as much sacrifice. Imagine the conversation you would have with that person. Hold the image of that person in your mind, and begin the dialogue.

Imagine the questions they might ask you. How do you answer?

Fast-forward to what hopefully will be many years from now, and imagine that person delivering your eulogy. What do they say you cared about most? What memories or anecdotes would they share to illustrate it? Do they remember you the way you wish to be remembered? Do the actions you have taken align with the words they share about what you stood for and how you showed it?

Ask yourself, are you ready to quit on them?

Grow Good

When Miriam was born, no one knew who she would be.
But when she died, the well ceased to exist, and similarly with
Aaron with the pillar of cloud, and Moses with the manna.
—RASHI

We are all given names when we are born. While we may be named after family members whom our parents wish to honor and whom they may hope we will emulate in some way, at birth our names are empty vessels waiting for us to fill with the deeds that over time will imbue our names with meaning—make them stand for something. In this, no two names are alike, even when people share the same ones.

This is what it means to make a name for ourselves: To take something that means nothing and turn it into what we want it to be. It is an opportunity given us all, and in the ancient rabbinic imagination it is quite literally the opportunity of a lifetime. As it is taught, "Three crowns may be worn in the world: the crown of learning, the crown of the [biblical] priesthood [to which one can only be born], and the crown of royalty. But a good name is a crown that surpasses the value of them all."

As we know, not all of us will be born with a combination of gifts and smarts that win Nobel Prizes, invent lifesaving vaccines, or split atoms. Not all of us will be born scions of powerful families; and precious few of us will be princes or princesses, dukes or duchesses, kings or queens by accident of lineage. But we all have a name to mold and shape in whatever way we see fit. And even if an Emily or a Jacob Junior come after us, our names will stand for something unique that we take with us when we die.

The rabbis of old say this was the case with Miriam, the sister of Moses. Miriam was one of only a handful of female prophets named as such in the Hebrew Bible. The Bible calls her brothers, Moses and Aaron, prophets, too. All three figure prominently into the Israelites' evolution from slavery to freedom, and the forty-year sojourn through the desert meant to lead them out of Egypt and into the Promised Land.

Yet neither Miriam nor Moses nor Aaron made it to the destination—the journey to which had been their life's work. Still, their contributions along the way helped sustain generations of Israelites throughout the challenging trek—contributions without which the Israelites could not have survived long enough to bring forth the generations that would one day see that storied land.

Some of those things that Miriam, Aaron, and Moses brought to the journey ceased to exist upon their deaths. According to the prolific eleventh-century French exegete Rashi, Miriam's Well, the life-giving water source that accompanied the Israelites through the desert while Miriam was alive, vanished when she died, causing fear and upheaval among the community, which instantly cried out that they were doomed to die of thirst.

Rashi and other ancients in their commentaries agreed that this wondrous portable spring went with the Israelites everywhere due to Miriam's uniqueness as a leader—that potable water existed in abundance for the community in mile after mile of arid land on Miriam's merits.

While on the one hand, it is a tribute to Miriam that something so vital and essential to sustaining all life would disappear at the end of her own. On the other hand, what befalls the collective purpose of a people marching toward freedom and to its own greater purpose in creating a world of freedom for all if the loss of one person spells the end of the journey for everyone? From the story of Miriam's life-giving well we draw another challenge for any change-maker: make yourself redundant.

We have talked about discovering the need that needs you most, and about finding what you, and you alone, are uniquely equipped to do that can be done by no one else. Yet part of your unique path to making the world a better place is to bring people along with you who can do good better.

I first encountered this notion while riding the subway to the VisionSpring offices one day. The car jerked back and forth in time to a loud and maddeningly incessant clanking noise as we hurdled forward at an unusually fast clip. I knew the chances of the train derailing were slim, but my thoughts drifted toward the macabre: What if the brakes fail? What if we derail? What if we crash? What if this is how I die?

Minutes later the train pulled into the station and the other passengers and I spilled out onto the platform, business as usual. Once above ground and grateful to be on terra firma, I kept thinking about what it would have been like if that really had been it for me.

This was my "What if Jordan gets hit by a bus?" moment (yes, it would have made more sense for me to have thought of this as my "Jordan gets thrown from the A Train" moment, but I'd gone to a pretty dark place where consistent imagery wasn't top of my mind). When you choose to work for change in an area of need so big that it can require your energy over the course of your whole life, you also need to embrace the fact that it will take many others, during your lifetime and beyond your lifespan, to effect real change. So, dark as it may seem, part of caring about the work you do is asking yourself who could jump in to pick up where you left off if your life were to end today. Who are the people who not only can do the work, but also take the work well beyond where you ever could have taken it yourself? In this sense, making a difference also entails being a mentor.

When you mentor another person who hopes to do something good, not only do you foster the good for the sake of the future, but you also benefit from what often is their contagious enthusiasm, which can reignite that fire in the belly you once had if the flames have become barely glowing embers. As you encourage a mentee to find and make their own brand of difference, they can push you to take your change-making skills to the next level. And every once in a while, your mentee's path and yours may even converge, as you begin walking right alongside each other and, even better, find yourself following him.

The greatest example I can share of a mentee like this is Neil Blumenthal, who, along with his University of Pennsylvania Wharton School classmates, Dave Gilboa, Jeff Raider, and Andy Hunt, founded Warby Parker. Neil came to work for Vision-Spring in 2003, doubling VisionSpring's staff roster as our second employee. At the time he was a recent college graduate who didn't know exactly what he wanted to do next, but he did know that whatever it was he wanted to help others.

Neil's tenure at VisionSpring began as a happy accident. One of my patients knew I worked at the Council on Foreign Relations and told me she knew the "greatest young man," and he needed a job. She asked if I would meet with said greatest young man, aka Neil, to see if I could help find a job at the Council.

Despite my best efforts, a job at the Council didn't materialize. However, in the process of getting to know Neil, I saw all of the great qualities that had caused my patient to speak so highly of him, and because I'd had that chance to get to know him I invited Neil to come work with us.

Back then, VisionSpring was in its start-up phase and we were working on a pilot program in El Salvador that was riddled with challenges. I asked Neil if he would go there to assess what was happening on the ground and try to make it right. In exchange we would pay him a stipend to cover his expenses while he trained our first group of Vision Entrepreneurs.

While staying near our office in Santa Ana, Neil was involved in every part of the business. He learned how to conduct basic vision screenings so that he could teach the VEs how to do them in the field, and as he worked on sales techniques with the VEs, he gained a boots-on-the-ground understanding of the challenges inherent in creating a market that values vision. To do so he spent countless hours listening to VEs and the people whom Vision-Spring served to gain a better understanding of their priorities, their stories, their lives.

Neil also spent years becoming an expert in determining what styles, colors, materials, and pricing appealed to VisionSpring's customers and potential customers; and he immersed himself in the ins and outs of manufacturing. By 2008 he not only had helped us grow immeasurably in El Salvador, but he also had helped us initiate our work with BRAC and expand into ten other countries. He also helped grow our staff tenfold.

When Neil decided to pursue his MBA, it was clear that whatever he chose to do he would be successful, and that most certainly has borne out to be the case. When Neil first shared his idea for what would eventually become Warby Parker, it was easy to be enthusiastic. He and his partners wanted to fill a hole in the market by offering high-quality frames and lenses at a fraction of the cost of what was available to most consumers. They wanted to take on optical industry behemoths, like Luxottica—a $25 billion company that manufactures most every high-end designer frame you can think of (Ray-Ban, Prada, Oakley, Versace, and Chanel, just to name a few) and owns LensCrafters, Pearle Vision, Sunglass Hut, and optical shops inside Sears and Target stores. They wanted to find a way to cut out the middleman to manufacture and sell glasses, complete with prescription lenses, for $95 in a variety of trendsetting styles that would appeal to everyone—from those for whom price was no object (read: Oprah) to cost-conscious students on tight budgets. And the one thing Neil knew for absolute certain the day I met him remained of primary import in the creation of this venture. He and his partners wanted to build a business that would measure its success not only in dollars and cents but in human impact, too. Based on my experience with VisionSpring, none of this sounded crazy to me, and given what I'd already seen that Neil was capable of I had no doubt that he could do it.

Needless to say when *GQ* magazine ran a piece calling Warby Parker "the Netflix of eyewear" on the very same day that Neil, Dave, Jeff, and Andy scrambled to get the company's website to go live, I didn't see the overwhelming consumer response and demand as much of a surprise. It was a thrill and a privilege to have been one of the people they'd engaged to help bring them to that moment, and it remains one to this day.

People often think of mentoring as something you do when you have your work all figured out, or when you're older and more experienced than the person who could benefit from having a guide. But it's important to remember that when you're working on a complex issue with multiple moving parts, while you may have put in more time and learned more in the process, you never have it all figured out. And, while it's true that with age comes experience, experience in the social change space transcends age. If you have logged more time researching an issue, if you know more people in the change area that you've chosen, or if you have a particular skill or talent that you have been applying to an issue that you can share, you are perfectly equipped to be a mentor.

With that in mind, as I look back now I think that what I did my best to offer Neil, and then Neil and his partners, was what anyone can offer another person who wants to make a difference: an open door, constructive encouragement, experience, and room to grow.

Whether by talking about what you're doing, asking someone to join or shadow you as you do your work, or connecting them to others who can open doors to opportunities to get started when it's just not clear how, you are in a position to extend the invitation that may move a person either from thought to action or from action to greater impact. In Neil's case, once I listened to him and heard that he wanted whatever he did to make a difference, it was easy for me to open the door to VisionSpring.

Encouragement also is an easy thing to offer, but it should be more than just cheerleading. It should include asking tough questions and offering insights that build the excitement level without tanking the mentee's enthusiasm.

Offering this kind of constructive encouragement hinges on your experience and how you can best leverage it in service of the mentee's goals. By pinpointing what piece of your expertise fits the situation, you not only can be maximally helpful, but also can apply your limited time strategically.

For instance, when Neil, Dave, and Jeff came to me with their first set of prototype frames, I knew that Neil already had exceptional design chops and a keen eye for style. And as someone who'd never have been mistaken for Chief Cool Officer in any phase of my career, I understood that what I had to add to the mix at that juncture was my optometry experience. Having been in the business for decades, I knew I could be helpful introducing them to glasses frame manufacturers in China and lens labs in New York who could put the lenses in the Warby frames and keep them at the price point Warby was targeting. I also could tell how different lens types would fit inside frames and fast-forward to what the finished product would look like on people's faces.

Along these lines, while some of the oversize-shaped glasses Neil, Dave, and Jeff had in their sample collection had a sort of geeky chic quality, the most common prescription lenses (-2.00 or -3.00), once inside the frames, would take on a thick Coke-bottle look that I suspected would take the look from ironically nerdy to genuinely awkward. In the end, probably not something too many folks would be eager to wear. This observation helped Neil,

Dave, and Jeff tweak some of the designs that they would roll out to customers as they established the brand.

In addition, because with Neil's help, VisionSpring had begun hitting its stride as Warby Parker began taking its first steps, with VisionSpring I also had an established mechanism for Warby to achieve its goal to be a business that drove social change. Through VisionSpring, Warby could confidently implement its Buy a Pair, Give a Pair program by helping us do what we did best. This made room for Neil and his partners to focus on growing their company, making their vision a reality, and expanding and building upon their success.

By knowing where and how to be present as a mentor, and also knowing where and when to get out of the way, VisionSpring now has its largest strategic partner in Warby Parker. With their help—and that of anyone who buys a pair of Warby Parker glasses—we have served almost six million people.

In addition to being our biggest donor, Warby also provides the VisionSpring team with ongoing, reliable support in a variety of areas that they do best, including information technology, marketing, and communications.

A Talmudic sage once said, "I have learned much from my teachers and even more from my friends, but from my students I have learned more than from all of them." I can safely say that when it comes to Neil, this more than applies, although I think at this point Neil has been my teacher for at least as long as I was his. When we have dinner, our conversations run the gamut from work to family. As a husband whose wife also is a successful professional and as a father of two, Neil now faces many of the same challenges I once had, and still do, in integrating the work that animates our spirits and being there for the people who are our heart. In this sense, at times I remain the teacher, and in others Neil teaches me. In everything we strengthen each other, and we both are better change-makers and better people for the bond we share.

It is in large part because of Neil that about five years ago I decided to start setting aside one hour a month dedicated to mentoring. I schedule four fifteen-minute calls with budding social entrepreneurs and do my best to answer their questions. There is never a day that I don't come away inspired by the conversations.

One of my mentees, Abhi Nangia, is a first generation American who had his "dare to matter" moment when he was eleven years old. Abhi's parents had taken him to Delhi to visit family, and while there Abhi encountered a world that he never knew existed—a world that he brought home with him to the United States.

In one of our first conversations Abhi quoted Mark Twain, who said: "The two most important days in your life are the day you are born and the day you find out why." Abhi has explained to me that he discovered his why on that family trip, even though it was a long time before he found the how.

"I didn't know what poverty was," he said. "I didn't know there were people without opportunity, and I thought it was something that someone already should have taught me about by then."

Now at the age of twenty-eight, Abhi has taken that experience and is living his "how" through a global initiative he started called Better World Ed. Better World Ed is an organization dedicated to helping teachers integrate lessons in empathy and social change into their existing curricula.

To achieve this goal, Abhi and his team collect day-in-the-life video diaries of children and adults in cities throughout the United States and in the developing world. Then they weave those stories into lesson plans for teachers of math and literacy in kindergarten through eighth-grade classrooms across the globe.

Abhi hopes that by educating students at an early age about poverty through the individual stories of people they would never otherwise meet, he can help build children's empathy muscles and show them how they can use their math skills down the road to make extreme poverty a thing of the past.

Your Neils and your Abhis are out there. But don't wait for them to come to you, especially if you find yourself in a place on your path where you may not be able to dedicate as much time to your change work as you'd like. Even then, if you can carve out a fifteen-minute phone call or a thirty-minute coffee with someone who shares your hunger for change, whatever small assist you may be able to offer is a way to continue growing the good you've committed to doing. By extending a hand to a person trying to find a way to make their life matter, you will inspire the change-makers of today and also ensure that the well of good never runs dry.

Go Barefoot

In the back of a Greyhound Bus
It'll take you far
In the back of a Greyhound Bus
You can be who you are
—MICHAEL FRANTI & SPEARHEAD

John McNulty was the global head of the investment management division of Goldman Sachs. The eldest of six children, he was born to Irish immigrants and grew up in Philadelphia. His father, Charles, worked as a landscaper and truck driver, while his mother, Nora, was a housekeeper for a wealthy investment banker. Both were dedicated to their children and to giving them every opportunity in the land of opportunity.

With his parents' dreams for his life fueling his own, John went to college, attended Wharton, and after working as a summer associate at Goldman Sachs during graduate school, he went to work for the firm full time after earning his MBA.

From there he proceeded climbing the ladder of success in true American dream fashion. Within ten years of being at Goldman, John had gone from being a broker to becoming a partner and co-head of asset management. Over the course of his two-plus decade career he increased the firm's assets under his management more than sixfold. John also believed in helping emerging leaders and professionals of all backgrounds and genders reach and exceed their potential, and took great pride in mentoring dozens of young associates at Goldman and beyond.

Although John and his wife, Anne—also from an Irish immigrant family, a Wharton MBA, and a successful investment banker—made a point of creating a philanthropic foundation in 1985 when they'd both just gotten their careers off the ground, in 2001 John, who was then forty-nine, and Anne both retired in order to dedicate themselves full time to not-for-profit work.

Within three short months into the life of service they'd dreamed of sharing together, they snapped into action immediately following the September 11 attacks to create a counseling and support program for children who had been affected by the trauma of 9/11, with a special focus on immigrant children and their families. They also expanded the social impact work they had been doing for years, including providing opportunities in higher education, believing wholeheartedly in education as a powerful catalyst for changing the lives of individuals who can then go on to change the world.

While John and Anne already had accomplished a great deal in their combined efforts to effect positive change, when John died of a massive heart attack at the age of fifty-three, they'd only just begun. That's why even in the wake of their own loss, Anne and her children, John, Brynne, and Kevin, barely took a beat before redoubling their efforts to honor John's lifelong commitment to social change by continuing his work in their lifetimes. The four of them are still doing that work today.

I'd never heard of John and I didn't know his story until I met Anne in 2008 when I was awarded the inaugural John P. McNulty Prize. Because of John and Anne's commitment to supporting leaders who they believed were poised to make a difference in the world, Anne and her family established the prize, which includes a $100,000 award that the recipient can use to strengthen the initiative that he or she has created. To date, the McNulty Prize has strengthened the efforts of some forty social entrepreneurs working everywhere from South Carolina to South Africa, Rwanda to Nashville, putting their ideas and talents to work to discover elegant, sustainable solutions to some of the world's biggest problems.

I have remained in close touch with Anne and her kids and think of them and of John often. Although John and Anne worked hard to be able to invest significant financial resources in their quest to make their lives matter, that they began doing what they could do to make a difference long before they had those re-sources stands out to me as a shining example of not waiting until the conditions are just right to do what you believe is right. I also see them as a powerful team who worked as hard, if not harder, to establish and then communicate their core values to their chil-dren and to everyone with whom they came into contact; this is evident in John's early dedication to mentoring, which didn't require money, just presence, care, and time.

And of course as I have entered my fifties, I think about John and the length of days he did not get. I think about how much is possible to do if you will it in a life cut short, and also of how much more you can do with every year you have on this earth if you do not take it for granted. In this sense, time is our great fortune, and with it, while nothing is guaranteed, anything is possible if we invest it wisely in ourselves and in the world.

As my children, no longer children, begin growing more and more into who they are and take their places in the world, I also see life as a puzzle that never is complete. It expands and con-tracts. Some pieces fall away as new pieces appear. A parent dies, a child goes off to college; that child finds a partner who becomes part of your family; they have children, you grow older, you die. Every day something valuable is gained and something invaluable lost.

Still grieving my mother's loss, Erica and I began preparing—although we realized it's not possible to fully prepare—for Bryce to go off to college. In these times of intense transition, memories flood the brain. There is Bryce as an infant, just home from the hospital, lying on our bed, his eyes chasing every detail, as I gazed at this tiny helpless baby who'd been entrusted to our care, mar-veling at his every movement and expression, knowing he would be ours forever.

There is Bryce telling me in summertime that I had many more seasons of my life to dedicate to my legacy work, again causing me to marvel at the boy who still needed us becoming a young man who needed us less and less.

There is Bryce sitting at the piano singing with his mom from whom he has inherited a beautiful voice and musicality, in addition to his emotional intuition.

And there I was in spring, right before Bryce's high school graduation, the countdown to his departure for college having begun in earnest, on the other side of the Atlantic in a roomful of hundreds of people listening to a song that surprised me by bringing me to tears, just as I had been surprised—although intellectually I shouldn't have been—that the time for my first child to leave the nest had arrived.

Once a year for the last decade, I have traveled to England to the University of Oxford to attend the Skoll World Forum, an extraordinary and extraordinarily inspiring weeklong gathering of thought leaders, artists, and agents of change of all kinds from sixty-five countries. A highlight of the conference is when several innovators in social change receive that year's Skoll Award for Social Entrepreneurship, which always includes one musical artist who then shares a performance, each one more memorable than the next.

That particular year the honor went to singer-songwriter Michael Franti (of Michael Franti & Spearhead) and Do It For The Love, the foundation he and his wife, Sara, founded. Because Michael and Sara believe that music has the power to do more than entertain, but to heal, they built Do It For The Love to bring adults and children living with life-threatening health challenges, as well as wounded veterans, their families and caregivers to live concerts to listen to and spend time with artists they have dreamed of meeting. Michael and Sara believe that while music may not save lives, it makes people come alive, brings light and joy to the darkest of times, and creates memories to last for all time.

I remember Michael sitting on a stool, barefoot, strumming his guitar before singing a song called "I Got Love for Ya." He dedicated the song to his adoptive mother, a public schoolteacher who for thirty-five years spent every day in the classroom giving her all to thirty students, and then came home to her own five children (two of whom, including Michael, were adopted) and gave her all to them.

"Michael," he told us that she used to say almost daily, "my job as a parent is to give you wings." He explained that she wanted him to understand that she was there to teach him how to do the basics for himself—clean his room, do his laundry, do his homework—and to give him love and safety and a solid launching pad in life.

Many years later when Michael became a parent, he asked his mom what she'd meant, and she told him that she'd wanted to show him how to be independent once he got out in the world on his own so that he would "be free for higher things." To care for others, do for others, change the world for others.

As he continued speaking over the guitar melody he played, the music connected his mother's words to the moment when his son left home for college. He recalled watching his son board the bus he was taking from San Francisco to New York for his freshman year, and how overwhelmed he was in that moment with a sense of loss seeing him go. In his sadness he reminded himself that his job, too, had been to give his own child wings, and he hoped he had done it.

When he began to sing his story, it resonated with where I was in mine. Seeing him barefoot, I thought of Moses, who was also raised by an adoptive mother. As a young man, Moses came upon a burning bush and stared at it with wonder as the flames licked up around it but didn't destroy it. A voice called to Moses, the voice of God, telling him to remove the sandals from his feet because he was standing on holy ground. Once Moses stood barefoot, God told him of his birth lineage as an Israelite and called him to lead the Israelites out of Egyptian slavery.

While we may not receive calls of such magnitude, we are all called to higher things that can be as great as we choose to make them. If we're fortunate, someone—whether a birth parent, an adoptive parent, a teacher, sibling, or friend—will have given us wings in the world of our childhood—the first world that greets us at the beginning of our lives. And they will have known that the world they create for us is but the anteroom to the bigger world, the world that awaits us and the people who need us.

And no matter how hard it is or how sad it makes them to let us go, they will also know that if we are to find our own holy ground, they must release us and let us discover the place where we must stand alone and learn who we are and where in this world we belong. And once we have learned where we belong, if we are wise, we will not stand there alone forever, because we do not have forever to heed that call.

As Michael played, his fingers moved up and down the frets of a beat-up guitar nowhere close to retirement. His bandmate added some electric guitar licks to the mix, and Michael led us from his own song into an up tempo chorus of U2's "I Still Haven't Found What I'm Looking For" that turned a lamentation into a celebration of the possible. Suddenly we were on our feet, dancing and clapping, singing a hymn to the infinite and the finite limned with comfort, consolation, and pure joy.

Take the Dare

On the day that you read this chapter, take Aristotle's deathbed test. Imagine that you are on your deathbed today as your present self, whatever age you are or stage of life you are in. Look at your life as if you are reviewing a résumé. As you review, what aspects of it give you the greatest sense of satisfaction? Which ones are you more apt to gloss over? Which ones did you dedicate time to that in retrospect you wish you had put into something else? What is missing?

When you have a quiet moment of uninterrupted time, write your own eulogy. Take note of what memories or anecdotes find their way into it. What do they tell you about how you hope you will be remembered, what you wish to be remembered for most, and to whom you hope your life will have had held the most meaning?

Keep your eulogy somewhere close, and schedule a time in your calendar as soon as you finish writing it when you will take it out and read it again. Every time you read it, schedule the next reading. Add to it if you wish. As long as you have time, you have opportunities to try and build the life you want to lead, the life that you hope will become the legacy you leave behind.

May the father of all mercies scatter light and not darkness in our paths, and make us all in our several vocations useful here, and in his own due time and way everlastingly happy.
—GEORGE WASHINGTON

9 Follow Your Thread

Men go out into the void spaces of the world for various reasons. Some are actuated simply by a love of adventure, some have the keen thirst for scientific knowledge, and others again are drawn away from the trodden paths by the "lure of little voices," the mysterious fascination of the unknown.
—SIR ERNEST HENRY SHACKLETON

Henry Worsley was a highly decorated officer in the British Army. A talented leader, he served in the Special Air Service, an elite commando unit requiring a level of physical and psychological toughness few possess.

From the time Worsley was a young boy in boarding school in southeastern England, he had been fascinated with the Irish-born explorer Ernest Shackleton. Shackleton is best known for his ill-fated attempt to become the first person ever to make a successful trans-Antarctica crossing.

In 1907 Shackleton set forth from Argentina on a boat named *Endurance* to do the impossible. Sadly for Shackleton and his men, the mission proved to be exactly that. With only ninety-seven miles left to go before reaching the South Pole, Shackleton surmised that if he and the group were to press on to the end, the weather conditions were sure to result in their demise. With that, Shackleton called the expedition to a close.

Whilst in the midst of planning another attempt at the crossing in 1922, a heart attack claimed Shackleton's life. He was forty-seven. Yet prior to his death, Shackleton had penned an account of the 1907 expedition in a book called *The Heart of the Atlantic*. It was this very account that Worsley, a natural athlete who loved nature and the outdoors, stumbled upon in the school library when he was thirteen.

Although he wasn't much of a student, Worsley spent a good amount of time reading any tale of adventure he could get his hands on. Yet when he read the first lines from *The Heart of the Atlantic*, they spoke to him in a way that no other book ever had. Instantly Shackleton became his hero and Worsley promised himself that one day he would complete his hero's journey.

Although I'd heard of Worsley before, I knew precious little about his adventures, and even less about the man himself, until learning more about him as detailed in author and *New Yorker* staff writer David Grann's excellent feature, "The White Darkness." Worsley's adventures captivated me, but his personal story also resonated in a visceral way: his struggles in school, the peace and exhilaration he discovered in nature, following in the footsteps of a successful father (Worsley's was a World War II war hero and high-ranking career officer in the British Army). He had a wife who understood that one of the things she loved and admired most about her husband required making sacrifices of her own. And just as the first lines of Shackleton's account had spoken to Worsley, Worsley's words from a book he published in 2011 called *In Shackleton's Footsteps* instantly spoke to me.

In Shackleton's Footsteps is Worsley's account of his successful attempt to finish Shackleton's expedition. Worsley takes the reader with him as he and his party follow Shackleton's route all the way until they walk the last bit that Shackleton and his men could not. Yet despite—or perhaps because of—Worsley's lifelong worship of Shackleton, making the decision to even begin planning the expedition was a process of months during which time he battled fear, self-doubt, and intimidation in the face of an undertaking of this magnitude. Despite these feelings, Worsley was not prepared to walk away from his dream. He writes:

> I didn't know when it would be but I was beginning to learn in life that if your heart lifts at the thought of fulfilling a dream

then all that stands in your way is to take the first step and enter the arena.

It seemed to me that these could be the words of any person who dreams of doing something extraordinary—not extraordinary by the standards of others, but in the sense that when you think about achieving that extraordinary thing as you conceive of it, your "heart lifts" at the thought of it.

If you want making a difference in and beyond your lifetime to be the expedition of a lifetime, having an impact and growing in impact requires that your heart lifts at the prospect of doing the work—not just once, but multiple times over the course of your journey. Does what you're preparing to do to get started spark your ambition? Does what you're doing now ignite your passion? Does what you plan to do next keep the wheels in your brain turning and fuel the fire in your belly?

The ambition, the passion, the fire in the belly are vital to the adventure, and are especially so when your commitment must be stronger than your fears and your determination more stubborn than your doubts. As long as your heart keeps lifting, you will choose action over inaction, no matter how great the challenge.

You Are Not Me

Said Rabbi Zusya: "In the world to come they will not ask me, 'Why were you not Moses?' They will ask, 'Why were you not Zusya?'"
—HASIDIC TALE

How many times has someone told you to just be yourself? It's the "just" that gets me, as if being yourself is a snap when in fact it's one of the hardest things to do. This self that we're told should be so readily accessible to us is elusive, often more shadow than solid. Just when you think you've wrapped your arms it, it vanishes.

The pursuit of this mysterious self that we should "just" be is also made more challenging because the self is a master of disguise. It appears as one thing at work and yet another at home—one thing when meeting new people, another in the company of old friends. And then there's the self we are when no one's watching and the self we think we ought to be and the self others want (or need) us to be.

And on that day when you step out of the funhouse mirror room of selves and at long last trade wondering who you are for proudly declaring, "This is who I am!" you're hit with the only other thing that's harder to do than just being yourself: staying you.

This struggle to stay you calls to mind an idea captured beautifully by the twentieth-century American poet William Stafford in "The Way It Is." In it, Stafford imagines that a thread runs through our lives, through every chapter and change. And while that thread may be invisible to others or hard to explain, as long as we follow our own thread and never let go regardless of anything that happens to us or around us, we will always find our way back to ourselves even when we're tangled up in confusion, even when we're sure we are completely lost.

Making a difference is my thread. It's so much a part of me that without it I would become untethered from myself. And it's great that I know this. You've made daring to matter a part of your thread, even by thinking about it with serious intention. But as Stafford suggests, just having your thread isn't enough. It's hanging on to it and following it that makes the difference between daring and doing. And as he also tells us that at times it will be difficult to make sense of it to others, I have found that the challenge of explaining it to others sometimes pales in comparison to the struggle to keep making sense of it to myself.

Reminding myself of my thread and not letting go is hard. Everywhere you look there's always someone more successful, better looking, more fit, more powerful, more connected. It's not a perpetual fixation, but when all I can see is who I'm not, I can quickly lose perspective. It's like one day I'm walking down the street feeling pretty good about myself, and then suddenly feel like I've shown up in a T-shirt and shorts to a glitzy black-tie affair where everyone else is perfectly coiffed and shiny, mingling and making merry without a care, while I'm desperately searching for the nearest exit or a large potted plant to hide behind.

I know I'm not the only one who feels this way. Perhaps you've felt it, too, maybe while scrolling through Instagram or when a quick peek at someone's Facebook page turns into an hour of unintended Internet stalking. You see happy families, dream weddings, amazing vacations—people living the best life ever. They look like they have it all, and sometimes you can't help wondering, if only for a second, what it would be like to be them instead of you.

This sudden case of FOMO fever, this invitation we readily accept to compare our lives to those of others, is not relegated to the digital realm of trending hashtags and perfect selfies. In fact, it is something I used to see all the time in real time among the people in my term membership class at the Council on Foreign Relations.

Over the course of five years, term members wind up spending lots of downtime together chatting and getting to know one another over meals and between lectures. No matter what the discussion topic was for the day, no matter who people were or how much they'd accomplished, some part of them wanted to be someone else. The well-heeled Wall Street and McKinsey Management Consulting types wondered what it would be like to be the academics, faith leaders, and NGO workers coming home every night knowing they'd dedicated their entire day to making a difference. And the academics, faith leaders, and NGO workers wondered what it would be like to have bank balances well north of meeting monthly expenses.

Of course the ways they saw each other were oversimplifications that glided past the nuances and complexities of the others' real lives. But in these moments of personal doubt, even knowing this is the case still doesn't keep us from losing perspective about ourselves as our energy goes into longing for someone else's life.

Dedicating my life to change puts me in rarified company multiple times a year at gatherings of the most powerful people in the world, including at World Economic Forum (WEF) annual meetings in Davos, Switzerland, and summits the world over where VisionSpring and my work to make a difference are my calling card. The experiences I have at WEF convocations are unfailingly thought-provoking and invigorating. I always come away having learned at least twenty new things and having met at least fifty new people.

Yet some years when I'm fortunate to be invited to participate in these tremendous WEF programs, I'm more aware of how despite how many people I speak to who find VisionSpring fascinating and our work inspiring, or how much they say they admire me and what I'm doing to make the world a better place, the sessions I lead are far less well attended than those of tech entrepreneurs and Fortune 500 executives. And while the entrepreneurs and executives are among the incredible people I meet, and they are among the people from whom I learn, and while I admire them, I'm also jealous because I want to be like them. In these moments, the entrepreneurial, business-motivated part of me that I have put to work solving a social need turns into a little devil on my shoulder, saying, "Look who you might have been if you'd put your business skills to work for you."

And after those events, on long plane rides home that feel even longer, I think about how they may admire me, may want to be like me, but they don't want to be me.

In these periods, my outward obsession with other selves makes incursions on all fronts. In my for-profit optometric work, for instance, my partners and I pride ourselves on being on the cutting edge of optometric advances. Whether we're treating patients with nearsightedness and farsightedness, those with keratoconus (a serious corneal structural abnormality that causes extreme vision impairment), or those who have had corneal transplants and require highly specialized corrective lenses to see that protect the health of their donor corneas, we work hard to offer everyone we serve the most innovative technologies available today.

So when I received a phone call that a highly regarded optometric magazine wanted to run a feature on me, I got excited. Yet when they told me they wanted to make the feature about Vision-Spring, I was less excited. This piece about me and VisionSpring would appear alongside articles written by and about practitioners doing what I thought of as the serious hard-core scientific work, like breakthrough research and groundbreaking treatments for people suffering with macular degeneration. And there I would be: the warm, fuzzy do-gooder guy. I felt the same as I have sometimes felt at Davos: the good guy, but not really one of the guys.

For better and for worse, I've let myself unravel and started letting go of my thread enough times to know how to snap myself out of it. Doing so begins with stopping and acknowledging to yourself what's happening: Yes, I admire him/her/them (it's all the better if you can identify the person or persons whose selves you have been glamorizing). Yes, I want to be like him/her/them. Then ask yourself, "Do I really want to be him/her/them?"

Never ask yourself this question in a vacuum. As a matter of fact, isolating yourself when you're diminishing who you are by obsessing over who you're not will cause you to drift into crisis territory when what's happening to you is a turning point—an opportunity to affirm who you are, reacquaint yourself with yourself, and stand taller in your own shoes.

Reach out to someone you trust and someone who knows you well, and say out loud everything you're feeling. Focus on the reality of your life rather than on your fantasy of someone else's. And because dwelling in comparisons is a dangerous and unproductive place to put down roots, get up, stop thinking, and start doing. Whether for fifteen minutes or an hour or a day, be with the people and in the places that pull you back to you. Do the things that remind you of your thread.

If you're already doing your make-a-difference work, make a special point of identifying an immediate opportunity to help, even if it's stuffing envelopes surrounded by others who are dedicating their time to the same cause. If you're still searching, do something that actively contributes to the search—whether it's visiting an organization you've identified as a place of interest or purposely putting yourself in a place where you can see, experience, and feel the need you think may need you most calling you. Or just do one simple thing for one person—neighbor, stranger, family member, or friend—that takes a talent or quality you possess, that inspires you to make use of something you have inside you, that focuses your mind and heart on what you have to offer, rather than on what you don't have.

You can also make a special point of having a family meal or reaching out to a favorite teacher or treasured mentor whom you haven't been in touch with for a while. Visit a place that brings you joy in your town or neighborhood, like a nearby park or bookstore; get some exercise; look at a community calendar and attend a program that builds upon your interests. Any activity or setting that makes you feel content, makes you feel that you are enough by your own standards, that lets you see yourself in perspective rather than in relationship to someone else is a surefire way to get back to your guiding principles and ideals, to you, and to the life you love already in progress.

Gut Check

I am in Birmingham because injustice is here.
—DR. MARTIN LUTHER KING JR.

In the spring of 1963, the Reverend Dr. Martin Luther King Jr. led a protest march in Birmingham, Alabama, to encourage local consumers to boycott white-owned stores for the Easter holiday. The authorities arrested Dr. King for conducting the protest despite having been denied a permit. During his imprisonment, he wrote his famous "Letter from Birmingham Jail."

Dr. King's letter was a response to a statement drafted by eight white clergymen in *The Birmingham News* criticizing the march for which Dr. King had been arrested and questioning the wisdom of civil rights protests in general.

In the letter, Dr. King explains that he is responding to the clergymen's criticisms not out of a desire to justify to them why protests were both necessary and wise, but because he had faith that they were "men of good will," a real opportunity for mutual understanding was alive in that moment.

When Dr. King writes, "I am in Birmingham because injustice is here," it would seem to be a most obvious statement even in a communication to the most unenlightened reader. Yet I think that Dr. King wrote this line not as a statement of fact (which it was), but as an affirmation of purpose. I believe that while he sat behind bars for the sake of advancing justice, writing his some seven-thousand-word reply to eight men, Dr. King, even as committed and resolved as he was, had to have been writing some of those words to himself.

There was and always will be only one Dr. King, and but a relative handful of leaders—past, present, or future—have the strength of will, power of spirit, and ability to inspire and effect the kind of positive change that earns them a place in history books and a permanent place in the collective heart of the world. Yet he believed, as I do, and as anyone who insists that we can do better does, that every person is called to bringing about change and is capable of doing it.

In that spirit, "I am in Birmingham because injustice is here," represents the work within the work for change that every change-maker must do in order to have an impact and grow in impact in the face of ongoing challenges, including the challenges that come from within that distract us or draw us away from our commitment to making a difference—like losing perspective, forgetting why we're committed, letting go of our thread. Whether you're just beginning to forge your path to making a difference or you're already moving down the long road to making one, every change-maker has to check in with herself.

Checking in is about no one other than you, and reveals to no one other than you whether you know why you're working for change and whether your path is moving you in the direction of the difference you aspire to make.

Checking in is as simple as it is crucial. All you have to do is ask yourself two questions:

What needs me?
What feeds me?

These are the questions I ask when I feel myself drifting away from myself and from the intrinsic value I place on working for good. Because the work itself is what keeps everything in perspective, I have to make sure that the work I'm doing at any given moment is the right work at the right time for who I am and where I am on my path.

Part of what keeps us in the fight to make a difference is the fight itself, which is why the need you're serving can't be the only challenge you're facing. The work you're doing in service of meeting the need also has to be challenging in much the same way as we want our remunerative work to be. Ideally we'd like our remunerative work to ask something of us and push us to grow—whether it's honing an existing skill or mastering a new one in order to rise through the ranks and take on more responsibility or tackle more complicated tasks. A learning curve keeps us interested and engaged; it makes the hours go by faster, narrows the gap between what we have to do and what we want to do, and makes us more productive.

In order to stay invested in what you're doing to make a difference in the same way as you would a paying job or career, periodically ask yourself if what needs you is vital. Am I still the best person for this task, or have I gained other skills and experience that I could be putting to better use by taking on a new one? If I took on a different role, would I have a greater impact? If I took on a different role, could someone else continue to make that same impact and possibly do the work I've been doing better?

Similarly, occasionally stopping and making a point of asking yourself what feeds me also will keep you energized and committed. When was the last time I felt a fire in the belly? What inspired it? What am I doing right now that gets my pulse racing? Can I do more of it exactly as things are? If not, what would spark that feeling again and how could I translate it into action?

Try this yourself. You don't necessarily have to focus it on making a difference. If you want, ask yourself what needs you and what feeds you with anything you're doing right now that you feel is causing you to drift away from yourself: school, job, relationship. The idea is just to get into the habit of checking in so that you eventually can apply it to your brand of making a difference.

For the next two weeks, ask yourself what needs you and what feeds you. If your schedule permits, do your check-in once a day. Alternatively if once a day is too difficult, do your check-in once a week. In either case try and keep check-in time to the same window each day, and, if you're going the once weekly route do your check-in on the same day each week. Consistency in scheduling will ensure that your check-in doesn't fall by the wayside.

In addition to adjusting your check-in to work with your schedule, you also can organize the process in whatever way works best for you, such as:

1. Spending both check-in weeks asking yourself both questions at the same time: What needs me? What feeds me?
2. Spending one check-in week focused solely on "What needs me?" and your second week only on "What feeds me?"

How you choose to structure your check-in process, and how often you determine that you're due for one, is entirely up to you. The only imperative is that you do it and that you keep a record of all of your answers.

As with all of our other gut check questions, do not self-edit. Just as honesty is essential in asking yourself how much is enough, your needs me/feeds me check-in will only work if you don't hide yourself from yourself.

In that spirit of transparency, try to keep your answers to one word. You can have as many answers as you'd like—could be two, could be ten, could be more. Nonetheless, challenging yourself to keep your answers concise will prevent you from overthinking because overthinking can inadvertently lead to justification. So for now, don't add "because" to your answers.

In order to keep your answers simple and honest, you should

also limit your check-in time to a maximum of ten minutes. The bounded time for the check-in also will keep you from wandering.

Once you have all of your answers, make a "What needs me?" list and a "What feeds me?" list. On each of them, select the answers from your two-week check-in that came up consistently. Does what you're generally spending your time doing truly need you? Does it feed you? If you discover that your honest check-in answers are in alignment with where you are now, then know you're on the right track and take the space to feel excited about that and reaffirm your commitment. If not, what can you change so that you're investing yourself in doing what needs you most and, in the process, will feed you most?

Pause for Effect

There is no miracle, just better vision.
—Rabbi Michael Strassfeld

Some check-ins require a little more time and may even take putting yourself where you think you want to be in order to understand better where you belong.

In 1999 a young man by the name of Sam Morgan founded a company called TradeMe, the eBay of New Zealand. Morgan, a college dropout, got the idea for TradeMe while looking online for a cheap used space heater to warm up his tiny apartment. Only one Kiwi classifieds site existed at the time, but it was just the online version of a print edition with ads that were already a full week old by the time they made it up on the web, so he was getting aced out of all the good deals. With no heat in his apartment but a giant light bulb going off in his head, Morgan created TradeMe. Seven years later a large Australian media company purchased TradeMe for NZ$700 million.

As is the case with stories such as this one, Morgan's success may have come in a relatively short period of time, but nothing happened easily or overnight. Morgan faced his fair share of trials and challenges along the way.

One of those challenges occurred when TradeMe was growing at its fastest and Morgan was working 24/7, barely keeping up. He knew that if he kept going at that clip he would fall apart and the company would fall apart along with him.

Fortunately Morgan had some people he trusted well enough to leave TradeMe in their hands while he took a break. His break didn't involve running off to an island somewhere to sip tiny umbrella drinks (he hadn't sold the company yet!). Instead Morgan took a nine-to-five job as an information technology technician in Britain that was a professional refuge and maybe even what he felt he was more cut out for. After all, he hadn't set out to become the founder and CEO of a start-up. He needed to breathe and figure out if where he'd landed was where he belonged.

The pause helped Morgan do two things: (1) Realize how much he missed the immense challenge of running and growing his business; and (2) Figure out what he thrived doing, and find people who thrived doing the things that he could do if he had to, but that drained him and kept him from giving his best. Once Morgan reconnected with what needed him and what fed him, he returned to TradeMe with the answers and took the company to a whole new level.

Anything you're going to do with your whole self is worth taking a pause to make sure your best self is showing up for the job. This not only means knowing that you're taking care of the work, but also that the work is taking care of you. What you learn when you explore what needs you and what feeds you may not always be something you can implement right away, but that's more than okay. It's okay—even necessary—to think about exactly what you want—and don't want—to be doing one year, five years, and ten years down the road, just as you would do in a remunerative job or career.

The goal of every business, including social enterprises, is to scale. For a social enterprise, the more successfully you expand, the greater your impact on people's lives. The need your business exists to meet and the problem it exists to change are the stakes, and the people whose lives will be made better based on your ability to create maximum impact are your shareholders. Their success is linked to yours.

In 2003 Graham Macmillan, VisionSpring's first senior director, and I sat down to envision what our team would look like five years down the road. Who would we need by 2008 to help Vision-Spring scale based on how we hoped to grow in the interim?

Graham and I based this visioning exercise on all of the roles he and I were playing, which after making a list totaled twenty. So we drew twenty boxes and started writing our names in each box that applied. My name went into the boxes for roles like CEO, Board Chair, and Director of Development. Graham's name went into pretty much every finance-related role, sales, operations, and human resources box.

But the fun part came when we did a joint check-in. We talked about what needed us and what fed us, not just at VisionSpring, but what made the days feel like hours, and hours feel like days, for each of us in general. As we spoke, we began crossing our names off the boxes we hated and knew we were the worst at doing, and keeping our names in the boxes of the roles we loved and did best.

As we winnowed things down, the visioning exercise revealed that my goal at the end of those five years was to be occupying only two roles: evangelist and chief fund-raiser. An evangelist tells the business's story and reason for existence. His palpable fervor and clear personal investment in engaging, and permanently eliminating, the social need his enterprise lives to solve makes him uniquely suited to getting the message out there in the world. An evangelist also helps build the culture of the enterprise from the inside by inspiring those around him. He creates a sense of community, ownership, and belonging so that everyone who dedicates their time and talent to the cause knows that they are vital to the success of the enterprise and absolutely essential to its impact.

Apropos of that, the other box left with my name on it was chief fund-raiser. Just as the evangelist's belief in the mission turns people into partners on the inside of the business, the fund-raiser's contagious conviction helps cultivate capital contributors who also understand that they, too, are critical partners in the challenging work of solving a thorny problem that, if solved, could change the lives of hundreds of millions of people for the better.

This clarifying exercise that Graham and I did is another form of check-in that any person committed to making positive change can and should do at any point along her change-making path.

Using your needs me/feeds me findings, draw your own boxes. In what roles are you functioning or would you like to be functioning in your work to do good? Of those roles, which ones do you do best? Which ones do you do worst? Which ones do you hate, even though you can do them in an okay fashion? Which ones are you entirely ill-suited to do at all? And if you were to keep working on making a difference in the area you've chosen for the next five years, what roles would you like to be filling at the end of those five? Where are people who can fill those roles needed most? What do you need to begin doing or learning now in order to serve in those roles?

I Statements

I hold that a man should strive to the uttermost for his life's set prize.
—ROBERT BROWNING

Lawyer and playwright Wajahat Ali wrote a compelling *New York Times* opinion piece about approaching forty and feeling like he hasn't made a real difference in the world. He talks about the heightened sense of urgency he feels to "do something that matters," and the heightened sense of anxiety that he is not doing it yet.

Ali describes interviewing a teen activist half his age who has done more to make a difference than Ali worries he will do in a lifetime, and Ali concedes to feeling defeated as he watches his high school celebrity crush use her Twitter feed as a tool for social justice. He also details his feelings of guilt and embarrassment when he sees his friends dedicating weekends to canvassing for political candidates they believe in while he's "deciding whether to take my kids to the mall or Chuck E. Cheese's."

In what I would call his midlife mattering crisis confessional, Ali candidly captures something most people feel: a jumble of angst and optimism, hope that collides with reality—ours and the world's; the desire to do something that to us signifies that we're making a real contribution to humanity and to the demands of the times in which we're living, feeling called and motivated, yet also corralled by time constraints, family responsibilities, professional responsibilities and aspirations, and any number of other important bucket-list goals. Ali adds to this shared jumble, looking around at how other people already are making a difference, as if making a difference is a race or a competition, and rather than being inspired by them, getting ideas from them, or learning more about issues that may lead you to the need that specifically needs you, their mattering only trains the white-hot spotlight on our inaction and melts our enthusiasm and sense of urgency into a sad puddle of great expectations.

Yet the realization at which Ali arrives also applies to more lives than his own when he writes, "A crisis, once confronted honestly, can become less overwhelming."

A mattering crisis—whether midlife, late in life, or just starting out in life, the feeling that we haven't taken meaningful action to make a difference—is less about what we haven't done and more about not having a concrete action plan for doing. And by the way, part of combating this crisis also is knowing that no one who has lived among other human beings for any reasonable period of time—family, friends, neighbors, strangers—has failed to do something that really matters. You matter. You have mattered.

Again, when we're talking about a crisis of mattering, what we're really talking about is consciously digging in to a problem that moves you, that's bigger than you, and then working consistently and strategically to make positive, lasting change in your chosen area of need over as much of your lifetime as you're willing and able to dedicate to it.

When it comes to dismantling crises of mattering in order to build lives of service that matter to us and the world beyond us, Ali and I share something invaluable in common: smart and supportive wives. Taking one of those crucial steps in confronting these all-consuming crises that can be converted into turning points by sharing his struggle with his wife, she reminds him, "This moment, now, is the best years of our lives, which will never come back and people with much less than I have, have managed to make a mark on the world."

Wherever you are on your life's path, any moment that moves you to transform a crisis of mattering into an action plan that puts you on your own path to your something that matters has the power to turn life as you know it into the best life you know.

We've talked about different ways that you can move from daring to matter, which I've shared is the easy part, to the work of mattering itself, which is the most difficult part. Another way to make that move is by taking an action pledge. An action pledge gives your dare a more specific focus to help you take your desire to make a difference out of the realm of aspiration and into the realm of perspiration.

An action plan should be tough but also achievable; long-term enough that it requires constant effort, but realistic enough that you can achieve it. It also should begin with an *I* to make you the CEO of the change you want to make and the person with whom the buck stops when you evaluate yourself based on the standards you have set.

When you start out on your path to make a difference, your action pledge should reflect the reality of where you are. As such, tailor it to the life you're living so that you can do good on a steady basis:

> I will dedicate five hours this month to finding a way to discover how I want to make a difference.
> I will spend seven hours this month learning about a problem that resonates with me.
> I will find the need within that problem that needs me most by the end of this year.
> I will spend seven hours a month working on the need that needs me most.

Alternatively, if you've already found the need that needs you most and you're into the work, then tailor your action pledge to focus on your specific goals in your action area. These should be more detailed and should raise the stakes even higher—also in a challenging, yet realistic fashion—on what you're doing to make a difference now.

I took my first action pledge in 2013 as part of the Aspen Global Leadership Network Action Forum. The Action Forum brings together business leaders, social entrepreneurs, philanthropists, and others invested in social change. They come from dozens of countries across the globe to share their visions, reflect on their work, gain perspective, and recover their own, as well as recommit to what they've set out to do to make a difference in the world.

The action pledge itself is "a public commitment to help tackle a specific challenge." Mine was, "I will provide one million people a year with affordable eyeglasses in over twenty countries by 2016." My pledge obviously wasn't something I could achieve alone by a long shot. It was my pledge through my work with VisionSpring, and that of our staff, Vision Entrepreneurs, and local heroes at the grassroots level in every country, town, and village we served, as well as with our funders and strategic partners. I'd also made another nearer term pledge that I would ensure that 500,000 people who needed eyeglasses in the developing world not only had access to them, but had them, by 2014.

By 2014 we had in fact achieved that goal in twenty-two countries and had exceeded it by another 48,000 people. Although we didn't reach our one million people a year goal until 2018, the action pledge gave us a concrete benchmark for incremental success.

In taking my action pledge, I joined hundreds of others doing absolutely remarkable things of every size and scale in issue areas that I'd never otherwise have known anything about. People like Patricia Musoke, a scientist and project management specialist at the International Atomic Energy Agency (IAEA), whose 2016 action pledge was "to motivate at least 200 teenage Ugandan girls to pursue careers in Science, Technology, Engineering, and Math by 2020."

In the furtherance of her goal, Musoke founded an annual weeklong science camp for Ugandan girls in the hopes of pointing them in the direction of Science, Technology, Engineering, and Math (STEM) careers. Women make up more than 50 percent of the population in Uganda, yet few have access to the education or the encouragement they need to pursue STEM careers, which offer opportunities to lead financially independent lives. In Uganda, financial independence for women can be the difference between having to stay in abusive marriages and having the freedom to get themselves and their children out of abusive situations without worrying about financial vulnerability.

My action pledge experience has helped me in the process of squaring off with a specific social need in a targeted way. By taking your pledge, your work for good will go from something hazy (which can happen even when you're deep into your efforts to create change, because you're so deep into the work that you've gotten lost in its easily all-consuming nature) to something clearly stated that feels, and is, real and manageable. By zooming out and zeroing in on the practical, you impose structure on an imposing issue and on the imposing goal to make your life matter, which also helps keep you from feeling overwhelmed when you're trying to do something big and decidedly bigger than you.

In addition, once you've taken an action pledge and armed yourself with your own set of specifics, when you look around and see what other people are doing to take action you will feel more motivated, not less. Rather than feeling like the problems of the world are too vast and too difficult for you or anyone else to make a dent, or feeling like others have lapped you in the race to do something that matters, with an action pledge the only thing that will overwhelm you is how good it feels to see so many others who not only believe that real change is possible, but who also are proving it through their commitment, resolve, optimism, ingenuity, and action every day.

Community in Action

I celebrate myself, and sing myself,
And what I assume you shall assume,
For every atom belonging to me as good belongs to you.
—WALT WHITMAN

Prior to Jen's visit to sit in on the QUESTion Project classes that I talked about in chapter one, she'd had a fair amount of e-mail correspondence with the QUESTion Project's program director, Gabriel Gonzalez, to prepare for the day.

Jen told me that she and Gabriel had arranged to meet in the lobby of BCSM, the first stop of the day. When she arrived, she went directly to the reception desk and asked where she could find Mr. Gonzalez, whom she'd imagined was a guy in his fifties or sixties. Before the gentleman at the desk could answer, however, Mr. Gonzalez tapped Jen on the shoulder and identified himself. As it turned out, Jen had seen him when she first walked in but he looked so young that she thought he was a student.

Gabriel was kind enough to accompany Jen throughout the day, and during that time she learned that he was twenty-five and that his job with the QUESTion Project was his first out of college. Jen said it was clear that Gabriel enjoyed his work, but he shared with her that he knew he wouldn't be with the QUESTion Project forever. Nevertheless he also expressed that he had little idea of what to do next.

During a short cab ride between the two high schools, Jen asked Gabriel what he liked the most about his current job.

"I think it's seeing what happens when the students start trusting each other and they become a community of people struggling with the same questions," he replied. "Some of the questions are scary to ask, but they aren't afraid to face them because they know they're not the only ones asking, and they aren't asking them alone."

Gabriel then returned to the question of what he wanted to do next and recalled a time in college toward the end of senior year when he, his friends, and classmates became so wrapped up in what their next moves would be after graduation that they stopped asking the big questions about what they hoped to make of their lives, not just what they were going to do with them. He added that since joining the work world, and now focused on taking another next step, that hadn't changed. Now, he explained, with work responsibilities, rent to make, and the question of whether to go back to school or how to continue making inroads in the job market, even less bandwidth existed for the big questions.

Jen said that Gabriel had spoken with a hint of wistfulness (something you don't expect to see in a person in his midtwenties) about how much he wished he had his own community of questioners, like his QUESTion Project kids, where the same people he talks to and hangs out with now would speak just as honestly and openly as his students do about what they fear most in life, how they feel about the lives they're leading, what they find meaningful, how they hope to make a difference, and how they aim to do so.

Gabriel's wish called to mind a verse from Psalms: "How good and how pleasant it is when brothers and sisters sit together." What Gabriel wanted and needed was something we all need, something simple and yet for some reason something less easily attained. The verse highlights the simplicity of people just being together, gathering in and sharing the same space. Yet the verse also draws our attention to how easily we overlook the inherent power of community and the strength we derive from connection, as if to say, "Don't forget that there is beauty in fellowship."

Just as we need fellowship and community in our lives in general, we need fellowship and community in our individual quests to make our lives matter. Taking on the world requires the strength and support of others, the power that comes from connecting and knowing that you're not in it alone.

I know this because without the social entrepreneurial networks in which I've had the privilege of participating, like the Crown and Skoll Fellowships, without these circles of safety, support, friendship and inspiration, I'm not certain I would have grown in impact, as a change-maker, and as a person, in the same way.

My friend Ben Dunlap—author, distinguished academic, and past president of Wofford College in Spartanburg, South Carolina—whom I met through the Aspen Institute, once coined a phrase that has stayed with me ever since. When speaking about the Henry Crown Fellowship Program, Ben referred to its participants as "the army of the just."

I love this phrase because it captures what it means to be part of a group of people of all backgrounds and ages, men and women called to serve different needs, united by the same mission to make their lives stand for something bigger than themselves. The troops in this army who have put their life energies into healing the world are people with degrees from top universities who could be doing absolutely anything they want, but who choose to put their skills, talents, and brilliance to work to serve humanity. They motivate me through their example of how to match goodness with grit and the hard work it takes to bridge the chasm between the world as they envision it and the world as it is.

Because I have experienced the power of community in the pursuit of positive change, I believe that everyone committed to making a difference should have an army of the just of their own—to provide inspiration and guidance, to keep the tank full, and also to have an even greater impact than you ever could alone.

The last time I did a serious check-in, as you'll find is the case when you do yours at varying moments on your path to making a difference, I learned that some things were the same, but some things had changed enough that I had to pay attention.

When I asked myself what feeds me, my answers reaffirmed what I knew, what I've always known:

1. I derive great satisfaction in helping people.
2. I derive great satisfaction from working to right a wrong.
3. I derive great satisfaction when I receive positive feedback and validation for a job well done.
4. I derive great satisfaction from solving a difficult business problem.

When I asked myself what needs me, the fact that more than a billion people in the developing world still need glasses to stay in school, earn a living, and lead safer, fuller, more independent lives still instantly came to mind.

Yet some other sobering realities that had drawn more and more of my focus also landed on the "needs me" list, like:

1. Nearsightedness, farsightedness, astigmatism, and presbyopia are the leading cause of visual impairment in the world and the second leading cause of blindness in the developing world.

2. More than 2.5 billion people in the world could stay in school, earn a living, and lead safer, fuller, more independent lives if they had a simple pair of glasses and access to affordable eye care.

3. No global initiative exists focused exclusively on eliminating these simple, uncorrected refractive errors of the eye (nearsightedness, farsightedness, astigmatism, and presbyopia) by making affordable eye care and eyewear readily available to the people and in the places that need it.

4. If things continue at this rate, more than 50 percent of the world's population (including 65 percent of the population in East Asia) will need glasses to see, go to school, or go to work.

Reflecting upon these realities, I knew that VisionSpring still needed me and still fed me, but Liz Smith, a VisionSpring colleague, pushed me to think more boldly. This led to our deciding that without a serious global initiative, VisionSpring alone would never, ever be able to meet the need and solve the problem entirely. We also knew that if it hadn't happened by now, there was little chance that this kind of global initiative would magically appear, that we couldn't allow what remained a serious global health crisis another thirty years to get as bad or even worse than projected, and that we wouldn't be content to leave it all to chance. And so in 2014, with VisionSpring's blessing and support, Liz and I decided to create EYElliance.

EYElliance is a multistakeholder initiative that recognizes that NGOs are great at creating innovative solutions, but that they also require partners from the private and governmental sectors to increase their impact and go from affecting millions of lives to changing billions of lives. Our first step was to bring leaders in the optical industry, international NGOs, academics, donors, and health specialists together to explore whether there was an appetite for tackling this challenge on a global scale.

The first time we convened this new and diverse community of partners and stakeholders, we were thrilled that Secretary Albright agreed to join us and speak to the group. She emphasized how challenging it was to draw attention to one issue of global importance with so many other pressing global issues competing for attention and funds, particularly if the issue isn't viewed as a life or death problem. As a result, her central recommendation was that we demonstrate that uncorrected vision is more than a global public health issue. Rather, it's a global development issue that no initiative has ever existed to fight and to which no significant funds have ever been allocated.

Secretary Albright made it clear to us that if we wanted to start effecting change on this level, we would have to make clear on an even grander scale that when people can't see, they lose their livelihoods; that when children can't see to learn, they lose their path to an education that eventually leads to earning a living; that when people die in car accidents because they can't see it not only is senseless and tragic, but also comes with its own attending economic consequences.

This means that the need for glasses leads to greater income disparity due to chronic unemployment and underemployment. And according to a World Economic Forum study, extreme poverty and income disparity pose more dangerous threats to the world than earthquakes, tsunamis, water shortages, terrorism, pandemics, geopolitical instability, and the collapse of nations.

With fifty-three founding members, including a growing team

of for-profit industry leaders like Essilor and Alcon, international financial institutions like the World Bank, governmental organizations like the US Agency for International Development (USAID), philanthropic foundations like Skoll, Draper Richards Kaplan, and Horace W. Goldsmith, traditional NGOs like the Brien Holden Vision Institute and Helen Keller International, and not-for-profit social enterprises like VisionSpring, EYElliance has succeeded in taking a number of exciting steps forward.

For instance, we copublished a report, *Eyeglasses for Global Development: Bridging the Visual Divide,* with the World Economic Forum to make the cogent argument, as Secretary Albright suggested, that correcting vision is an essential part of global development. Once published, we had the opportunity to share the report at Davos and frame this issue for leaders in business and government for the first time.

We also have had the opportunity to work with Congresswoman Nita Lowey, the ranking Democrat on the House Appropriations Committee (the first woman, Democrat or Republican, ever to lead her party on the Committee) to insert language in the 2017 Foreign Appropriations Bill stating the importance of including vision screening and vision services in schools already receiving general aid across the globe.

And in 2018, for the first time in history, the US Government's Development Assistance Budget included a distinct line item for providing eyeglasses to those without access to them.

Another exciting step forward for EYElliance that strengthened the case for why vision is critical for global economic development was the publication of EYElliance stakeholder Dr. Nathan Congdon's findings in *The Lancet Global Health Journal* from the first-ever randomized trial to measure the impact of reading glasses on productivity. Congdon worked with VisionSpring to conduct a study on a tea estate in Assam, in northeastern India, where they gave nonprescription reading glasses to half of the 751 tea-pickers over age forty working on the estate. Over the course of eleven weeks, the productivity of those under the age of fifty who received the glasses increased by 21 percent, and for those over fifty by 32 percent—the highest ever scientifically recorded increase in productivity by a medical intervention (even greater than interventions such as mosquito nets and micronutrients). And 95 percent of those workers who experienced the benefit of corrected vision reported that if they had access to affordable glasses (the kind that currently VisionSpring sells), they would pay for them in the future.

Real change requires community—people coming together to combine talents, connections, and resources to get deeper into solving a problem because all problems are connected, as is the case with glasses, to a complex array of forces that without an array of committed change-makers will remain resistant to real and lasting change.

You don't have to be a social entrepreneur to create an army of the just, a community of change-makers who support one another, nourish one another's energy and commitment, and multiply their mattering quotient exponentially.

Start by gathering people who, like you, are trying to make their lives matter, and try to include people who are in different places on their paths. Gather for the good, share experiences and best practices about everything from time management to other places and people you should know to help you work on your individual action pledge. Are there ways you can combine forces or complement one another's work? Share highs, lows, lessons learned, and remind yourselves and one another that no one can or should do the heavy lifting of healing the world alone. Challenge one another, encourage one another, and enjoy being in one another's presence, laughing, sharing stories from any and all aspects of your life, just being.

And there's no need to reinvent the wheel in order to convene your army of the just. Create one out of a group you're already a part of, like a church, synagogue, temple, mosque, or community center, work, school, a parents' group or book club—a gathering you've already allocated time to so that you don't have to find more time in your already busy schedule. If you go this route, simply create a purpose for the gathering within the group's general purpose by focusing just one meeting on the topic of bringing about positive change. If you're connecting through a book club, try selecting a book that you think will lead to a lively conversation about making a difference.

The point isn't how you gather, but that you gather. The rest, like you, will grow in good naturally.

Take the Dare

If you don't have time to answer your needs me/feeds me questions right now, try starting your day simply by asking yourself the questions out loud:

What needs me?

What feeds me?

Ask yourself as you're getting dressed in front of a mirror. Press pause on the podcast or music you're listening to while you're on your way to work or school or while you're exercising, and ask yourself these two questions.

I challenge you to do this every day for a week, and see how it changes the way you see and experience your day.

With or without making your needs me/feeds me lists, as you move through your days with these questions, think about what you do throughout the day that supports the answers as you encounter them. What is one thing you've done during the day that supports your answers? What is one thing you've done during the day that does not?

Also try to notice when your heart lifts at the prospect of fulfilling your dream of making a difference. When it does, what is the catalyst for the feeling? Who is the catalyst for the feeling? What is the first step you can take towards making it happen? What stands in your way of making it happen? What will it take for you to remove the obstacles or to make it happen despite the obstacles?

Write an incremental action plan consistent with that dream on a Post-It, and put it somewhere where you will see it in your home every day. Take another Post-It with the same incremental action plan and put it somewhere where others will see it: at work, on your bicycle, on your jacket. Start holding yourself account-able to achieving your near term benchmark for progress not just by reminding yourself what it is, but by letting others know, and encouraging them to ask you how it's going.

If you want to take this one step further, give a blank Post-It note to a small group of people you see every day, and encour-age them to write down an incremental action plan for making a difference of their own. Convene an informal gathering every couple of weeks or once a month to check in with each other and compare notes on progress.

*Who is the person who craves life, who loves his days
and lives to see the good?*
—Psalm 34:12

10 Love Your Days

With each new initiative, your skill and confidence as a changemaker grows. You never need be afraid. And all through life you will have the power to express love and respect in action at ever more significant levels—and this, as both the prophets and scientists say, is what brings health, longevity, and happiness.
—Bill Drayton

One day a traveling salesman stopped in a small hamlet. He set up his wares, then stood by his wagon and began shouting, "Who wants to buy the elixir of life?"

A rabbi and scholar whose study window faced the village square heard the peddler's voice. The rabbi had been puzzling over the same verse for hours and having yet to arrive at what he deemed a satisfactory interpretation, he decided it was as good a time as any to take a break. Following the peddler's calls, he ventured out into the street to investigate.

"Who wants to buy the elixir of life?" the peddler bellowed.

"I'd like to buy," the rabbi said.

"It isn't something you need," he replied.

"But why?"

"You already have it."

Seeing the puzzled look on the rabbi's face, the salesman reached into his cart, fished out a book of Psalms, and pointed to the very verse the rabbi had been wrestling with all morning: "Who is the person who craves life, who loves his days, and lives to see the good?"

The rabbi thanked the peddler and ran back up the stairs to his study, just as eager to return to the verse that had frustrated him as he had been to leave it. He stopped short of his desk where the book lay open exactly as he'd left it. And then it came to him: he'd spent the whole morning challenged, engaged, and doing what he loved, just as he had the day before and the day before that and the day before that. Who is the person who lives with zest for tomorrow? The one who loves his days today.

The rabbi went to the window, searching the square for the peddler, only to find that the peddler was gone. He smiled, sat down at his desk, and turned the page.

Working for change is a strange thing. It requires forward thinking and a "someday" mentality.

Yet if we walk through our days focusing on the someday perfect world, we inadvertently cancel out the good right here in our midst. As we keep our eyes on the prize of the someday, we've committed ourselves to coaxing and commanding into being the someday when needless suffering is a matter of history rather than a matter of fact. The someday when our vision for the world as it should be matches the world as it is. It's easy to lose sight of the gifts that abound in the here and now.

The same goes for the way we walk through our own personal worlds. Someday I'll be happy; someday I'll have the money; someday I'll have the time; someday I'll be wiser, more present, healthier, more fulfilled.

While we cannot live without a someday inclination, without goals and the promise of future rewards and the efforts to achieve them that ennoble and invigorate the present, a someday preoccupation can undermine our efforts to achieve those goals. Whether in how we see our personal lives or in the way we view the world, loving our days as they are, seeing the good, recognizing what we have rather than fixating on what we lack is the elixir of life. Taking joy and pleasure in the present in fact makes us more optimistic about, and more effective in, the future.

According to Northeastern University professor of psychology and author David DeSteno, this bears out to be the case when it comes to keeping New Year's resolutions. DeSteno says, "By January 8, some 25 percent of resolutions have fallen by the wayside. And by the time the year ends, fewer than 10 percent have been fully kept." Oftentimes we attribute our failures to keep resolutions to lack of willpower, lack of self-control, and the inability to deny ourselves pleasure in the here and now. Yet as DeSteno explains, the punishing "I will do better, I will muscle through, I will wake up earlier" approach to self-improvement, while playing some role in our capacity to achieve our goals, can hurt more than help. As a study by DeSteno's colleague, Greg Miller, suggests, "willing oneself to be 'gritty' can be quite stressful" and put considerable physical and emotional stress on an individual.

According to DeSteno, Miller studied three hundred socially and economically disadvantaged teenagers, and indeed found that while the ones who succeeded at exerting self-control were more successful in denying themselves in the short term for the sake of accomplishing future oriented tasks, "their bodies suffered not only from increased stress responses, but also from premature aging of their immune cells."

DeSteno's takeaway from Miller's analysis as well as from his own work on the subject is that we're not naturally wired to grit our way to the future by effectively shutting off the valve that supplies us with good feelings in the here and now. He observes that the way human beings have managed to successfully do what it takes to get from "old you" to "new you" is through "social emotions": feelings like gratitude, patience, connection, generosity, pride in abilities one already possesses, and satisfaction in objectives already achieved. DeSteno explains that studies have shown that many of these emotions lead to better physical health in and of themselves, including lowering blood pressure and decreasing anxiety and depression. He further underscores the value of these emotions in the present and their connection to shaping our future selves by highlighting their link to increased academic performance and, specifically in the case of feeling pride, "an increase in perseverance on difficult tasks by over 30 percent."

It's clear that valuing today goes a long way to shaping tomorrow across the board. And when you have committed some part of your life to making a positive difference in the world—a resolution spanning multiple new years with results far less tangible than a smaller number on the scale or a higher grade on a test—taking care to experience these healing and regenerative emotions is a most necessary tonic. Fostering and cherishing these feelings is not selfish, but essential—for a change-maker who loves his days, who feels good and sees good and experiences goodness desires the same for others and won't quit, no matter how hard it gets, until he has done all he can in his own way to make it so. Like a person who has just fallen in love, the change-maker who loves his days wants the whole world to be in love, too.

Thanking Out Loud

Quoth Siddhartha: "What should I possibly have to tell you, oh venerable one? Perhaps that you're searching far too much? That in all that searching, you don't find the time for finding?"
—HERMANN HESSE

A few days and hundreds of patients after I'd diagnosed Chitra's cataracts at Aravind, I had the good fortune of having been assigned to the post-op station where I checked patients' healing processes by removing their bandages to rule out infections. While Chitra was still blinded by the cataract in her left eye, the bandage on her right was ready to come off.

Chitra's grandson had accompanied her on this visit and stood next to me as I peeled away the layers of gauze, sterile pad, and protective shield. When the light flooded her eye for the first time in almost twenty years, Chitra looked at her hands, studying them with intense curiosity and wonder almost as if she were on a hallucinogenic drug. Then she looked up at her grandson, whose face she hadn't seen in twenty years, and asked, "Doctor, will my vision last?"

"Grandma, it's me," he said. She quite literally couldn't believe her eyes.

As all three of us began to cry, what struck me as I observed Chitra taking everything in after having been without her vision for so long was how grateful she was for everything she could see right then and there. When she cried, her tears weren't for all of the years she missed watching her grandson grow from a child to a young man, but for the joy of simply being able to look at him as he was. With her sight restored, Chitra only saw what was right, what she'd gained, what she had, and not what she'd lost. Every single person and object before her was a revelation, and my heart filled with gratitude for the gift of being there to witness her pure and perfect delight.

Over the years, I have learned that gratitude is an art, a practice, a conscious pause. Sometimes the opportunities for gratitude greet us with little effort on our part—we luck into them and can't help but welcome them as a reflex. Yet in order to sustain ourselves and reinforce our love of life, expand our joy, and focus our gaze on the good—particularly when we're dedicating ourselves to creating good and can fall into the habit only of seeing its absence—we have to summon gratitude from within. We have to choose gratitude rather than leave gratitude to chance.

Choosing gratitude is training ourselves to be on the lookout for opportunities to give thanks in moments and for people we may unintentionally take for granted. We need to turn routine into revelation. Much like we take our vision for granted, choosing gratitude is like briefly removing our glasses, taking a look about, and then putting them back on—noticing the world of difference between how we see without them and how much we see with them. Or think about it in terms of the way many of my adult patients who've never worn glasses before describe how they experienced the enormity of the change upon seeing a tree and watching it go from lime-green blob to verdant array of individual leaves after their vision is corrected. (Try this yourself. Look at a tree with glasses or lenses and without. If you have 20/20 vision, move far away and note what you see, then move close until you can see fine detail.)

Inviting gratitude is like standing on the beach watching a watercolor sunset with only your senses to take it in—no camera or video. Just your eyes to see the streaks of red and purple in varying hues not replicable on any color wheel or in any Crayola box against the blue sky relaxing into the dimming of the day's light. Just your ears to hear the crashing of the waves on the shore and the seagulls' animated conversations. Just your nose to smell the seaweed and place the taste of the salt air on your tongue. Only your breath to draw in the peace and return it to evening calm on the exhale. No holding a phone skyward like a crossing guard raising a stop sign as it happens because no picture or video will capture the experience exactly as it is, as it was, as it never will be—at least not exactly—again. The moment exists solely for the moment's sake, and is cherished as such.

How you invite gratitude is personal. For instance, I know people who keep daily journals, and I admire the practice. Yet I also know myself, my schedule, my energy levels, and how I organize my life, and as such I also know I'm not a journal person. I am an information gatherer, a researcher, a processor. I need to take things in, zoom out and observe the lay of the land from thirty thousand feet, and then zoom back in to do a thorough exploration of the terrain before I speak about things. I also have a tendency to be in perpetual "go" mode, consumed by my tasks and lengthy daily to-do lists, relying heavily on others (which admittedly and justifiably sometimes gets on their nerves) to help pick up the shortfall. What all this means is that I know I have to work extra hard at awareness, and for me working at awareness means scheduling it and treating it in the same way I treat any task.

So when it comes to gratitude, I schedule a Gratitude Day. Gratitude Day takes places annually sometime between Christmas and New Year. On Gratitude Day I generally call between ten to twenty people (although I don't have a set number from the get-go—quality, not quantity, is the goal) for whom I'm grateful to talk to them and tell them so.

I know that taking one day out of 365 to express my gratitude may seem like a small thing when compared to keeping a daily record, but it is the practice I've created that works for me, and at which I know I can succeed. And it turns out that Gratitude Day has had the added effect of focusing me on gratitude during the other 364.

In many ways I am preparing for Gratitude Day all the time, with my preparation intensifying as Gratitude Day draws closer.

In order to know who I'll spend Gratitude Day calling, I have to reflect seriously on the year that has passed. Who comes to mind when I think about what has transpired between last Gratitude Day and this one? Who am I especially grateful for when I imagine the highs and the lows, bars set and bars raised, what I've learned and how I've learned it, how I've grown? In the process I think of moments for which I'm grateful—some of which I knew at the time, but many of which it took thought to identify. These questions and this review as I look to Gratitude Day give me a real chance not only to recognize everything for which I'm thankful, but to share it in a conscious way.

Once I have generated my gratitude list, which often is a mix of family members, colleagues, and friends—people I've known for years and some I've only just met—I prepare for the calls themselves by noting exactly why I'm calling each person. I want each person I speak with to know what it is about them that I am grateful for—what they did, how they did it, what it evoked in me, and what they mean to me. It is in this way that I get to what I believe is actually the most important part of gratitude: sharing it.

While feeling gratitude is of great value, it's not enough to be quietly thankful, to keep the gratitude you conjure to yourself, for yourself—especially when it comes to people. If feeling gratitude can increase our emotional and physical health, brighten our outlook, and give our productivity a bump, imagine what knowing that you're appreciated can do. Imagine how you've felt when someone has taken the time to thank you for something you did that to you was just second nature, but to them made all the difference on a dark day or in a time of struggle. What effect did the expression of gratitude have on you? Did it give you a boost when you were feeling low yourself, doubting your own accomplishments or diminishing your value? How did you comport yourself with others or in other facets of your life after receiving those thanks? Were you more generous with others? Did you find yourself energized and more prepared to take on a task?

By sharing gratitude you do more than mark a moment for yourself. You also create a moment for someone else—something they might cherish, that might make them smile for a bit, that reminds them—as we all need to be reminded—that they make a difference, sometimes make *the* difference, just by being who they are.

Anything Could Happen

Our goal should be to live life in radical amazement . . . get up in the morning and look at the world in a way that takes nothing for granted. Everything is phenomenal. . . . To be spiritual is to be amazed.
—Rabbi Abraham Joshua Heschel

I've invoked the teachings of Rabbi Heschel throughout this book because his wisdom never ceases to inspire me, and when it comes to sustaining and strengthening ourselves as we work to make the world a better place, Heschel's conceptualization of what he calls "radical amazement" is more than an idea that informs my life. It's a daily practice.

Radical amazement is Heschel's call to wonder and the celebration of awe that he unpacks in his book, *God in Search of Man*. Published in the mid-1950s in the wake of the horrors of the Holocaust and the invention of the atomic bomb, in the same year when fourteen-year-old Emmett Till was lynched while visiting family in Mississippi on summer vacation and Rosa Parks went to jail for refusing to move to the back of a Montgomery, Alabama, bus, and just as the United States entered the Vietnam War, Heschel held that people should allow themselves to reengage with the mystery of life. He encouraged people to marvel at small things, like a simple sunrise or the way that there are billions of people in the world yet no two human faces are exactly alike. It was Heschel's hope that he would succeed in persuading his readers to see everything around them as an opportunity to be dazzled by the workings of the world beyond our comprehension—to be dazzled by the fact that much of the world functions in a realm we cannot reach, but that we can, if we choose, behold.

Selling wonder, as it were, to humankind at a time when the abject failure of science, philosophy, and rational thought enveloped recent history and current events in an ominous cloud was no easy feat. The belief that the Enlightenment, scientific advances, and moral philosophy had placed humanity on a linear fast-track to a better world, that Kant's Categorical Imperative promising that rational thought would lead to the universal human enactment of the Golden Rule, had taken on the force of religion. And then so-called enlightened human beings did unfathomably inhuman things, and the religion of reason died, as did God and traditional religion—not for all, but for many.

In that climate of advanced disillusionment, Heschel did not shy away from reality, but rather suggested that the death of reason wasn't the death of the world or the negation of the human spirit. He wrote:

> As civilization advances, the sense of wonder declines. Such decline is an alarming symptom of our state of mind. Mankind will not perish for want of information, but only for want of appreciation. The beginning of our happiness lies in the understanding that life without wonder is not worth living. What we lack is not a will to believe but a will to wonder.

To me, Heschel's notion of radical amazement is one of the most enduring spiritually subversive acts we can perform in a world with more mind-blowing technological advancements and more readily accessible information than Heschel ever could have imagined sixty years ago, yet still a world, just like the one he lived in sixty years ago, in which more and better remain two dramatically different things.

When you choose to spend your life walking toward a problem, rather than looking away from it, radical amazement is a soul-saving grace. I have discovered that staying amazed allows me to see the beauty in my life and the world around me without pretending that I don't see the ugliness, the small-mindedness, the brokenness, the pain. It helps me maintain a positive outlook, look forward to even the most difficult of days, and allows me to continue to cherish my time on this earth, maintain perspective, and stay connected to my commitment not just to making positive change in the world but to genuinely believing that positive change is possible.

Staying amazed means letting life pleasantly surprise you. For me this means being pretty much anywhere in nature. Drawing my attention to the perfect balance of an intact ecosystem, the built-in interconnectedness, the way the earth is recreating itself at all times, the seasons and cycles of life.

But I don't need to be in the forest or in the mountains to let nature surprise me. Oftentimes I'll make a point of taking a long walk outside when the weather is bad, allowing myself first to feel the cold or wet, the wind—all of the natural forces I can't control, rather than avoid them or rush through them.

From there I draw my awareness to doing nothing more than putting one foot in front of the other. When the ground is saturated with rain, slick with ice, or buried in snow, I walk more deliberately, look more carefully, so as not to trip or fall. When I walk in inclement weather I say to myself, "Now I am walking," and I think of nothing else. Just by walking, I start to marvel at all the mechanisms in my body and brain that know exactly how to work in unison to achieve a seemingly simple step. The more focused I become on walking, the more I begin to feel my breath and hear it. The inhale in, the exhale out. And soon I'm marveling at this thing I do thousands of times a day, in waking and nonwaking moments, without thinking or trying, yet without which I would cease to be alive. Is walking a surprise? No. Is breathing a surprise? No. But by opening myself to wonder, these mundane things become a true source of amazement.

What amazes you? What leaves you awestruck when you allow it? If you don't yet know, that's okay. Experiment with something that doesn't feel forced or inorganic to you. If you don't meditate, don't meditate. If you associate the great outdoors with mosquito bites, not majesty, don't look for wonder in nature. Put yourself in a place you know well or do something you do frequently, but change one aspect of what is routine so that you're slightly off-kilter. Let yourself be until that ordinary experience is transformed—until you see something you never noticed, hear something you never listened for, react in a way you otherwise wouldn't. Let yourself be until you the commonplace becomes uncommonly remarkable.

Being amazed also can be as simple as putting your head on the pillow at night and waking up in the morning, bookending your days with built-in wonder. I do this by drawing on two Jewish rituals that I have adapted for myself and incorporated into my life.

For many of us, worry and fear are a regular part of bedtime. When we lie down and close our eyes, our to-do lists grow longer and more intimidating, and any worries or problems we may have always seem worse. While by day we can successfully evade the awareness of how little of life is in our control, somehow it always manages to catch up with us at night.

Our busy minds may also be our way of stalling, like kids who keep asking for one more bedtime story so they don't have to go to sleep. Our hesitance, even when we're dog-tired, may stem from our unconscious sense of how vulnerable we are when we are asleep.

In that vein, the Talmudic sages went so far as to describe sleep as "one-sixtieth of death." Erica also talks about sleep from a psychoanalytic standpoint as a "mini-death." As in death, in sleep we have no agency. We are defenseless. Yet if we really want to enter a state of nighttime rest, we've no choice but to temporarily loosen our grip and relinquish control.

And relinquish control we must, because all beings need sleep. According to the *Oxford Handbook of Sleep and Sleep Disorders*, "sleep is by no means an exclusive feature of human physiology and behavior. All other mammals sleep, too, albeit in some cases with adaptations." Yet unlike some species that have to periodically defer sleep to avoid being gobbled up as prey or unlike mammals, like the blind Indus dolphin who must power nap in order to safely navigate the sea, ever since the Neolithic period we humans have required good old-fashioned monophasic sleep (sleep at night, awake by day).

Not only do we need sleep for restorative purposes, but many current studies demonstrate that not getting enough of it can slowly kill us. As Matthew Walker, a neuroscientist, Director of the Center for Human Sleep Science at the University of California, Berkeley, and author of *Why We Sleep*, says, "No aspect of our biology is left unscathed by sleep deprivation."

As sleep is truly a matter of life and death, the Jewish sages created a bedtime ritual to counteract bedtime fear with the recitation of a liturgical poem (or *piyyut*) called Adon Olam. Adon Olam is the grown-up's lullaby to the self, in which we make peace with the darkness and entrust our souls to God's safekeeping until daylight appears. And having placed our bodies and spirits in God's safekeeping, we are free to sleep peacefully, unburdened if only for the night of any fear.

So when I find myself starting to make my bedtime lists, all the things I failed to accomplish that day and everything I have to do the next, I consciously replace each item with the last words of Adon Olam: "I will not fear." I repeat them like a mantra until I fall asleep.

While truly restorative sleep can be somewhat miraculous in and of itself, it is this nighttime practice that prepares me to start my day with wonder when I wake up in the morning.

When I first open my eyes, I pause before diving into the fray by acknowledging that the mere act of waking up is a miracle. I do so in the spirit of a prayer traditionally meant to be uttered instantly upon waking before your feet even hit the floor. The words are: "I stand before you and offer thanks, Sovereign of all living things, for graciously returning my soul to me. Your faith in me is great."

While I don't say the prayer, I do spend five minutes stretching and slowly reinhabiting my body as I think about what I'm looking forward to that day. I reflect with wonder on what it means to awaken to another day of life, to know that something greater than me has put its faith in me, and that I have just received the gift of more time to make my time in this life count. The more I think about this, the more I get excited for what lies ahead. The more I think that absolutely anything could happen today—that everything is possible.

As the day unfolds, I walk into the kitchen and enter the Kassalow morning chaos and see Erica preparing breakfast for the kids, Sofia and Jonas grabbing backpacks and tossing dishes somewhere in the vicinity of the sink, and Griffey positioned underfoot hoping for a surprise from one of those plates. We are all here, all safe, together; our bellies are full, and we're about to venture out into the world to fill another day with more life. And although this morning really is no different than any other, when I wake up ready for wonder, it never ceases to amaze me that at least five miracles have already happened in my home—all before seven thirty.

Labor of Love

Wisdom says that I am nothing. Love says that I am
everything. Between these two my life flows.
—SRI NISARGADATTA

A few years ago, I received an invitation to participate in a program called the Wellbeing Project. The Wellbeing Project brings social entrepreneurs together for three retreats over the course of eighteen months. The retreats are aimed at giving social entrepreneurs a chance to do some soul work in order to stay connected to who they are and the kind of lives they want to lead, and also to avoid burnout. I signed up instantly.

At the first retreat, I met a fascinating group of people. Among other activities we had the opportunity to work with movement specialists, Gestalt therapists, and other practitioners in order to focus ourselves and, in some sense, come back to ourselves by pinpointing where we'd gotten off course. I walked away from the experience grateful for the chance to be involved and looking forward to the next gathering.

When I received a follow-up e-mail from the program about just that, it was a bright spot in my inbox and in my day. As I went to enter the next retreat dates in my calendar, though, I noticed that part of it conflicted with Rosh Hashanah, the Jewish New Year. I reached out right away to bring it to the organizers' attention, and while they apologized profusely, they said unfortunately it was too late for them to change the date.

Rosh Hashanah is part of an important season in the Jewish calendar year. It also traditionally is a family holiday, and of course our custom is for me and Erica and the kids to observe together by going to synagogue and enjoying festive meals with our extended family and friends.

With that in mind, I faced a serious dilemma. As much as I didn't want to be away from my family or from our rabbi and synagogue community at the start of the New Year, I wanted to go to the retreat more. I couldn't explain it, but I just knew I had to go.

A tense conversation with Erica followed, but when she heard how important the retreat was to me, we agreed that I would go. That's not to sugarcoat the process because even though she supported my decision, Erica was pretty upset.

Despite rocking the boat on the home front, the retreat turned out to be just as worthwhile as I'd expected. What I discovered in the quiet and in the conversations was that the part of the path I'm on in my life now as I've moved beyond the half-century mark requires me to consciously and deliberately love the people I cannot live without.

The more I thought about this, the less of a coincidence it was to me that the retreat that gave me the space and time to realize that while the problem in the world that needed me remained a priority in my life, at this particular time in my life the people who are my world needed me more. I didn't overlook the irony that I chose to be away from them in order not to miss out on the retreat, only to find that I couldn't be true to where I was in my life or to myself if I kept missing out on moments for us to be together. But sometimes you have to go away to remind yourself where you belong.

One of the first things I did when I got home was sit down with Bryce. Before I left, he and I had looked at his basketball game schedule. Of eighteen games in his senior year season, my schedule was such that I'd committed to being at only three of them.

Upon my return, we took out the game schedule and went through it again until I'd found a way to be at nine. Still only half the season, but by letting go of other commitments I wanted to show Bryce through action that loving him is one of the great privileges of my life, and my number one priority. It wasn't a big thing, but it was a start.

While I'd missed celebrating the New Year, I did observe Yom Kippur (the Day of Atonement) with my family. One of the main themes of Yom Kippur is taking an inventory of your life—looking at where you've hit the bull's-eye and examining where you've missed the target.

The archery metaphor appears many times in the Yom Kippur prayers, and it resonated especially deeply that year. Living a life of doing good and doing well, and really any life well lived at all, is a perpetual process of knowing what you're aiming for and why. It's the courage to keep reaching into your quiver with humility and hope, knowing that more often than not you're going to miss the mark.

About the same time, I read a book called *The Miracle of Mindfulness* by Thich Nhat Hahn, a renowned Vietnamese Buddhist monk and Zen master. Known to his students as Thay ("teacher" in Vietnamese), he originally wrote *The Miracle of Mindfulness* in the midseventies as a manual to help young nuns and monks living in war-ravaged Vietnam shore up their souls after having faced death, suffering, and untold destruction every single day for years.

In the book, Thay calls to mind a short story, "The Three Questions," by our old friend Tolstoy. In it, an emperor wakes one day and determines that he has three questions; if he could find the answers he would never veer off his life's path. The emperor's questions were:

What is the best time to do each thing?
Who are the most important people to work with?
What is the most important thing to do at all times?

Having established his goal, the emperor sends forth a decree throughout his kingdom, calling on anyone who thinks he has the answer to come directly to his palace to present it, promising a sizable reward in return for the right ones.

Many flocked to the palace in the hopes of delivering the correct answers and filling their coffers with the reward, but the emperor found all of the answers lacking.

Convinced that no one in his whole kingdom would ever arrive with the answers he sought, the emperor went forth to seek the wisdom of a hermit who lived high in the mountains and who was known to be an enlightened soul.

After some time and many trials, the hermit finally offers the emperor the wisdom the emperor had come seeking.

The hermit said, "Remember that there is only one important time and that is now. The present moment is the only time over which we have dominion. The most important person is always the person you are with, who is right before you, for who knows if you will have dealings with any other person in the future? The most important pursuit is making the person standing at your side happy, for that alone is the pursuit of life."

Thay shares why he included Tolstoy's words in *The Miracle of Mindfulness*, a book that Thay originally intended to reach just a small group of people whom he knew well and who were living in the service of others. He explains:

> We talk about social service, service to the people, service to humanity, service for others who are far away, helping to bring peace to the world—but often we forget that it is the very people around us that we must live for first of all. If you cannot serve your wife or husband or child or parent—how are you going to serve society? If you cannot make your own child happy, how do you expect to be able to make anyone else happy? . . . The word service is so immense. Let's return first to a more modest scale: our families, our classmates, our friends, our own community. We must live for them—for if we cannot live for them, whom else do we think we are living for?

Making a difference, making your life matter, can seem like such a faraway thing—far beyond your reach, far beyond your abilities, far beyond the outskirts of your time and circumstances. It begins when something within you stirs. When that something tells you that this faraway thing is, in fact, not far from you at all. When this something promises you that who you are, who you will be, who you can be is a person who leaves the world a better place because you were in it because you were created in part to be a creator: a creator of healing, of hope, of justice, of change—real, positive, lasting change.

And then you find the change that's calling you. Whether you find it at twenty-five, fifty-five, or seventy-five doesn't matter. Once you find it, you set about getting to the heart of the need whose gravitational pull has a hold on you. You make your sacrifices, you dedicate your time, you offer the skills you have, you acquire new skills so you can keep growing in the good you hope to do over time.

But what will make the realest of real differences in who you are and who you become as a change-maker, whatever shape being a change-maker takes for you, is and always will be how well you love the people closest to you.

The great eighteenth-century Hasidic storyteller, the Dubner Maggid, tells the tale of a man traveling through the forest who happened upon a clearing where he saw a large wall with several dozen arrows stuck in it. Each arrow was smack-dab in the middle of the bull's-eye.

When the man spotted the archer placing an arrow in his bow and preparing to take aim again, he sprinted over and breathlessly said, "Sir, I have never seen such amazing accuracy and skill. You have hit the bull's-eye every time! Please tell me your secret. How did you become such a perfect shot?"

"It's simple," the archer replied. "First, I shoot the arrow and then I draw a bull's-eye around it."

Without love, even when you know the kind of difference you want to make, even when you're working hard to bring about the change you want to see, you'll spend all your energy running around drawing arbitrary bull's-eyes.

As crazy as it may sound, sometimes the unwieldy task of making a difference in the world can actually be easier than showing up for the people right in front of you. Because loving your partner, your spouse, your parents, your children, your siblings, your friends, your neighbors, and the people you serve with takes time and patience, commitment and care, even when we don't have it to spare. Loving them and seeing them in a way no one else can—at their best and at their worst; helping them become who they don't yet believe they can be, and letting them become who they know they really are takes focus and presence, humility and sacrifice.

Loving the people closest to us better and loving them more is ultimately how you'll make good on your dare to matter, because love is what matters most. It keeps you strong and makes you stronger. It teaches you how to forgive others and yourself. It keeps you plugged into joy and laughter and tears—the things that let you know you're alive. Loving reminds you every day what it means to have something worth fighting for and growing for. It is the hardest and the easiest thing we'll ever do.

When making a difference is your goal, always aim for love.

Take the Dare

If you wear glasses or contact lenses, pause for a moment each day and notice the difference in your vision with and without them. Think of all you can do and all you can see because of them, and be grateful for the simple gift of sight.

Let your gratitude muscles grow stronger from this one small practice until you are seeing your world through the eyes of a person who can recognize everyone and everything that makes you who you are and imbues your life, and your days, with meaning.

But don't just keep this account to yourself. Pick your Gratitude Day. Maybe it's the birthday of a person you loved who is no longer alive, but by whose example you try and live. Perhaps it's a holiday or time of year that you feel lends itself naturally to observing your Gratitude Day.

No matter what date or time of year you choose, be generating your phone call list for the year all year long. Create a Gratitude entry in your contacts list, and keep the log there in the notes sec-tion. When Gratitude Day arrives, before you call the people on your list, make sure that you have written down everything about them for which you are grateful with specificity and detail.

And love the people you love not just with words, but with action. Let them know through your deeds, no matter how imperfect, that they make all the difference in your world.

Acknowledgments

This book would not have seen the light of day if it were not for Jen Krause. I thank her for her belief that my journey was worth sharing and for the patience and persistence that were necessary to bring this book to life. I am indebted to her for helping me uncover how my faith animated my work and led to my desire to leave the world a bit better because I was a part of its miraculous unfolding. This book came alive because of her wisdom and writing skills. I am particularly grateful to her for helping me help the reader find their unique path to make a difference.

Our lives are made up of a symphony of people. It is with them that we make the music of our days. I am most fortunate to be part of a large symphony. I will do my best to thank all the players, but alas I will fail. I apologize in advance for not including you because if you are looking for your name, you warrant a mention.

First, I must thank the entire team at Drs. Farkas, Kassalow, Resnick & Associates for affording me a home base that has anchored my personal and professional life. I owe a particular debt of gratitude to my father, Dr. Ted Kassalow, as well as Drs. Paul Farkas, Barry Farkas, Susan Resnick, and Kevin Rosin for graciously giving me the latitude to spend half of my professional life on endeavors beyond our practice walls.

To my colleagues and friends at VisionSpring: you have made my dreams come true. Your dedication to spreading the gift of sight across the world leaves me in awe of each of you. I want to give special thanks to Lily Dorment, our first employee, and Graham Macmillan, Neil Blumenthal, and Miriam Stone, who I consider our founding team. To Peter Eliassen, Nira Jethani, and Anshu Taneja for their years of concentrated dedication. To Kevin Hassey, for his years of leadership, and last, but certainly not least, to our dynamic and fearless leader Ella Gudwin.

Appreciation also goes to VisionSpring's entire team, past and present, and to our Board of Directors for their strategic guidance and stellar governance under the capable and remarkable leadership of our board chair, Reade Fahs.

On behalf of VisionSpring, I also want to thank our major donor partners whose financial support and guidance have been a steady source of strength. These include Warby Parker, the Mulago Foundation, Sam Morgan and Jasmine Social Investments, Peery Foundation, The Skoll Foundation, USAID, the Horace W. Goldsmith Foundation, Alcon Foundation, Bohemian Foundation, and the David Weekley Family Foundation.

In addition, I would like to thank the many other organizations and individuals who have generously contributed to VisionSpring's efforts over the years. This includes our key field partners, with a special mention to BRAC and its remarkable founder and vice chairperson Mushtaque Chowdhury, who have collectively helped us deliver vision services and eyeglasses to nearly six million individuals.

I also owe a deep debt of gratitude to my colleague and friend Liz Smith with whom I co-founded EYElliance. Her undaunted resolve and keen strategic mind made the whole effort possible. Special thanks to the founding members of EYElliance's steering committee, Jayanth Bhuvaraghan, Chris Jurgens, Kovin Naidoo, Alex Sloan, and Andy Tembon. Many thanks, as well, to the generous donors who helped us bring EYElliance to life, including USAID, The Skoll Foundation, Alcon Foundation, Essilor, Draper Richards Kaplan Foundation, Horace W. Goldsmith Foundation, the Crown Family, the McNulty Foundation, Jeff Walker, and Rachel Tiven.

I have been incredibly fortunate to be nurtured by a host of fellowships that focus on supporting, celebrating, and improving social entrepreneurs and their endeavors. These include the Draper Richards Kaplan Fellowship, The Skoll Foundation Fellowship, The Schwab Foundation for Social Entrepreneurs, the Ashoka Fellowship, and the Henry Crown Fellowship at the Aspen Institute. I am deeply indebted to each of these extraordinary organizations, the people who fund and manage them, and especially to my friends and colleagues in each of these groups. They remain a source of strength and inspiration in my life.

I'd like to express thanks to my teachers and colleagues from the WellBeing Project. You have given me the gift of silence and space and the realization that the best way to see and hear is in quietude.

To my lifelong friends from high school, I'd like to express how much I love you guys. You have always been so encouraging and proud of my work and that means the world to me. You will always be my brothers.

I have been blessed with several mentors to whom I will be forever grateful. They include, Rabbi Ammiel Hirsch, Les Gelb, John Palmer, Dr. Govindappa Venkataswamy, R.D. Thulasiraj and David Green.

Jen and I would like to express our sincere gratitude to our amazing agent Jane von Mehren at Aevitas Creative Management whose genius enabled us to distill the essence of this book, build a compelling proposal, and find it a wonderful home at Kensington Publishing.

To the Kensington Publishing family, under the inspired and inspiring leadership of president and CEO Steven Zacharius and publisher Lynn Cully, thank you for believing in us and for your willingness to donate 15 percent of the book's profits to Vision-Spring to help bring sight to the underserved people worldwide.

Special thanks, as well, to our thoughtful and skillful editor Denise Silvestro, and to the entire talented Kensington team, including Jackie Dinas, Vida Engstrand, and Ann Pryor.

Finally, I would like to thank my incredible family. To my supportive and loving sisters, Julie and Jennifer, your shining examples give me hope for the world. I can't express how important you are to me.

To my father, who has always been a beacon of strength in my life, and to my mother, who although no longer with us in body will forever glow at the center of my spirit.

To my beautiful children, Bryce, Jonas, and Sofia, perhaps this book is really for you. I love you. May you find the remarkable gifts that bloom when you serve others.

Finally to my wife, Erica, who is the true star of this book. You have taught me what it means to love. You have taught me the power of love. I am forever grateful to you, and I will love you forever.